P9-CLQ-294

LEARNING TO BE A SAGE

LEARNING TO BE A SAGE

Selections from the
*Conversations of Master Chu,
Arranged Topically*

By Chu Hsi
Translated with a Commentary by
Daniel K. Gardner

University of California Press
Berkeley   Los Angeles   London

Portions of Part One appeared in Daniel K. Gardner, "Transmitting the Way: Chu Hsi and His Program of Learning," *Harvard Journal of Asiatic Studies* 49, no. 2 (June 1989): 141–172, and are reprinted here with the permission of the journal.

Cover: The first column of the title page
of the 1880 edition of the *Chu-tzu yü-lei.*

University of California Press
Berkeley and Los Angeles, California

University of California Press, Ltd.
London, England

© 1990 by
The Regents of the University of California

Library of Congress Cataloging-in-Publication Data

Chu, Hsi, 1130–1200.
    [Chu-tzu yü lei. English. Selections]
    Learning to be a sage: selections from the Conversations of
Master Chu, arranged topically / by Chu Hsi; translated with a
commentary by Daniel K. Gardner.
        p.   cm.
    Selected translation of: Chu-tzu yü lei.
    Includes bibliographical references.
    ISBN 978-0-520-06525-3
    1. Philosophy—Early works to 1800.   I. Gardner, Daniel K., 1950–
II. Title.
B128.C52E5   1990
181'.11—DC20   89-39348
                                                              CIP

Printed in the United States of America

13   12   11   10   09   08
12   11   10   9   8   7

The paper used in this publication is both acid-free and totally chlorine-free
(TCF). It meets the minimum requirements of ANSI/NISO Z39.48-1992
(R 1997) (*Permanence of Paper*). ♾

Contents

Acknowledgments

It is perhaps fitting in a book on learning to begin by acknowledging those people who were so important in teaching me the pleasures of studying China's past; were it not for Willard J. Peterson of Princeton University and Benjamin I. Schwartz of Harvard University this book would surely never have been written.

The study of Sung China involves deciphering sometimes indecipherable Chinese texts. Yüan-chu Lam of Wellesley College and Tao-chung Yao of Mount Holyoke College were untiring in their efforts to keep me from going too far astray; both gave hours of their time in reading over drafts of translations. Their ears and eyes were especially helpful in making sense of some of the more colloquial and idiomatic passages in the records of Chu Hsi's conversations with disciples.

Every writer should be as fortunate as I have been to have a reader with patience, unerring good judgment, and a sense of humor. Cynthia J. Brokaw of the University of Oregon has been subjected to countless drafts of this book: her reading of the last draft was as fresh and insightful as that of the first. Whatever value this book may have owes much to her.

Of course, without time no book can be written. I would like to thank the National Endowment for the Humanities for a grant that gave me the time to do the research for this book, particularly Part One.

Finally, this book is dedicated to Claudia, who on the good days helped me to feel the joy of discovery and progress and on the worst encouraged me to be mindful of the cosmic insignificance of it all. Her understanding and companionship have meant everything.

Abbreviations

I-shu   Ch'eng Hao and Ch'eng I. *Ho-nan Ch'eng-shih i-shu. Kuo-hsüeh chi-pen ts'ung-shu* edition.

Nien-p'u   Wang Mou-hung. *Chu-tzu nien-p'u. Ts'ung-shi chi-ch'eng* edition.

SJCC   Ch'ang Pi-te, Wang te-i, Ch'eng Yüan-min, and Hou Chün-te, eds. *Sung-jen chuan-chi tzu-liao so-yin.* 6 vols. Taipei: Ting-wen Shu-chü, 1974–1976.

YL   Chu Hsi. *Chu-tzu yü-lei.* Ed. Li Ching-te. Ch'uan ching t'ang edition, 1880; Peking: Chung-hua Shu-chü, 1986.

Wen-chi   Chu Hsi. *Hui-an hsien-sheng Chu Wen-kung wen-chi. Ssu-pu tsung-k'an* edition.

Preface

Few students of China would question the importance of Chu Hsi (1130–1200) in the Chinese cultural tradition. It was his brand of Confucianism that was taught in the public schools, in most of the private academies, in the Imperial University, and even in the imperial household. And it was his understanding of Confucianism that served as the basis of the prestigious civil service examinations. From the fourteenth century until the early decades of the twentieth century, Chu's teachings constituted a sort of orthodoxy. Indeed, to be fully literate was to be educated in the thought of Chu Hsi. Although some scholars might reject the system constructed by Chu, none could avoid reading or memorizing his works, for the entire educational structure of later imperial China was built on them. Arguably, then, even those who did take exception to the orthodoxy could not but be influenced by the ideas and values transmitted in those works on which they had spent so much of their childhood and adolescent training.

As crucial a figure as Chu Hsi might have been, as influential as his writings most definitely were, only one limited and now out-of-date volume of English translation of his works (J. P. Bruce, *The Philosophy of Human Nature, by Chu Hsi*, 1922) exists. The reason for this neglect is quite simple: no one text written by Chu succinctly and coherently presents his philosophical position. Never did he write a sustained philosophical treatise outlining for readers his system of beliefs. Rather, Chu's ideas have been left to us in interlinear commentary on the Confucian canonical texts, in essays, letters, poetry, and so forth, which survive in the *Collected Literary*

Works of Master Chu (Hui-an hsien-sheng Chu Wen-kung wen-chi) and in conversations with his disciples, written down by them, then collected together and edited in 1270 as the *Conversations of Master Chu, Arranged Topically (Chu-tzu yü-lei)*. Since no one of his commentaries on the canon presents Chu Hsi's Confucianism fully, and since the *Collected Literary Works of Master Chu* comprise 121 chapters and the *Conversations of Master Chu, Arranged Topically* 140 chapters, the translator of Chu's writings is confronted with a mass of material whose coherence and systematic underpinnings are exceedingly difficult to get at.

The problem thus becomes: How can Chu's writings be presented so that his philosophical message is accessible and intelligible to the English reader? That is to say, what organizing principles can be used in preparing a translation of Chu Hsi's works?

Chu's central concern was how man could learn to be a sage, that is, to be fully moral. All men, of course, were born with the same good nature, the same principle (*li*), but few men were able to make that nature, that moral principle, manifest in their daily lives. For just as men were born with a nature, they were also born with a physical and psychic endowment. This psychophysical endowment (*ch'i*) was different in each individual. And it was the quantity and quality of this endowment that would determine whether the individual's nature would emerge or remain obscured. But even in the worst, most evil of people, the originally good nature never disappeared, never lost its perfection; it simply was badly obscured. Thus for Chu the dilemma was how to refine and perfect one's psychophysical qualities so that one's good nature, the basis of one's humanity, would be fully realized.

It was to this dilemma that Chu gave most of his philosophical attention, developing for his disciples a systematic, step-by-step program of self-perfection. The very first step in this program, and certainly the most crucial one in Chu's mind, was "apprehending the principle in things" (*ko wu*); one had to engage in the study of things in the world out there—books, nature, history, human relationships—if one hoped to refine oneself. Since man shared moral principle with everything else in the world, study of other things and apprehension of the principle inhering in them would lead to an understanding of the same principle inhering in oneself. Study was thus the road to self-awakening, the process of returning to one's true self; for Chu Hsi its aim was never the acquisition of knowledge for its own sake.

Indeed, so important was *hsüeh*, "studying" or "learning," to Chu Hsi that the editor of the *Conversations of Master Chu, Arranged Topically* devoted a full seven chapters (7–13) to Chu's comments on the topic. In this translation volume I have taken these seven chapters on learning as the main text. Because of their length (114 double-leaf folio pages), I have translated selected passages, in the order that they appear in the chapters. In deciding which particular passages to translate, I have followed the standard abridged version of the *Conversations of Master Chu, Arranged Topically*, edited by Chang Po-hsing (1651–1725) in the early eighteenth century (*Chu-tzu yü-lei chi-lüeh*), adding passages not included in Chang's abridgment that seemed to me especially illuminating and significant.[1]

As I intended this book to present a general picture of Chu's philosophical system, many of these passages on learning are followed by annotation, both Chu's and mine. For instance, if Chu's passage on learning talks about the importance of the mind in learning or self-cultivation, I have followed it with translated passages from Chu's writings, principally the *Conversations of Master Chu*, that help to explain what Chu Hsi meant by mind and its role in his overall philosophical scheme. Or, if the passage on learning deals with the principle that students might hope to uncover in their reading of canonical texts, I have followed it with selected passages from Chu's writings on principle. My aim has been to allow Chu to speak for himself as much as possible, to let him elucidate his philosophical system in his own words. To his annotation I have added my own commentary when necessary.

So that the reader is clear about what is what, Part Two uses two distinct typefaces, one for the passages from the chapters on learning and one for Chu's and my annotations following the passages. The passages from the chapters on learning are numbered chronologically, and their location in the original text is given in paren-

1. To my knowledge, Chang Po-hsing himself never articulated his principles of selection. I have not detected any obvious prejudices in his abridgment of the chapters in question. Indeed, in general, I have found his selection from these chapters to be admirably evenhanded, that is, a fair representation of Chu Hsi's main ideas.

theses at the end of each translated passage (as is the location of Chu's comments cited in the annotation). In footnotes I give biographical information, cite textual references, and discuss some of the more technical points of translation raised by Chu's comments.

This format will enable the reader, if he so chooses, to read only the passages from the chapters on learning in the *Conversations of Master Chu*, thereby approximating the way in which a literate Chinese would have read this influential text by this influential philosopher. But the reader can also read "outward" from Chu's comments on learning to comments about the many other aspects of his thought for a more comprehensive understanding of Chu Hsi's philosophical system.

To prepare the reader for the translation, I have provided an introduction in five sections. In the first section I present a brief biography of Chu Hsi to acquaint the reader with the highlights of Chu's life. In the second I argue that Chu's interest in education grew out of his conviction that Chinese society and culture in the twelfth century were in a state of crisis; only if the proper values were transmitted in the proper way might this crisis be resolved. In the next section I summarize Chu's various efforts to improve the transmission of proper values to different levels of the Sung population. In section four I analyze in detail the program of learning Chu Hsi designed for his students: What did he mean by learning? What constituted the ideal curriculum? How should students read the texts in this curriculum? And, what was the relationship between reader and text? I close this section by outlining Chu's philosophical system, placing the issue of learning in the context of his metaphysics and program of self-cultivation. Finally, in section five I discuss in broad terms how Chu Hsi's understanding of learning compares with that of other prominent thinkers of the Sung: What was original in Chu's understanding? What did he have in common with these other thinkers? And, how did his program of learning signal a transformation in the Confucian tradition?[2]

2. Throughout this book "Confucianism" refers broadly to any teaching grounded, either directly or through received tradition, in interpretations of the Confucian Classics. "Neo-Confucianism" refers more narrowly to the metaphysically oriented Confucianism that first emerged in the Sung; it includes the school of principle (*li-hsüeh*) and the school of the mind (*hsin-hsüeh*).

Part One

Introduction

A Brief Biography of Chu Hsi

There is not a Chinese thinker since Mencius (fourth century B.C.) who is better known than Chu Hsi (1130–1200) or who has had more influence on Chinese culture—indeed on East Asian culture—than Chu Hsi.[1] Drawing on ideas raised by his predecessors, Chu developed a systematic metaphysics that dominated the Chinese intellectual world until the early years of the twentieth century. Chu also wrote commentaries on the Confucian Classics, which in the fourteenth century the Chinese government declared orthodox: from then on all candidates for the prestigious civil service examinations, in answering questions on the Classics, were required to accord with Chu Hsi's interpretation of them. And since most Chinese with any education aspired to pass the examinations, most Chinese capable of reading read and tried to master Chu's commentaries. Although some of these people no doubt remained unconvinced by Chu's interpretations of the Classics, few could escape their influence altogether. Chu Hsi has thus cast a long shadow over the literate culture of China for the last eight hundred years.

Chu was born on 18 October 1130 in Yu-ch'i County, Fukien.

---

1. The following are among the most useful scholarly studies on Chu Hsi: Chan, "Chu Hsi's Completion of Neo-Confucianism"; Chang Li-wen, *Chu Hsi ssu-hsiang yen-chiu*; Ch'ien Mu, *Chu-tzu hsin hsüeh-an*; Fan Shou-k'ang, *Chu-tzu chi ch'i che-hsüeh*; Gardner, *Chu Hsi and the Ta-hsueh*; Morohashi and Yasuoka, *Shushigaku taikei*; Schirokauer, "Chu Hsi's Political Career"; and Wang Mou-hung (1668–1741), *Chu-tzu nien-p'u*. In preparing this biography, I have consulted most of these works, particularly the *Chu-tzu nien-p'u*.

The family's native home was Wu-yüan County (in present-day Anhui), but Chu's father, Chu Sung (1097–1143), had moved the family to Yu-ch'i to assume the post of subprefectural sheriff.

Chu Hsi entered elementary school in 1134 at the age of five. In 1140 his father, forced from office because of his outspoken criticism of Prime Minister Ch'in Kuei's (1090–1155) policy of appeasement toward the Jurchen Chin, began to instruct the young Chu at home. Here, for the first time, Chu Hsi was taught the ideas of Ch'eng I (1032–1107), the Neo-Confucian master of the Northern Sung, and the relatively brief canonical texts, the *Greater Learning* (*Ta-hsüeh*) and the *Doctrine of the Mean* (*Chung-yung*), which later would become so central to his philosophical program.

When Chu Sung died in 1143, Chu Hsi, following his wishes, continued his studies with three of his father's close friends—Hu Hsien, Liu Tzu-hui, and Liu Mien-chih (whose daughter he would eventually marry). We do not know precisely what Chu studied with these men, but he would later complain that they had been fond of Buddhist teachings as well as Confucian ones, and, in fact, it was while studying under them that Chu began frequenting Taoist and Buddhist schools. According to his own comments, his fascination with Buddhist teachings continued for ten or so years, ending when he was twenty-six or twenty-seven. The degree to which his Neo-Confucian teachings may have been directly influenced by this exposure to Buddhist ideas remains problematic for scholars. But there is little doubt that the vigor with which he would later refute Buddhist teachings was affected by what he personally knew their allure to be. The man usually credited with showing Chu the errors of his Buddhistic ways and bringing him firmly into the Confucian fold is Li T'ung (1093–1163), a friend of his father who had studied under Lo Ts'ung-yen (1072–1135), a disciple of Yang Shih (1053–1135), who, in turn, had studied under Ch'eng I. Chu Hsi visited Li T'ung on four separate occasions (1153, 1158, 1160, and 1162), formally becoming his pupil in 1160.

In 1148, his commitment to Confucian teachings still not altogether firm, Chu Hsi, only nineteen years old, passed the *chin-shih* examination. That he received the degree at so young an age perhaps helps to explain his prodigious scholarly output. For Chu could devote those years that most literate Chinese spent preparing for the civil service examinations to independent scholarship. Having passed the examinations, Chu was appointed subprefectural registrar of T'ung-an in 1151, a post he took up in 1153 and held until 1156. He conscientiously supervised the local registers there, promoted education, built a library, strengthened city defenses, and reported on public morality. After leaving this post, he maintained himself in sinecures for roughly twenty years; not until 1179 did he take up another important office.

This period from 1156 to 1179 was extremely productive for Chu the scholar. He wrote and edited about twenty works and, at the same time, developed close associations with the most prominent scholars and philosophers of the day. With Lü Tsu-ch'ien (1137–1181), a devoted friend, he compiled *Reflections on Things at Hand* (*Chin-ssu lu*) (1175), which would later become the primer of Neo-Confucian teachings. He carried on an extended exchange, in letter and in person, with Chang Shih (1133–1180) and Lu Chiu-yüan (1139–1193), largely over aspects of the self-cultivation process: with Chang he discussed the meaning of equilibrium and harmony (*chung-ho*) of the mind (first described in the *Doctrine of the Mean*) and how such states could be attained, and with Lu he debated, most famously at the Goose Lake Temple (1175), the relative importance in the self-cultivation process of "following the path of inquiry and study" (*tao wen-hsüeh*) and "honoring the moral nature" (*tsun te-hsing*). Chu and Lu would never reconcile their philosophical differences, Chu insisting that inquiry and study were essential in guiding the mind to moral rectification, and Lu that the mind is moral of itself and in little need of external guidance. The consequences of these differences were profound: Neo-Confucianism would later split into what has conventionally been characterized as Chu Hsi's school of principle (*li-hsüeh*) and Lu Chiu-yüan's school of the mind (*hsin-hsüeh*).

In 1179, Chu became the prefect of Nan-k'ang (in present-day Chiang-hsi). There his commitment to education continued, evidenced best by his efforts to revive the White Deer Hollow Academy. The "Articles of Learning" (*hsüeh-kuei*) he compiled for the academy reflect his zealous devotion to learning for the sake of moral improvement, not for the sake of worldly success. These "Articles of Learning" were to be extremely influential, serving as a model for academies throughout much of East Asia down through the present century.

The well-known invitation Chu extended to Lu Chiu-yüan to lecture at the White Deer Hollow Academy in the spring of 1181 points up Chu's interest in making the academy a place of serious intellectual reflection for students—after all, Lu was an outspoken philosophic rival of Chu's. In fact, so pleased was Chu in the end with Lu's lecture, which treated the distinction between righteousness and profit, that he asked Lu to write it down and later had it inscribed on stone.

Chu Hsi's term at Nan-k'ang expired in 1181. In 1182 he assumed the duties of intendant for ever-normal granaries, tea, and salt for Eastern Liang-che (present Chekiang), an area suffering from famine. To alleviate the suffering, he instituted the community granary (*she-ts'ang*), the purpose of which was to provide grain loans to peasants at low rates of interest. Unlike Wang An-shih's (1021–1086) more famous "green sprouts" program, the community granary system lent the peasantry grain, not money, and was to be managed voluntarily by prominent men on the village level, not by the state. It is difficult to know what success Chu might have had with the community granary system, for he had but brief opportunity to implement it. In 1182, having indicted T'ang Chung-yu (ca. 1131–1183), the prefect of T'ai-chou and a relative of the prime minister, for misconduct in office, he found himself an enemy of some of the most powerful men in the empire. Not only Chu but the entire school of thought with which he was associated, called Tao-hsüeh ("Learning of the Way") by contemporaries, now came under attack by high-ranking supporters of T'ang. Shortly thereafter Chu Hsi withdrew from office.

Chu would later hold, albeit briefly, two other important posts, serving as prefect of Chang-chou (Fukien) in 1190–1191 and prefect of T'an-chou (in present-day Hunan) in 1194. In late 1194 he was invited to become lecturer-in-waiting at court, where he lectured to Emperor Ning-tsung on the short Classic, the *Greater Learning*. This lectureship lasted a mere forty-six days, for Chu became embroiled in a conflict with the influential imperial relative Han T'o-chou (1151–1207) and returned to Fukien. The attack on Tao-hsüeh, as a result, now intensified. In 1195 political adversaries equated it with Wei-hsüeh, "false learning," and a year later the emperor himself proscribed the teachings of the school.

During his lifetime, Chu Hsi declined many more offices than he accepted; he served in public office for only nine or so years, much of the rest of the time holding temple guardianships. Chu's apparent unwillingness to serve has been called the defensive reaction of an insecure person.[2] More likely, it was the considered reaction of a person who in his childhood had witnessed his father's abrupt and painful dismissal from office over a policy difference with a powerful statesman. Perhaps, too, Chu simply wished to avoid what he viewed as the corrupt and unethical politics of the day; to serve when the Way did not prevail might have compromised his moral purity. Moreover, Chu may have also calculated that he simply would be of better use to society transmitting the Way to others in classrooms and writings than in holding government office. In any case, by avoiding office Chu Hsi was no doubt able to devote a great deal more time to teaching and writing.

This, of course, is not to suggest that Chu had little interest in the political order. For not only did he acquit himself with distinction in the offices he did hold but he also submitted sealed memorials to the throne (in 1162, 1180, and 1188) and even went to the capital for personal audiences with the emperor (in 1163, 1181, and 1188). Certain themes ran through these memorials and personal audiences: the emperor, Chu argued, must rectify his mind and only then might the empire become tranquil; the military must be made strong so that the central plain, the traditional heartland of Chinese civilization, might be recovered from the Chin (1115–1234), who had settled there in the early twelfth century; and the emperor must establish sound personnel policies, selecting only worthy and talented men for government service. Finally, we should not forget that although Chu may have spent much of his life developing and teaching a highly elaborate program for the self-cultivation of the individual, his assumption and hope were that the moral cultivation of the individual would lead to social and political harmony.

Still, teaching and writing were clearly dearest to Chu. Throughout his life he exhibited an almost missionary zeal to pass the Confucian Way on to others. The numerous years he spent discussing Confucian teachings with students, the record of which is found in the *Conversations of Master Chu, Arranged Topically*, attest strongly to

2. Schirokauer, "Chu Hsi's Political Career," p. 188.

his commitment to transmitting the Way; so too do his voluminous writings, particularly his many commentaries on the Confucian Classics, which he hoped would help to illuminate the Way embodied in the sacred canon.

Of all his writings perhaps the most significant and influential were the commentaries on the Four Books—the *Greater Learning*, the *Analects* (*Lun-yü*), the *Book of Mencius* (*Meng-tzu*), and the *Doctrine of the Mean*—known collectively as the *Collected Commentaries on the Four Books* (*Ssu-shu chi-chu*).[3] Convinced that the kernels of Confucian teachings were to be found in these four works, Chu spent much of his adult life reflecting on their philosophical significance and preparing commentaries for them. As a result of the great weight he gave them, a major shift in the Confucian tradition occurred: from Chu's time until the early twentieth century the Four Books would be the essential texts in the Confucian curriculum, replacing the long-authoritative Five Classics—the *Book of Changes* (*I ching*), the *Book of Poetry* (*Shih ching*), the *Book of History* (*Shu ching*), the *Book of Rites* (*Li chi*), and the *Spring and Autumn Annals* (*Ch'un-ch'iu*). It was the Four Books, together with Chu Hsi's commentaries, that would serve as the basis of the civil service examinations.

Indeed, one of Chu Hsi's most widely recognized achievements, the elaboration of a systematic metaphysics, derived largely from his reading of the Four Books. This reading, in turn, was influenced by ideas advanced by the great Neo-Confucian thinkers of the Northern Sung, men such as Chou Tun-i (1017–1073), Chang Tsai (1020–1077), Ch'eng Hao (1032–1085), and particularly Ch'eng I. The metaphysical synthesis worked out by Chu represented a new

3. Among the many books Chu Hsi wrote, edited, or annotated, in addition to those mentioned in this brief biography, were *The Surviving Works of Messrs. Ch'eng of Honan* (*Ho-nan Ch'eng-shih i-shu*), *An Outline for the Comprehensive Mirror for Aid in Government* (*Tzu-chih t'ung-chien kang-mu*), *An Explanation of the Western Inscription* (*Hsi-ming chieh-i*), *An Explanation of [Chou Tun-i's] Explanation of the Diagram of the Great Ultimate* (*T'ai-chi t'u-shuo chieh*), *Records of the Origins of the School of the Two Ch'engs* (*I-lo yüan-yüan lu*), *Collected Commentaries on the Book of Poetry* (*Shih chi-chuan*), *Original Meanings of the Book of Changes* (*Chou-i pen-i*), *Lesser Learning* (*Hsiao-hsüeh*), *Collected Commentaries on the Elegies of Ch'u* (*Ch'u-tz'u chi-chu*), *A Commentary on the Chou-i ts'an-t'ung-ch'i* (*Chou-i ts'an-t'ung-ch'i k'ao-i*), and *Collected Commentaries on the Book of History* (*Shu chi-chuan*). His numerous essays, letters, prefaces, postscripts, tomb inscriptions, and other literary documents were collected together in the *Collected Literary Works of Master Chu*.

development in Confucian philosophy: it was an attempt to give the traditional aim of Confucian teachings—the moral cultivation of the individual—an ontological foundation. Man could become perfectly moral because the nature with which he was born was itself always moral; his endowment of psychophysical stuff, however, had the capacity—if it was turbid, dense, or impure enough—to obscure the moral nature, and thus it had to be refined if the moral nature was to become manifest. Chu Hsi's program of learning, at the heart of which lay the concept of *ko wu*, "apprehending the principle in things," was intended by Chu to be the means by which man would refine himself and connect with his originally moral nature.

Chu Hsi would continue to polish his commentaries on the Classics and elaborate his philosophical system until his death on 23 April 1200. Nine years later, after Han T'o-chou had passed from the scene and the attacks on Tao-hsüeh had run their course, Chu was honored with the posthumous title Wen. In 1230 he was given the title state duke of Hui; and in 1241 his tablet was placed in the Confucian temple. In the early fourteenth century Chu Hsi's thought was declared state orthodoxy and remained so until the early years of the twentieth century.

Chu Hsi and the Crisis of the Way in the Twelfth Century

Chu Hsi was not happy with the state of affairs in the China of his time. Although to the casual observer of some eight centuries later China of the Southern Sung period seems culturally sophisticated and materially prosperous, to Chu Hsi the problems of the day seemed quite profound. Indeed, to Chu's mind China faced something of a crisis.

Since the beginning of the Sung, foreigners had occupied territory traditionally belonging to the Chinese. First, in the mid-tenth century the Khitan tribespeople from Mongolia extended their control over sixteen northern prefectures centered around Peking. In the early years of the twelfth century the Jurchen tribes of Manchuria in turn extinguished Khitan power; but not content with the northern prefectures of the Khitan alone, Jurchen forces continued south, subjugating all of North China. Henceforth, from 1125 until the fall of the dynasty, Sung control over China was limited to the area south of the Huai River. Chu, along with other officials and literati of the Southern Sung, expressed displeasure with this occupation of the north and, even more, with the government's decision in 1141–1142 to sue for peace with the Jurchen rather than to fight for repossession of land that was rightfully Chinese.[1]

The occupation of the north clearly represented a political and

---

1. For Chu's views on the Sung restoration of North China see Tillman, *Utilitarian Confucianism*, pp. 169–171.

territorial threat to the Chinese people. But for some, like Chu Hsi, it represented a cultural and moral threat as well. The Confucian assumption that when the true Way prevailed in China those who came into contact with it would feel a great sense of awe and happily submit to it was one that Chu fully shared. That the Jurchen had not submitted to the Chinese but had in fact overrun them, establishing their own Chin dynasty (1115–1234) in the north, demonstrated that the great Way, the Way that set the Chinese apart from (and above) all other people, had all but disappeared in the Central Plain, the heartland of Chinese civilization. The question posed for Chu by the "barbarian" subjugation of the north, then, was not simply how to strengthen China's military forces—though this was a concern of his—but how to reinvigorate a weakened cultural and moral tradition.

If the Way was in decline, surely the emperor and the ruling elite bore much of the responsibility. And Chu was not shy about pointing a finger at them. In memorials and letters to acquaintances he berated emperors and the bureaucracy for their moral turpitude; his refusals to accept official appointment were often cast in the form of a protest against a corrupt and immoral government.[2] Chu's own involvement in the factional disputes of the late twelfth century and the official condemnation of his learning as "false learning" in the 1190s did nothing to disabuse him of his low opinion of the ruling order of the day. But as severe as Chu may have found the ills of government to be, the cure for them, he was convinced, remained simple: the ruler merely had to rectify himself. Once the ruler became rectified, his majestic example was sure to inspire those around him to become rectified; and with a ripple-like certainty moral example would exert its power from one person to the next, until the entire realm achieved moral perfection. And thus the great Way would again prevail.[3]

The popularity of Buddhist teachings was also for Chu evidence that the times were out of joint. The Confucian Way, which to him was synonymous with the Chinese cultural tradition (or at least

2. See Schirokauer, "Chu Hsi's Political Career," particularly pp. 177–179, 186.

3. See, for example, Chu's memorial in *Hui-an hsien-sheng Chu Wen-kung wen-chi* (hereafter *Wen-chi*) 11.18b–40b, discussed in Schirokauer, "Chu Hsi's Political Career," pp. 177–179.

with the best parts of it), was losing ground to Buddhism, particularly the Ch'an school. Chu Hsi knew that Ch'an teachings were
seductive, because he himself had engaged in a study of them for
more than ten years, beginning at age fifteen or sixteen.[4] Indeed,
his writings and conversations with disciples evince a rather deep
fear of Buddhism's allure for the people of his time: "Be they adults
or children, officials, farmers, or merchants, men or women, all enter the Buddhist gates."[5] He once remarked that although families
might have the wherewithal to resist Buddhist teachings for a generation or two, after the third generation they were sure to be
"turned around by them."[6] What particularly worried Chu Hsi
was the appeal Buddhist teachings seemed to have to the intel-
ligentsia.[7] It was these men he counted on to keep the Confucian
Way alive and well. If they surrendered to the foreign creed, whom
could he depend on? "In the world there are but a few great men,
and they've all been drawn into Buddhism—how detrimental!"[8] So
attractive was Buddhism that even disciples of the great Ch'eng
brothers, Chu's spiritual heroes, had turned to it.[9] For Chu this was
strong proof of the power of Buddhist teachings and cause for deep
concern over the survival of the Confucian Way.

In Chu's view, then, the "barbarian" occupation, the ineptitude
in government, and the widespread popularity of Buddhist
teachings all reflected a serious spiritual and moral malaise. Chu
devoted his life to the cure of this malaise, or as he might have put

---

4. E.g., *Chu-tzu yü-lei* (hereafter *YL*) 104.9b–10a/vol. 7, p. 2620. Throughout
the footnotes, references to *YL* are to *chüan* and folio numbers of the Ch'uan ching
t'ang edition and to volume and page numbers of the Chung-hua Shu-chü edition.
I give references to both because even though I find the Ch'uan ching t'ang edition
the best available and base my reading of the text on it the Chung-hua Shu-chü
version is now the most readily available.

5. *YL* 126.30b/vol. 8, p. 3037. The Ch'eng brothers had also been greatly dis-
turbed by the allure of Buddhism; see Kasoff, *Thought of Chang Tsai*, p. 15. Hymes,
Statesmen and Gentlemen, pp. 177–199, discusses the pervasiveness of Buddhism in
Chinese society during the Southern Sung.

6. *YL* 126.34a/vol. 8, p. 3041.

7. See, for example, comments in *YL* 126.29b–30a/vol. 8, pp. 3036–3037,
24.20b/vol. 2, p. 587, and 126.24b/vol. 8, pp. 3030–3031.

8. *YL* 132.20a/vol. 8, p. 3183.

9. *YL* 24.20b/vol. 2, p. 587 and 126.30a/vol. 8, p. 3037; see also *YL*, *chüan* 101,
passim, and Ch'ien Mu, *Chu-tzu hsin hsüeh-an*, vol. 3, pp. 160–197, passim.

it, to the resuscitation of the great Chinese Way. Learning—defining it and transmitting it—was at the heart of Chu Hsi's life-long mission. Serving in official positions would never have the same urgency for him, for in his mind China's well-being depended ultimately on the sort of learning pursued by the people of the day: the right sort would lead to a revitalized China in which the true Way prevailed, the wrong sort to the continued decline of Chinese politics and society and the demise of the Way.

The learning going on around him clearly was not the right sort. Muh of Chu's writings and recorded conversations with disciples read as harsh indictments of the contemporary learning pursued by Confucians. To him their learning was nothing like that promoted by the great sages of the past. According to Chu, the sages had taken as the one express aim of their learning "to understand moral principle clearly in order that they might cultivate their persons, thereafter extending [their perfection] to others." But contemporary students of the Way seemed to abandon this aim completely as they scrambled to achieve far less noble goals—reputation for profound thinking, literary renown, or even wealth and rank.[10]

Inspired by a remark made by Confucius in the *Analects*, Chu drew a distinction between two antithetical kinds of learning: learning done for one's own sake or moral betterment (*wei-chi chih hsüeh*) and learning done for the sake of others (*wei-jen chih hsüeh*), with a view toward impressing others and winning their acclaim.[11] He wanted students to become sensitive to the vast differences between them:

The important thing for students today is to distinguish between the paths. What's important is the boundary between "doing it for one's own sake" and "doing it for the sake of others." "To do it for one's own sake" is to grasp the essence of things and affairs firsthand in reaching an understanding of them—you want to understand them for yourself. It isn't to understand them recklessly, nor is it to understand them in a way that makes you look good, so that people will say yes, you have indeed understood; if this is how you were to go about it, even supposing you did under-

10. Chu makes this argument in *Wen-chi* 74.18b.
11. In *Lun-yü* 14/24, it is recorded: "The Master said: 'In antiquity men studied for their own sake; nowadays men study for the sake of others.'" See de Bary's discussion in *Liberal Tradition*, pp. 21–24.

stand them 100 percent accurately, they'd still have no effect on you at all. (2.49)[12]

Learning then had to affect the student to have any merit. If it had only a cosmetic value, beautifying the wearer in the eyes of beholders but not changing the inner self in any way, it was not the learning pursued by men of antiquity—it was not true learning.

To Chu Hsi's great dismay it was "learning for the sake of others" that had become prevalent in the world of learning in twelfth-century China. First, literati had become intent on cultivating a reputation for "loftiness" and "ingenuity" and made little effort to reach true understanding. The effect this trend had on the reading of the Classics was particularly troubling to Chu:

> Those who discuss the Classics these days are usually guilty of one of four vices: raising up what's originally lowly so that it becomes lofty; reading meaning into what's originally shallow so that it becomes profound; pushing away what's originally near at hand so that it becomes remote; and invariably making what's originally clear obscure. These are the great evils plaguing current discussions of the Classics. (5.61)

Thus Chu routinely admonished his own students and friends not to be seduced into "abstruse and profound"[13] explanations of things, for "not only will others not understand you, but you yourself won't understand either."[14] Students too prone to the abstract and lofty risked an even greater danger, that of "swerving from the right path and entering into heterodoxy."[15] This, Chu said, is precisely what had happened to Hsieh Liang-tso (1050–1103), one of the Ch'eng brothers' outstanding disciples.[16]

An equally pernicious practice from Chu's point of view was the too great emphasis students had come to place on literary expres-

---

12. References to passages that appear in the translation of *YL* in Part Two are given in parentheses. Reference is to the Part Two chapter and passage numbers (not to the *YL* chapter numbers). References to passages from *YL* not translated in Part Two are placed in footnotes.

13. *Wen-chi* 56.1a.

14. *Wen-chi* 39.22b; cf. *YL* 8.3a/vol. 1, p. 131 (2.14). Chu even leveled criticism at his good friend Chang Shih and the Hunan school for their tendency to speak much too abstractly; see Ch'ien Mu, *Chu-tzu hsin hsüeh-an*, vol. 3, pp. 244–247.

15. *Wen-chi* 39.10a–11a.

16. See *YL* 101.12a/vol. 7, p. 2567. Despite Chu's charge, Hsieh has long been regarded as one of the Four Masters of the Ch'eng school.

sion. Although Chu Hsi was certainly capable of admiring a refined literary style, he was deeply concerned by what he saw as the contemporary obsession with belles lettres at the expense of content. Ambitious to write well—or at least to be thought good writers— the people of his day were given to the "novel," "unusual," and "lofty" in expressing themselves; they did not particularly care about what they wrote, nor were they at all interested that what they write accord with the true meaning of the Classics.[17] From an early age students were encouraged in this tendency, to the point, Chu feared, that they were in danger of neglecting their moral character: "Nowadays, beginning in their early youth, people are taught to compose couplets. As they get somewhat older, they are taught to compose showy prose. Both [these practices] spoil their originally good natures" (1.9).[18] There was even a type of belletrist, Chu remarked, who never bothered to read the Confucian Classics at all.[19] The purpose of writing, thus, was not what it had been; no longer was it to make manifest the Way and its subtleties but rather to flaunt one's skills and to gain social acceptance as a cultivated person, a man of breeding: "In recent times those who write or do calligraphy and painting struggle to produce the novel and unusual in order to please the censors of social customs."[20]

Chu thought much of the blame for this literary overaestheticism was to be placed at the feet of Su Shih (1036–1101). Su, along with Han Yü (768–824), Ou-yang Hsiu (1007–1072), and others, had been almost solely concerned with literary style and only occasionally happened to touch on moral principle.[21] In short, Su had made the grave, and to Chu unforgivable, error of separating writing from the Way:

The Way is the root and trunk of *wen* [literary writing]. *Wen* is the branches and leaves of the Way. Only if it [*wen*] has its root and trunk in the Way will whatever is expressed in *wen* be the Way. The writings of the sages and worthies of the Three Dynasties were all done with this convic-

17. *Wen-chi* 37.20a and *YL* 139.19b/vol. 8, p. 3316, 139.21a/vol. 8, p. 3318, and 139.23b/vol. 8, p. 3320.
18. Although Chu here is quoting Lu Tzu-shou, he clearly shares Lu's sentiments.
19. *YL* 139.8a/vol. 8, p. 3304.
20. *Wen-chi* 81.26a.
21. *YL* 137.25b/vol. 8, p. 3276.

tion, and thus their *wen* was one with the Way. Now, [Su] Tung-p'o has said, "What I call *wen* must go together with the Way." This is to take *wen* as *wen* and the Way as the Way and to wait until composing *wen* to look for a Way to put into it. This is the great flaw in [Su's] writing. . . . He does not first reach an understanding of moral principle and then compose *wen*.[22]

And unfortunately, according to Chu, Su strongly influenced literati of the Southern Sung, encouraging "a tendency toward the crafty and illusory."[23]

Striving after a refined literary style, then, was yet another way of learning for the sake of others rather than for one's own moral betterment: "To practice a thoroughly studied, ornate style in the hopes of pleasing others is for a purpose other than one's own—it's shameful."[24] It was also a great waste of time and energy,[25] for if students were to turn their attention first to "learning in order to understand principle, as a matter of course they would produce good writing."[26] That is, good writing would flow spontaneously from a sound understanding of principle.[27]

Still, for Chu Hsi the gravest contemporary threat to true learning was, ironically, posed by the Confucian-based civil service examinations. The prospects for worldly success that they offered

22. *YL* 139.22a–b/vol. 8, p. 3319; cf. the translation in Lynn, "Chu Hsi as Literary Theorist," p. 338.

23. *Wen-chi* 37.20b. He also remarked (*YL* 139.12b/vol. 8, p. 3309): "Since the literary writing of the Three Su's appeared, students on the first day rush toward the artful." It should be noted, however, that Chu's criticism of Su was occasionally tempered by praise for his literary talent; see, for example, *YL* 139.12b/vol. 8, p. 3309 and 130.19a/vol. 8, p. 3113. On Chu's views of Su Shih see Gōyama, "Shu Ki no Sogaku hihan, josetsu"; Chang Chien, *Chu Hsi te wen-hsüeh p'i-p'ing yen-chiu*, pp. 8–12, 97–100; Bol, "Literati Learning," pp. 177–183; Lynn, "Chu Hsi as Literary Theorist," pp. 337–341; and below, Part One, "Chu Hsi and the Transformation of the Confucian Tradition."

24. *YL* 139.22a/vol. 8, p. 3319. Elsewhere (*YL* 11.6b/vol. 1, p. 182 [5.27]) Chu rather cynically observed: "Once [people] pass the examinations, they read for the sake of [learning to] compose miscellaneous prose. As for the eminent among them, they read for the sake of [learning to] compose ancient-style prose. In [both] these instances they're reading not for themselves but for other reasons."

25. *YL* 139.10a/vol. 8, pp. 3306–3307.

26. *YL* 139.10a/vol. 8, p. 3307.

27. *YL* 139.22b/vol. 8, p. 3320. For general discussions of Chu's literary theory and criticism see Chang Chien, *Chu Hsi te wen-hsüeh p'i-p'ing yen-chiu*, and Lynn, "Chu Hsi as Literary Theorist."

diverted students from the real aim of learning;[28] after all, the rewards for success in them could be immense—prestige, official status, authority and power, and substantial wealth. Students thus easily became preoccupied with studying to pass them, and "learning for one's own sake" all but disappeared. Chu complained: "In learning, we have to read for ourselves, so that the understanding we reach is personally meaningful. Nowadays, however, people read simply for the sake of the civil service examinations" (5.27; cf. 7.68). Elsewhere, he put his criticism more sharply: "Today [students] covet wealth and office, not the Way and righteousness. They want to become men of high position, not good men."[29] In fact, Chu's sense here that his contemporaries found the examinations especially appealing is borne out by recent historical research. During the twelfth and thirteenth centuries, competition in the civil service examinations seems to have increased dramatically; it is estimated, for example, that two hundred thousand candidates took the prefectural examinations in the late twelfth century, though the chances of succeeding were a slim one out of a hundred.[30] And as the competition increased, so naturally did the candidates' efforts at preparing for the examinations.

28. Chu was by no means the only Sung thinker to be critical of the effects of the examination system on learning. For instance, Ch'eng I earlier had expressed his displeasure with those who in pursuit of examination success lost sight of true learning. See, for example, the comments in Chan, *Reflections*, p. 199, and idem, *Source Book*, p. 551. Yeh Shih (1150–1223), a philosophical opponent of the Ch'eng-Chu school, was equally if not more disturbed by the effects that the examinations seemed to have on learning. In *Shui-hsin hsien-sheng wen-chi* 3.14a, he wrote rather sharply:

A harmful corollary of using the examination to select governmental personnel is to convert all scholars to aspirants of governmental positions. A healthy society cannot come about when people study not for the purpose of gaining wisdom and knowledge but for the purpose of becoming government officials. . . . Nowadays . . . beginning with childhood, all of a man's study is centered on one aim alone: to emerge successfully from the three days' examinations, and all he has in his mind is what success can bring to him in terms of power, influence, and prestige.

This translation is from Li, *Essence of Chinese Civilization*, p. 167; this passage is partially cited in Chaffee, *Thorny Gates*, p. 88. For a general discussion of literati reaction to the examinations see Nivison, "Protest against Conventions."

29. *Wen-chi* 74.25a.

30. See Chaffee, "Education and Examinations," pp. 55–61, and idem, *Thorny Gates*, pp. 35–41.

Literati, then, at least as Chu Hsi saw them, were engaged in an almost single-minded pursuit of success in the examinations. This pursuit tended to aggravate the flaws in learning already mentioned—the striving for profundity and the quest for literary reputation. In preparing for the examinations, students cared little about apprehending the true meaning of the Confucian Classics; rather, in order to attract the attention of the examiners, they strained to discover "novel and unusual" interpretations of them.[31] And even more important to them than the canon of sacred texts itself was the examination-style essay, the form in which they were supposed to write their answers. Chu complained, perhaps with some exaggeration, that students spent more time learning to master it, in order to impress the examiners—the arbiters of style—than they did studying the sage words in the Classics (6.31; cf. 7.55). This sort of "examination learning" was precisely what Chu meant by "learning for the sake of others," and it certainly was a far cry from the "learning for one's own sake" advocated by Confucius.

This is not to say, however, that Chu Hsi condemned the examinations as a method of official recruitment. He regarded them, in fact, as a reasonable means of bringing talented and moral men into government service and acknowledged that students could legitimately devote some of their attention to studying for them. He even wrote an essay that, although criticizing contemporary examination standards and practices, also proposed, as a way of strengthening the examination system, an ideal curriculum for examinees.[32] To Chu's mind the real problem was simply that stu-

31. *YL* (Chung-hua shu-chü edition), vol. 7, pp. 2693–2694. (From *chüan* 109, which is missing from the Ch'uan ching t'ang edition available to me.) This passage is cited in Chang Li-wen, *Chu Hsi ssu-hsiang yen-chiu*, p. 638. Cf. *YL* 10.14a/vol. 1, p. 175 (4.53) and 11.15a/vol. 1, p. 191 (5.48).

32. "Hsüeh-hsiao kung-chü ssu-i" in *Wen-chi* 69.20a–28b. The curriculum that Chu proposed in this essay contained a wide range of texts, including not only the Classics but also commentaries on them by a variety of scholars representing different schools of interpretation, historical writings such as the *Tzu-chih t'ung-chien* by Ssu-ma Kuang (1019–1086), and the philosophical works of the Taoists and Legalists. For a brief summary of this essay and a description of the contents of Chu's proposed curriculum, see de Bary, *Liberal Tradition*, pp. 40–42, and Nivison, "Protest against Conventions," pp. 189–190.

dents gave the examinations too much attention; anxious to get ahead, they compromised true Confucian learning.[33] Chu advised:

Scholars must first distinguish between the examinations and studying— which is less important, which is more important. If 70 percent of their determination is given to study and 30 percent to the examinations, that'll be fine. But if 70 percent is given to the examinations and 30 percent to study, they're sure to be overcome by the 70 percent—how much more if their determination is completely given to the examinations! (7.54)

Chu saw no reason, then, why students could not engage in true learning and examination preparation at the same time. One did not preclude the other. In fact, on occasion Chu Hsi suggested that when done in the proper spirit true learning and examination preparation were one and the same:

It isn't that the examinations are a trouble to men, it's that men become troubled by the examinations. A scholar of superior understanding reads the texts of the sages and worthies and on the basis of his understanding of them writes the essays required in the examinations. He places aside considerations of success and failure, gain and loss, so even if he were to compete in the examinations every day he wouldn't be troubled by them. If Confucius were born again in today's world, he wouldn't avoid competing in the examinations, and yet they wouldn't trouble him in the least. (7.64)

Unfortunately, what commonly seemed to happen, in Chu's view, was that students lost the will to pursue true learning as they got caught up in the pursuit of examination success. It was this will that had to be preserved in the face of preparing for the examinations:

Someone asked whether preparing for the examinations interferes with one's efforts at true learning. Chu said: Master Ch'eng has said that one shouldn't fear that it will interfere with one's efforts at true learning but only that it will rob one of one's will to learn. If one spends ten days of every month preparing for the exams, one still has twenty days to cultivate true learning. But if one's will to learn is shaken by the preparation for the exams, then indeed there's no cure.[34] (7.61; cf. 7.65 and 7.63)

33. This point has been made by Chaffee, "Revival of the White Deer Grotto Academy," p. 15.
34. Ch'eng I's comment can be found in Ch'eng Hao's and his *Ho-nan Ch'eng-shih wai-shu* 11.5a; it is translated in Chan, *Reflections*, p. 199.

In the end, then, Chu was not advising students not to participate
in the examinations; never did he discourage students from taking
the examinations or doing the necessary preparation for them.
He was simply warning them not to neglect true learning as they
worked toward the examinations.[35]

Chu Hsi placed at least some of the responsibility for the
"examination mentality" of Sung students on the government-
sponsored local schools. The spread of government schools in prefectures and counties had begun in the late tenth and early eleventh
centuries, picked up momentum in the eleventh and twelfth centuries, and continued apace through the Southern Sung period.[36]
Taking as their mission the training of future officials, local schools
generally offered a curriculum designed to prepare students to pass
the civil service examinations.[37] And thus they only added to the
great pressure most students no doubt already felt to concentrate
their efforts on examination learning. To Chu this state of affairs
was especially reprehensible. It was the job of schools to teach the
true Confucian Way, not the way to succeed in the examinations;
moreover, by focusing on examination learning, schools engendered an unhealthy competitiveness. Discouraged by the sort of
education he found in these local government schools,[38] Chu Hsi
would give a great deal of his thought and time to education in
private academies.[39]

Most students of the Sung, then, were not engaged in true learning. And Chu was concerned that, in the end, the few who were

35. Chu on occasion poked fun at those around him who made much of their
decision not to participate in the exams: "Not sitting for the examinations is a
small matter. But these days when people say they aren't going to sit for the
examinations, they regard it as some fantastic achievement" (*YL* 13.23a–b/vol. 1,
p. 245 [7.60]; cf. *YL* 13.24a/vol. 1, p. 246 [7.63]).

36. For a discussion of state schools in the Sung, see Chaffee, *Thorny Gates*,
pp. 73–88.

37. Under the Three Hall System (*san-she fa*), implemented at the turn of the
twelfth century, schools had the dual responsibility of educating students and
selecting *chin-shih* from among them. When the Three Hall System was abolished
in 1121, the schools no longer had a formal connection with the civil service
system, but they continued to serve as centers for examination preparation. See
Chaffee, *Thorny Gates*, pp. 77–88; see also Lee, *Government Education*, pp. 107–112.

38. See, for a good example, *Wen-chi* 79.23a–b; Bol, "Literati Learning,"
pp. 8–12, discusses Chu's views of schools.

39. See Terada, *Sōdai kyōikushi gaisetsu*, pp. 269–271, and below, Part One,
"Restoring the Way: Chu Hsi's Educational Activities."

might not be prepared to make the effort necessary to master the Way. The Buddhists, to his mind, had created an atmosphere in which almost all students of the day had come to believe that learning was easier than it actually was, that there were timesaving shortcuts to true understanding. Even Confucians had come to find the "laborsaving" methods of Buddhist learning appealing; in fact, according to Chu, it was precisely because the learning process in Buddhism was so much less arduous that Buddhism had become so popular.[40] Chu ridiculed the Buddhists' naive approach to learning, making clear to his students how ineffectual and misguided he thought it was: "In their method, before anything else, they place a large ban on reading books and probing principle. They forever want their students to fix their minds on some unclear, unknown place and one day, by chance, suddenly to become enlightened."[41] Chu believed there simply were no shortcuts to true understanding. Rather, learning was a long, rigorous process, which, if done in the proper spirit, following the proper sequence, might in time result in a total understanding of the one true principle underlying the universe. He pleaded with students not to be hasty, not to expect understanding to come without effort: "In studying the teachings of the Sage, there's an orderly sequence to be followed. You shouldn't look for enlightenment at the very beginning."[42] Chu was trying to counter the expectations he feared Buddhist teachings had created in men of the Sung.

Finally, as he surveyed the landscape of late twelfth-century learning, Chu Hsi became troubled by what he perceived to be the insidious effects of the printing revolution on learning. Printing with woodblocks had been invented sometime before or during the eighth century by the Buddhists; in the tenth century the government had used the technique to produce standard, orthodox editions of the Confucian canon. During the early Sung, the revolution in printing gained momentum, until by the twelfth century printing technology had spread throughout the country: the government, temples, county and prefectural schools, and large-scale commercial printers and publishers were all printing books in their own shops. The printed book was now available just about every-

---

40. *YL* 126.29b/vol. 8, p. 3036; cf. 126.30a/vol. 8, p. 3036.
41. *Wen-chi* 60.5b; cf. *Wen-chi* 46.3b and *YL* 14.11b/vol. 1, p. 260.
42. *Wen-chi* 53.2b.

where.[43] In fact, Chu himself seems to have been involved in the printing business as a sideline.[44]

Printing on such a scale no doubt made books far more economical and thus accessible to a larger number of people; and it may well have abetted a rise in literacy. Chu, however, seemed to be at least as worried as he was pleased about the consequences of this printing revolution. Books, ironically, had become almost too readily available. Students no longer had to commit texts to memory since they now had easy access to them. Their reading, thus, had become far less disciplined and penetrating. Chu commented: "Because nowadays the number of printed texts is large, people don't put their minds to reading them. As for the Confucians of the Han period [206 B.C.–A.D. 220], in instructing one another in the Classics, they just recited them from memory. Hence, they remembered them well" (4.42). Chu often compared reading by contemporary students with that of their less technologically advanced predecessors:

The reason people today read sloppily is that there are a great many printed texts. . . . It would seem that the ancients had no written texts, so only if they had memorized a work from beginning to end would they get it. Those studying a text would memorize it completely and afterward receive instruction on it from a teacher. . . . For people today even copying down a text has become bothersome. Therefore, their reading is sloppy. (4.43)

Because of the availability of the printed book, people had become lazy; they had stopped reading as they should. Perhaps such laziness derived from more than just the convenience the availability of books afforded them; it may be that confronted with all the books now circulating people felt overwhelmed and simply gave up—the burden of culture had grown too great. In any case, Chu was deeply dismayed by the sloppy reading habits of his contemporaries and expressed the hope that they would learn to approach the great texts in the cultural tradition in the same conscientious manner as had the ancients.

43. This brief summary is based upon Twitchett, *Printing and Publishing*; Carter, *Invention of Printing*, pp. 23–81; and Goodrich, "Development of Printing."
44. Ch'en Jung-chieh, *Chu-hsüeh lun-chi*, pp. 220–222, and Chan, "Chu Hsi and the Academies," p. 412.

Restoring the Way:
Chu Hsi's Educational Activities

In Chu Hsi's eyes, then, the Way was in decline, and customs had degenerated. The learning of the day not only had not helped solve the problems confronting society but had itself become a problem. And yet, discouraged as he was about the state of learning he found around him, Chu never lost faith that it was through education that the Way ultimately would be revived and customs reformed.

This faith in the reformative powers of education rested on a rather comprehensive understanding of what education entailed. For Chu education meant not just formal schooling or book learning but also the transmission and absorption of cultural values, customs, and modes of proper behavior. Correct learning, then, could make the individual student morally perfect, but beyond that it could transform the society as a whole, making it less vulnerable to outside attack, either from "barbarian" peoples or "heterodox" religions. To have this effect, education—in this broad conception—had to be available to all social statuses, and although Chu Hsi's main interest may have been with the education of the relatively small group of his philosophical followers, he by no means ignored the education of other members of society. Education, in Chu's hands, took different forms to suit what he believed to be the needs and concerns of different audiences in a variety of different social and intellectual contexts.

One of his most influential educational efforts was the compilation of the *Family Rituals* (*Chia-li*), a work apparently intended to

23

guide both scholar-officials and commoners in the practice of family ceremonies.[1] This text, which was based on texts of the Northern Sung, particularly the *Etiquette for Letter-Writing and Other Occasions* (*Shu-i*) by Ssu-ma Kuang (1019–1086) and the imperially sponsored *New Forms for the Five Categories of Rites of the Cheng-ho Period* (*Cheng-ho wu-li hsin-i*), outlined in considerable detail what family members were to do in family ceremonies; a chapter was devoted to each of the four family rituals—coming of age, weddings, funerals, and sacrifices. This work, then, was a prescriptive one telling people how to behave, not a philosophical one explaining why people were to behave in a certain way.[2]

The *Family Rituals* was thus not related to what we would consider formal education; it was not taught in schools or academies. But as a manual that provided instruction to the people in familial matters, its function was indeed educational. Likewise, Chu Hsi's "community compact" (*hsiang-yüeh*) was not a work taught in the schools; it too was more a "how-to" manual of instruction, offering guidelines for how people were to behave in their interactions with others in the community. Based on the earlier compact of Lü Ta-chün (1031–1082), Chu's compact called for people to enter voluntarily into a contract with other members of their local community, agreeing to the following general terms: (1) to encourage one another to behave virtuously and perform worthy acts; (2) to correct one another's faults; (3) to associate with one another according to the proper rites and customs; and (4) to aid one another in times of misfortune and difficulty.[3] Under each of these four major provisions Chu Hsi presented a detailed list of the deeds and rituals members of the compact were expected to perform. The specificity of these deeds and rituals can be striking. For instance:

If you are riding on horseback and a venerated or senior person is on foot, as soon as he comes into view, dismount and make a low bow before him.

1. The authorship and the audience of this text have been open to question. Patricia Ebrey, basing her work on recent Chinese and Japanese scholarship, accepts attribution to Chu Hsi; she also concludes that the contents were intended to be applicable to the entire populace. For a lengthy discussion, with partial translation, of the *Family Rituals*, see Ebrey, "Education through Ritual."

2. This summary is based on Ebrey's "Education through Ritual." Ebrey (pp. 296–297) concludes that of all Chu's writings the *Family Rituals* "may be the one most often consulted by people of little formal education."

3. *Wen-chi* 74.25a.

If he has already given way to you, you still salute him in the same way, and only after he has passed a considerable distance beyond you do you remount the horse. If the venerated or senior person orders you to remount the horse, you steadfastly refuse. If you meet a peer and you are both on horseback, riding on opposite sides of the road bow to each other and pass. If he is on foot and gives way to you before you reach him, dismount and make a low bow to him. When he has passed by, remount the horse. If you meet a junior[4] or someone still younger and you are both on horseback, should he give way to you before you reach him, make a low bow and pass. If he is on foot and gives way to you before you reach him, dismount and make a low bow. (With a young person you need not dismount.)[5]

In the Chinese context, of course, the performance of the sorts of ritual acts detailed here did more than bring order to the community; it was thought to breed in the individual an inner correctness. That is, by acting as one should, in accord with the rules of etiquette appropriate to one's station in life, one was cultivating one's own morality.

If a person failed to perform the deeds and rituals outlined in the compact, even after being reprimanded, he faced expulsion from the compact.[6] The compact thus served for its members as a kind of constitution, an elaborate set of prescriptions for proper conduct in the local community.[7] The community compact envisioned by Chu was not widely adopted during his lifetime, but in later dynasties as well as in other countries of East Asia its influence would be considerable.

Chu's efforts to instruct people outside the formal classroom setting took other forms as well. He had libraries built[8] and shrines and monuments erected that commemorated distinguished personages, including the great Neo-Confucian masters of the Northern Sung.[9] Such shrines, he hoped, by honoring those men who in their

---

4. I.e., a person no more than ten years younger than oneself.

5. *Wen-chi* 74.28a; this translation is based on Übelhör, "Mr. Lü's Community Pact," pp. 11–12.

6. *Wen-chi* 74.26b.

7. On the community compact see Übelhör, "Community Compact," and Hymes, *Statesmen and Gentlemen*, pp. 132–134.

8. E.g., Wang Mou-hung, *Chu-tzu nien-p'u* (hereafter *Nien-p'u*), pp. 10–11; cf. *Wen-chi* 75.1a–b.

9. E.g., *Nien-p'u*, pp. 12, 78, 194; cf. *Wen-chi* 20.1a–b, 77.3a–b, 86.4b–6b,

lifetimes had displayed exemplary moral qualities, would have the power to transmit those qualities to later generations. For Chu the shrine was a natural extension of the traditional Confucian belief in the power of moral example, the belief that a good man, through an almost "magical charisma," would transform those around him into morally superior individuals.

In addition, Chu, in his capacity as an official, issued more than one hundred public proclamations (*pang*),[10] the purpose of which was to instruct both the educated and uneducated populace under his jurisdiction not only in practical matters, such as the community granary, the community compact, drought and famine relief, taxation, local defense, and the reclassification of land, but in matters of morality, rites, and customs as well. The proclamations exhorted people, for example, to maintain good human relations, both inside and outside the family; to follow the proper decorum in daily life and in family ceremonies, particularly marriage and mourning; to practice with devotion filial piety and brotherliness; to help improve the quality of local students and schools; and not to engage in certain religious or superstitious practices, many of which were associated with Buddhism.[11] To give the reader something of the flavor of these proclamations, I quote the following excerpt from a proclamation Chu published in Nan-k'ang as he assumed the prefectural duties there in 1179:

Now I entreat you, literati, commoners, and community elders under my jurisdiction, to gather together each season of the year and to give instruction to the people and on occasion, when circumstances call for it, to offer repeated injunctions. In this way our youth will all know to practice filial piety, brotherly respect, loyalty and faithfulness; within the household to serve their parents and older brothers and outside of it to serve their elders and superiors; to be generous toward relatives and friendly toward neighbors; to offer assistance to others in need and to aid them in times of

---

78.22b, 19.46b–47b. For a summary of Chu's shrine-building efforts see Schirokauer, "Chu Hsi as an Administrator," pp. 211, 216–217. Cf. also Chu's numerous accounts applauding the construction of shrines and libraries in *Wen-chi, chüan* 77–80, passim.

10. This figure was arrived at by Ron-Guey Chu, "Public Instruction," p. 255.

11. See *Wen-chi, chüan* 99–100, for many of Chu's proclamations. Ron-Guey Chu's "Public Instruction" is a study and translation of Chu's proclamations relating to public morality and ritual observances; Schirokauer, "Chu Hsi as an Administrator," pp. 218–219, presents a summary of one important proclamation.

misfortune and difficulty. It may be hoped thereby that our customs, in their excellence, will not suffer in comparison to those of the ancients and that we will be able to assist the sage Emperor in his wishes to enrich custom.[12]

Chu's intention clearly was to use the public proclamations to nurture proper moral behavior among the people at large; they became a sort of "pulpit" for him, from which he could lay down moral guidelines for those under his jurisdiction.

A considerable part of Chu's efforts to ensure that people of the day were properly educated was devoted to improving the conditions in the local government schools. As the subprefectural registrar of T'ung-an (1153–1156) and the prefect of Nan-k'ang (1179–1181) and Chang-chou (1190–1191), Chu Hsi took a deep personal interest in the schools in his regions.[13] As noted earlier, he found the students in those schools to be lazy and concerned primarily with success in the state examinations, not with true Confucian learning. He sought to attract better students and admonished them to put aside ambitions of wealth and power and set their sights instead on the true Way; he made a practice of visiting the schools to look over the students' work and hold discussions with them.[14] Chu also invited distinguished scholars to come lecture at the schools[15] and himself taught there when his schedule allowed.[16] He hoped thus to make the local schools in the areas under his supervision centers of serious Confucian study and to free them from their past preoccupation with examination learning. Chu's commitment to reinvigorating local schools is evident from the proclamation issued in Nan-k'ang cited earlier:

In recent years the scholarly tradition [in this prefecture] has declined, with the school supporting a mere thirty students. . . . Now I entreat the village elders to select young men who are dedicated to learning and send them to the school. They will be given assistance and be eligible to attend lectures and participate in classes. Meanwhile, the prefecture will take various steps to provide more support for schooling. And the prefect himself, when official duties permit, will visit the school regularly and discuss

---

12. *Wen-chi* 99.2a.
13. See Schirokauer, "Chu Hsi as an Administrator," pp. 208–219.
14. See *Wen-chi* 74.1b–2a and *Nien-p'u*, pp. 9, 171.
15. E.g., *Wen-chi* 20.1a and *Nien-p'u*, p. 9.
16. *Nien-p'u*, pp. 78, 171.

the meaning of the Classics with the school officials and in a variety of
ways guide and encourage them. It may be hoped thereby that in time
talented people of outstanding ability will appear and that we will be able
to assist the sage Emperor in his wishes to develop men of talent.[17]

It is recorded that Chu, in fact, visited the Nan-k'ang commandery
school every four or five days and engaged tirelessly in discussion
with the students there.[18]

But Chu apparently was never fully satisfied with the education
offered in the local schools.[19] Even as he was attempting to improve
the quality of the Nan-k'ang commandery school, he began to
search elsewhere for the sort of education he believed the people
needed. In 1179, as he took up the post of prefect of Nan-k'ang, he
initiated the revival of an academy scenically situated on a mountain a few miles north of the commandery capital. Known as the
White Deer Hollow, its history could be traced back to the late
eighth century, when it served as a residence for an official of the
T'ang. In the tenth and eleventh centuries, under the Southern
T'ang (937–975) and early Sung, it had flourished as an academy;
Sung T'ai-tsung (r. 976–997) had even presented it with a set of the
Nine Classics. But by the early Southern Sung the academy had
fallen into ruins.

Chu revived the White Deer Hollow Academy not as a replace-
ment for the government school but rather as a supplement to it.
And to his mind the supplement was necessary. Buddhist and
Taoist temples were overrunning the countryside, he argued. There
were more than one hundred on Lu Mountain alone, but only three
government schools were to be found in the entire prefecture.[20]
This sort of saturation, by the Buddhists in particular, posed a danger to Confucian learning;[21] only if schools and academies that
transmitted the proper Way became a stronger presence in the
area could heterodox teaching be kept at bay. For Chu Hsi, then,

17. *Wen-chi* 99.2a–b; loosely based on Ron-Guey Chu, "Public Instruction,"
p. 261.

18. *Nien-p'u*, p. 78.

19. For a scathing attack by Chu on this education see, for example, *Wen-chi*
79.23a–b; cited in Terada, *Sōdai kyōikushi gaisetsu*, pp. 270–271.

20. *Wen-chi* 16.19b, 20.9b; cf. *Wen-chi* 13.21b. See also Hymes, *Statesmen and
Gentlemen*, pp. 177–199.

21. Chan, "Chu Hsi and the Academies," p. 402, and Terada, *Sōdai kyōikushi
gaisetsu*, pp. 267–268, touch on this point.

academies would help serve to offset the powerful influence Buddhism had at the time.

The White Deer Hollow was only one of the academies with which Chu was associated during his lifetime. Records show that he founded eight of them, taught or lectured at another dozen, wrote accounts for three, and left plaques for at least nine.[22] But he is best remembered for his work at the White Deer Hollow Academy. In addition to restoring the buildings and finding the personnel, the revenues, and the books for it, Chu became actively involved in the instruction there; in fact, it was there that he attracted a number of his loyal disciples.[23] What in particular has tied Chu's reputation to the White Deer Hollow Academy is the set of articles of instruction he formulated for it in 1180. From that time on these articles served as a model for academies not only in China but throughout East Asia.[24] Though they have been cited often,[25] it is worth quoting them again here, in their entirety:

> Affection between parent and child;
> Righteousness between ruler and subject;
> Differentiation between husband and wife;
> Precedence between elder and younger;
> Trust between friends.[26]

The above are the items of the Five Teachings. When Yao and Shun appointed Hsieh to be Minister of Education and to set forth reverently the Five Teachings,[27] it was precisely these teachings. Students should study these and nothing more. In studying, there is a proper sequence, which likewise involves five items, listed separately below:

> Study extensively, inquire carefully, ponder thoroughly, sift clearly, and practice earnestly.[28]

22. These figures are from Chaffee, "Revival of the White Deer Grotto Academy," p. 49, and Chan, "Chu Hsi and the Academies," p. 411.

23. Chan, "Chu Hsi and the Academies," p. 396, and Chaffee, "Chu Hsi in Nan-K'ang," pp. 424–427.

24. For a brief discussion of the articles' influence see Chan, "Chu Hsi and the Academies," pp. 398–399.

25. For example, Meskill, *Academies in Ming China*, pp. 50–51; Chaffee, "Revival of the White Deer Grotto Academy," pp. 13–15; de Bary, *Liberal Tradition*, pp. 35–36; Chan, "Chu Hsi and the Academies," p. 397; and Terada, *Sōdai kyōikushi gaisetsu*, pp. 297–298.

26. From *Meng-tzu* 3A/4.

27. See Legge, *Chinese Classics*, vol. 3, p. 44.

28. *Chung-yung* 20/19.

The above is the proper sequence for studying. Studying, inquiring, pondering, and sifting are the means by which to probe principle. As to earnest practice, its essence is present in every step from self-cultivation on down to handling affairs and dealing with others, as follows:

> Be loyal and true to your every word, serious and careful in all you do.[29]

> Curb your anger and restrain your lust; move toward the good and correct your errors.[30]

The above are the essentials of self-cultivation.

> Accord with the righteous, do not seek profit; illuminate the Way, do not calculate the advantages.[31]

The above are the essentials for handling affairs.

> Do not do to others what you do not want done to you.[32]

> Whenever you fail to achieve your purpose, look into yourself.[33]

The above are the essentials for dealing with others.[34]

"The Articles of the White Deer Hollow Academy," then, is not a detailed set of instructions prescribing how students were to conduct themselves from hour to hour at the academy. Rather, it is a general outline, setting forth first the content of learning, then the method of learning, next the aim of learning (i.e., self-cultivation), and finally the effects that proper learning would have on a student's dealings with others.[35] The articles are in essence nothing but a simple restatement of traditional Confucian values and social mores, which take the five human relationships as central. Indeed, with the exception of one remark by Tung Chung-shu (176–104 B.C.) from the *Han History* (*Han shu*), the articles are all simply quotations from the Confucian Classics. But Chu must have felt

29. *Lun-yü* 15/6; translation from Waley, *Analects*, p. 194.

30. From *Chou i*, pp. 25–26.

31. Statement of Tung Chung-shu (176–104 B.C.), found in *Han shu*, vol, 8, 56.2524.

32. *Lun-yü* 12/2, 15/24.

33. *Meng-tzu* 4A/4; adapted from Lau, *Mencius*, p. 119.

34. *Wen-chi* 74.18a–b; the translation here is loosely based on de Bary, *Liberal Tradition*, pp. 35–36.

35. Because the articles are so general, Chan believes that they probably were not influenced by the far more complex and detailed monastic regulations, such as the *Pai-chang ch'ing-kuei*, as other scholars have asserted. See Chan, "Chu Hsi and the Academies," p. 399.

that such values and social mores needed to be restated. In an essay he attached to the articles, he highlighted the necessity of returning to traditional Confucian learning:

I have observed that the sages and worthies of antiquity in teaching people to pursue learning had one intention only: to have them understand moral principle clearly in order that they might cultivate their persons, thereafter extending [their perfection] to others. The sages and worthies did not simply want people to engage in the memorization of texts and the composition of verse and essays for the purpose of winning a reputation and obtaining wealth and office. Those who today pursue learning go against [the wishes of the sages and worthies]. The methods used by the sages and worthies in their teaching are all to be found in the Classics. Dedicated literati really ought to read through them thoroughly, ponder them deeply, and then sift them with an inquiring mind.[36]

With the academy, then, Chu hoped he was creating a setting where students could engage not in a "vocational" preparation for examinations but in disinterested study.[37] The academy was to lead students back to the true message of the sages and worthies found in the Confucian canon. An important point to note here is the responsibility Chu placed on students at the academy to think about the Classics for themselves; this is a point he would reiterate over and over in conversations with his disciples. The "Articles of the White Deer Hollow Academy" thus represent an attempt by Chu Hsi to articulate in the face of the examination-oriented education of the time a general philosophy of Confucian education that called for the return to disinterested study of the tradition's fundamental values and texts.[38]

Chu Hsi's missionary zeal in educating the people of his day and ensuring the transmission of the Confucian Way perhaps finds its clearest testimonial in his prodigious scholarship and his lifelong commitment to the teaching of disciples. Chu wrote, compiled, and edited books throughout his entire adult life. His purpose was

36. *Wen-chi* 74.18b–19a.

37. Chaffee too makes this point in "Revival of the White Deer Grotto Academy," p. 56.

38. The number of academies that had sprung up by the late twelfth century suggests that they had a strong appeal; the competition in the examinations, which by that time was extraordinarily keen, had probably done much to alienate literati and turn them more toward the life of the mind and moral cultivation found in the academies. See Chaffee, *Thorny Gates*, pp. 89–91, particularly table 13, p. 89.

always the same: to highlight the Way and make it accessible to others. He wrote commentaries on all but one of the Five Classics,[39] on each of the Four Books,[40] and on the *Book of Filial Piety* (*Hsiao ching*).[41] For it was in these texts from the Confucian canon in particular that the Way could be found; after all, they had been written by the great sages of antiquity, men who themselves fully embodied the Way. Thus the message conveyed in them was certain to embody the Way as well. That message, however, given its subtlety and profundity, was difficult for most people to apprehend. Chu intended for his commentaries to make that task somewhat easier.

History too conveyed the Way, documenting as it did the Way in operation. Hence, Chu produced a number of historical works—one on famous statesmen of the Northern Sung, one on the development of the Ch'eng brothers school of Neo-Confucianism, and one a sort of summary of Ssu-ma Kuang's monumental *Comprehensive Mirror for Aid in Government* (*Tzu-chih t'ung-chien*)[42]—the purpose of which was not primarily to narrate historical events but rather to pass moral judgment on those historical events and personages and thus clarify for readers what the Way looked like in practice.

In addition to these scholarly writings on the Classics and history, Chu devoted much time to editing and commenting on the words of the great Neo-Confucian masters of the Northern Sung; he prepared editions of the Ch'eng brothers' and Hsieh Liang-tso's conversations[43] and commentaries on Chang Tsai's *Western Inscription* (*Hsi-ming*)[44] and Chou Tun-i's *Diagram of the Great Ultimate Explained* (*T'ai-chi t'u-shuo*).[45] Like the authors of the Classics these

39. For example, for the *I ching* he wrote the *Chou-i pen-i* and the *I-hsüeh ch'i-meng*; for the *Shih ching*, the *Shih chi-chuan*; for the *Shu ching*, the *Shu chi-chuan*, which was completed by his disciple Ts'ai ch'en (1167–1230) (see Ch'ang Pi-te et al., *Sung-jen chuan-chi tzu-liao so-jin* [hereafter *SJCC*], vol. 5, p. 3783, and Ch'en Jung-chieh, *Chu-tzu men-jen*, pp. 333–334); and for the *Li*, the *I-li ching-chuan t'ung-chieh*. For handy lists of Chu's writings see Chang Li-wen, *Chu Hsi ssu-hsiang yen-chiu*, pp. 82–87, and Chou Ta-t'ung, *Chu Hsi*, pp. 93–113.

40.The most famous and influential are the *Lun-yü chi-chu*, the *Meng-tzu chi-chu*, the *Ta-hsüeh chang-chü*, and the *Chung-yung chang-chü*.

41. *Hsiao-ching k'an-wu*.

42. Respectively, these are the *Ming-ch'en yen-hsing lu*, the *I-lo yüan-yüan lu*, and the *Tzu-chih t'ung-chien kang-mu*.

43. *Ho-nan Ch'eng-shih i-shu*, *Ho-nan Ch'eng-shih wai-shu*, and *Hsieh Shang-ts'ai hsien-sheng yü-lu*.

44. *Hsi-ming chieh-i*.

45. *T'ai-chi t'u-shuo chieh* and *T'ung-shu chieh*.

men of the Northern Sung, Chu believed, were sages and worthies who in their lifetimes had embraced the Way and whose words too therefore embraced the Way. They needed to be heard, for they could help make the Way clearer to the people of Chu's time. So important were these words that with the help of his trusted friend Lü Tsu-ch'ien, Chu compiled an anthology of them; in this anthology, *Reflections on Things at Hand*, he selected 622 comments by the four men of the Northern Sung he most admired—Chou Tun-i, the Ch'eng brothers, and Chang Tsai—as a way of making their ideas, scattered in voluminous writings and conversations, as accessible to people as possible. The conviction that their words truly conveyed the Way but that they needed to be pared down and anthologized to become accessible and meaningful to others was clearly what inspired Chu to produce the work. In the preface to it he wrote:

Together [Lü and I] read the works of Masters Chou Tun-i, Ch'eng Hao, Ch'eng I, and Chang Tsai and lamented over the fact that their doctrines are as extensive and broad as a sea without shores. Fearing that a beginner may not know where to start, we have selected passages concerned with fundamentals and closely related to daily application to constitute this volume, making a total of 622 items divided into fourteen chapters. . . . Thus if a young man in an isolated village who has the will to learn, but no enlightened teacher or good friend to guide him, obtains this volume and explores and broods over its material in his own mind, he will be able to find the gate to enter.[46]

The pedagogic concern expressed in this preface was one that lay behind all of Chu's scholarly work: to make the great Way manageable for others so that it might be preserved and passed on to later generations.

Chu Hsi's teaching of disciples would seem to have been at least as important to him as his scholarship. Even when writing, he never gave up teaching. Chu first attracted those who took him as master during his early years in T'ung-an (1153–1156); by the time of his death a half century later the number of his followers had reached nearly five hundred.[47] The *Conversations of Master Chu, Arranged Topically* is the record, in 140 chapters, of conversations

46. *Wen-chi* 81.6b–7a; translation from Chan, *Reflections*, pp. 1–2.
47. Ch'en Jung-chieh, *Chu-tzu men-jen*, pp. 1–27.

that took place over the years between Chu Hsi and his disciples. It constitutes a detailed chronicle of the master's pedagogic concerns and style. Also, preserved in the *Collected Literary Works of Master Chu* are a great many letters Chu Hsi sent to disciples during his lifetime. Chu's commitment to passing the Way on to others is nowhere better evidenced than in these two collections. It is in them that we find Chu as teacher and transmitter, instructing those of his age what in the Chinese cultural tradition was most precious and why. And it is in them that we come to feel the deep sense of mission this late twelfth-century intellectual had in reviving a Way he was convinced had become endangered.

Chu Hsi's Program of
Learning for Followers of the Way

Chu Hsi knew what he wished to accomplish as a teacher: to make the Confucian message, first articulated by the sages of the past, accessible to students of the present. For Chu this meant deciding which texts from China's long and rich cultural tradition would constitute the best curriculum for these students, which texts would most effectively and clearly transmit the Confucian message to them. Based on his experience as both student and teacher, he was convinced that certain texts more readily and more lucidly yielded up the Confucian truth than others. He would have students turn to these writings first. Indeed, one of Chu Hsi's great achievements as an educator was to develop a graded, rather precise curriculum designed to introduce students to the Confucian message.

But having observed what he perceived to be the dismal state of learning around him, Chu Hsi was equally convinced that texts—no matter how full of wisdom or inspiration—meant little or nothing if those coming to them did not possess the proper attitude. And so, in teaching others, he did more than establish a rigorous curriculum; he developed and lay before them a highly elaborate method of reading, which he hoped would enable them to absorb the message embodied in his curriculum. If he could induce students to approach the texts and their reading of them in the right way—a way he neatly outlined for them—the Confucian Way might be preserved. In the *Collected Literary Works of Master Chu* and the *Conversations of Master Chu, Arranged Topically* we find a devoted teacher preoccupied with the question of how man learns most effectively and with the related question of what enables him to learn. Chu Hsi, in teaching students, was as interested in epistemology and what we might call the psychology of learning as he was in the content of learning.

Chu's pedagogic outlook placed an enormous burden on his students, for he expected them to be ready to give their lives, just as he was, to preserving the Way. They were to be the educated and moral elite, the vanguard of his program to revive the great Confucian tradition. To Chu his students were a corps of true learners who, once they had themselves heard and embraced the word of the sages, would go and spread it throughout the rest of the world. Chu's goal of resuscitating and transmitting the Way thus depended quite heavily on them.

Those who studied under Chu Hsi, then, assumed something of the role of religious novitiates; for them Chu would provide guidance—through his choice of texts to be read, his discussion of them, and the disciplined methodology of learning he developed—in the apprehension of the truth embedded in the canonical tradition. It is clear from conversations with his disciples that Chu did not anticipate that they would necessarily translate the understanding they reached in their study with him into formal public service as officials, as traditional Confucian teachings might have demanded. That is to say, Chu's program of learning was not designed primarily to yield the archetypal Confucian official.[1] It was designed rather to lead those who followed him to a deep and personally meaningful understanding of the Confucian truth, which had been largely obscured for more than fifteen hundred years, since the death of Mencius.[2] Chu trusted that if his cohort of disciples embraced and practiced this truth for themselves it might once

1. In "Hsüeh-hsiao kung-chü ssu-i" (*Wen-chi* 69.20a–28b), Chu Hsi discussed the sort of learning that would be appropriate for those preparing for the examinations and government service; on this learning see de Bary, *Liberal Tradition*, pp. 40–42, and Nivison, "Protest against Conventions," pp. 189–190. But the program of learning that interested Chu far more, and that is presented throughout his writings and conversations, is one for devout Confucians hoping to embrace the Way and tread the true path—the sorts of Confucians who studied for moral and spiritual cultivation, not for examination or worldly success.

2. On the tradition since Mencius's death see the preface to *Ta-hsüeh chang-chü* 2a–b.

again prevail in the world: through their teaching of others, their writing, their exemplary lives, and if they so chose, their official service, these disciples might well pass the Way on to later generations, ensuring its survival into the future.

In setting up a curriculum for his followers, Chu Hsi, not surprisingly, made the Confucian Classics the core texts. Chu believed that the Classics had been written by the great sages of antiquity and hence fully embodied the truth, or, in Neo-Confucian terms, *li* (conventionally translated "principle")[3] (5.44 and 3.17).[4] Even though earlier scholars had also believed that the sages of the past had set down the truth in the Confucian canon, an important and essential difference between Chu Hsi and these scholars was in the sorts of truths they hoped to discover in the texts. Pre-Sung classicists had tended to look for limited, "situational truths," that is, prescriptions detailing how to behave in life's varying circumstances and how to govern the people most effectively; this is why they turned to the Five Classics. But in seeking *li*, Chu was looking for a truth more abstract and more universal; he was looking for the "principle" that underlay all things in the cosmos. Hence he chose to focus more on the Four Books. Thus, although the body of Confucian canonical texts remained largely the same from pre-Sung to Sung times, the approach to it and the message to be found in it changed markedly in Chu Hsi's hands.[5]

Of course, Chu was not suggesting that it was only in the Confucian Classics that truth or principle could be apprehended; it did after all inhere in all things and affairs in the universe. But the Classics, written as they were by the great sages of antiquity, manifested it more clearly than anywhere else. As Chu once remarked: "All things in the world have principle, but its essence is embodied in the works of the sages and worthies. Hence, in seeking principle we must turn to these works."[6] For those wishing to tread the true Way, there was simply no better guide than these texts:

---

3. For a discussion of *li* and its translation see the annotation that follows passage 1.4 and below, Part One, "Chu Hsi's Program of Learning for Followers of the Way."

4. See also *YL* 10.1aff./vol. 1, pp. 161ff. and 11.11b/vol. 1, p. 187 and *Wen-chi* 14.12a–b and 42.22b–23a.

5. I have made this point in *Chu Hsi and the Ta-hsueh*, pp. 48–49.

6. *Wen-chi* 59.5a.

The sages wrote the Classics to teach later generations. These texts enable
the reader to reflect on the ideas of the sages while reciting their words and
hence to understand what is in accordance with the principle of things.
Understanding the whole substance of the proper Way, he will practice
the Way with all his strength, and so enter the realm of the sages and
worthies. Although the texts are concise, they treat all matters under
heaven, the hidden and the manifest, the great and the small. If he who
wishes to seek the Way and thereby enter into virtue abandons the
Classics, he will have nothing to which to apply himself.[7]

Needless to say, reading the canon was important to Chu Hsi,
then, not principally as an intellectual exercise but rather as the
intellectual means to a moral, even a spiritual, end: through the
classical texts the sensitive reader could apprehend the principle
underlying the universe and hence "practice the Way with all his
strength, and so enter the realm of the sages and worthies." Indeed, contrary to the reputation for bookishness that he gained in
the Ming (1368–1644), Chu was determined that reading not
become excessively scholastic, devoid of moral and spiritual significance. When he announced to his disciples that "book learning
is a secondary matter for students" (4.1), he was warning them
that reading must never be an end in itself but merely a way to
come to know principle and thus follow the true Way.[8]

In fact, once principle was apprehended, Chu believed that even
the Confucian Classics and their commentaries could be abandoned. At times he sounded startlingly like Lu Chiu-yüan: "When
we read the Six Classics, it should be just as if there were no Six
Classics. We are simply seeking the moral principle in ourselves"
(5.41). Or: "We rely on the Classics simply to understand principle. Once we have grasped principle, there is no need for the
Classics" (5.52; cf. 4.2, 4.3, and 5.26).[9] In other words, reading the
Classics was of no consequence to Chu Hsi if it did not provide
moral and spiritual advancement for the reader.

7. *Wen-chi* 82.26a.
8. In *YL* 10.6a/vol. 1, p. 167 (4.29), Chu comments: "Reading is one way of
apprehending the principle in things." See also passages in *YL* 10.1a/vol. 1, p. 161.
Ch'eng I had held the same point of view; see, for example, Chan, *Reflections*,
pp. 47–48.
9. Lu Chiu-yüan once remarked (*Hsiang-shan hsien-sheng ch'üan-chi* 34.1b): "If in
our learning we understand what's fundamental, the Six Classics all are but footnotes to us."

Chu was aware, however, that reading the Confucian canon and apprehending its message were not necessarily easy matters. The texts were old and hence difficult to understand, particularly for beginners:

So great an expanse of time separates us from the sages that their discourses on the texts have become lost to us, and even our venerable teachers and scholars cannot fully understand the symbols and numbers, the designations and descriptions of things, the commentary, and the directions to the reader found in the Classics. How much less are the young novices, who hurriedly read through the texts, able to appreciate their general concerns and essential points.[10]

To make the classical texts less formidable, less incomprehensible, Chu, continuing the efforts of his predecessors the Ch'eng brothers, developed a graded curriculum.[11] At the very top of this curriculum he placed the *Greater Learning*, the *Analects*, the *Book of Mencius*, and the *Doctrine of the Mean*. To Chu's mind the "ease, immediacy, and brevity" of these works gave them an accessibility that other texts in the canon lacked.[12] As he wrote to an acquaintance: "If we wish principle to be simple and easy to appreciate, concise and easy to grasp, there is nothing better than the *Greater Learning*, the *Analects*, the *Book of Mencius*, and the *Doctrine of the Mean*."[13] Only after fully mastering these four texts—referred to commonly since the Yüan period (1279–1368) as the Four Books—were students supposed to turn to the previously authoritative Five Classics, the *Book of Changes*, the *Book of Poetry*, the *Book of History*, the *Book of Rites*, and the *Spring and Autumn Annals*.[14] Thus, with Chu Hsi, the Four Books came to displace the Five Classics as the central texts in the Confucian tradition. As such they now constituted the core teachings in the Confucian school; they would continue to do so until well into the present century.

10. *Wen-chi* 82.26a.
11. On the Ch'engs' curricular suggestions see Gardner, "Principle and Pedagogy," pp. 65–69.
12. *Wen-chi* 82.26a.
13. *Wen-chi* 59.5a. So certain was he of their effectiveness that in 1190 Chu published them together as a collection, giving it the title *Ssu-tzu*, the *Four Masters*. This was the first time these four texts, known commonly since the Yüan as the *Ssu-shu*, the Four Books, circulated together.
14. See, for instance, *Wen-chi* 82.26a.

The histories too were to be studied, according to Chu, but only
after the canonical texts had been completely comprehended. It
was simply that principle was not nearly so accessible in the histories. The Classics, in particular the Four Books, clearly revealed
principle; the histories were much more discursive, recording examples of how principle had actually operated in the past (5.42,
5.44, 5.65, and 5.66).[15] For Chu genuine understanding of principle
meant understanding it in actual practice, and thus a reading of
the histories was essential. But he cautioned his students against
reading them prematurely: "If you turn to the histories before
thoroughly mastering the *Analects*, the *Book of Mencius*, the
Doctrine of the Mean, and the *Greater Learning*, your mind will have no
measuring-stick and thus will be frequently misled."[16] In a more
elaborate comment:

People nowadays have yet to read much in the Classics or thoroughly
understand moral principle before they begin reading historical texts, inquiring into the order and disorder of the past and present and studying
institutions and the laws. This can be compared to building a dike to
irrigate the fields: a dike should be full of water before you open it, then
the water will rush out, nourishing all the crops in the field; if you hastily
open the dike to irrigate the field just when the dike has accumulated little
more than a ladleful of water, not only will this be of no benefit to the field
but you'll no longer have even the ladleful of water. Once you've read a
lot in the Classics and you've thoroughly understood moral principle,
your mind will be completely clear as to the standard of measure; if you
don't then turn to the historical texts, inquiring into the order and disorder of the past and present and studying institutions and the laws, it's
like having a dike full of water and not opening it to irrigate the field. If
you've yet to read much in the Classics or thoroughly understand moral
principle but eagerly make reading the histories your first order of business, it's like opening a dike with a ladleful of water to irrigate the field.
You can stand there and watch [the water] dry up. (5.65)

The reader had to apprehend principle from the Classics first; only
with an understanding of this principle would he have the standard
of measure for evaluating the events and persons of the past. Chu,

15. See also *Wen-chi* 77.22a.
16. *YL* 11.19a/vol. 1, p. 195; Ch'ien Mu, *Chu-tzu hsin hsüeh-an*, vol. 5, pp. 110–
114, cites passages from *YL* and the *Wen-chi* on the priority of the Classics over the
histories.

to be sure then, would have students include in their program of learning such standard historical works as the *Records of the Grand Historian*, the *Tso Commentary* (*Tso chuan*), the *Comprehensive Mirror for Aid in Government*, and the dynastic histories (5.66); he even ridiculed men—like Wang An-shih—for their ignorance of historical works (5.44). But the role of these texts in the program was secondary to and clearly less important than that of the Confucian Classics (5.43).[17]

Chu was persuaded that this curriculum for students of the Way contained a coherent message. He remarked to them: "Everything you read is of the same principle" (4.31; cf. 3.30). Each of the canonical texts and the important histories conveyed, more or less explicitly, the same Confucian truth; with work the reader would see for himself the interrelatedness of the texts Chu proposed they read. Over and over again in his writings we find Chu trying to reconcile various passages from the different texts, hoping to demonstrate to his students the essential unity of the Confucian message.[18] For example:

The words of the sages and worthies for the most part seem dissimilar. Yet, they've always been interconnected. For example, the Master said: "Do not look, listen, speak, or move, unless it be in accordance with the rites,"[19] "when abroad behave as though you were receiving an important guest and when employing the services of the common people behave as though you were officiating at an important sacrifice,"[20] and "be loyal and true in your every word, serious and mentally attentive in all that you do."[21] Mencius then said: "Seek for the lost mind"[22] and "preserve the mind and nourish the nature."[23] The *Greater Learning* then treated what is called "the apprehension of the principle in things, the extension of knowledge, setting the mind in the right, and making the thoughts true."[24] Master Ch'eng then concentrated on elucidating the word *ching*. If you simply read all this, it may seem like a hodgepodge, utterly confused. But

---

17. According to Kasoff, *Thought of Chang Tsai*, pp. 82–84, Chang Tsai would have learners read only the Classics and not bother with the histories at all.

18. Cf. Kasoff, *Thought of Chang Tsai*, pp. 17–19, where he talks about the Sung effort to "link concepts from different classical texts."

19. *Lun-yü* 12/1.

20. *Lun-yü* 12/2.

21. *Lun-yü* 15/5.

22. *Meng-tzu* 6A/11.

23. *Meng-tzu* 7A/1.

24. *Ta-hsüeh*, "Classic of Confucius," para. 4.

in fact it's all of the same principle. Tao-fu said: "Drifting around in the texts, I felt they were all different. It's only when I really applied myself that the principle running through them all became apparent." Chu said: "That's right. Just concentrate your efforts on one spot; all the rest inheres in that spot. The Way of the sages and worthies is like a house. Though there are different doors, you'll be able to enter it approaching it from just one direction. I fear only that you won't make the effort." (6.33; cf. 2.5)

The interrelatedness of the classical texts was an article of faith for Chu Hsi. Since these texts were all transmitted by the great sages—men who completely embodied the one Confucian Way—what they transmitted naturally cohered.[25]

Chu Hsi's pedagogic concerns went beyond telling his students *what* to read; he was just as anxious that they be taught *how* to read as well. Indeed, Chu devoted much of his life to developing a hermeneutics (or to use his own term, *tu-shu fa*), a comprehensive theory and method of reading and learning from what to him were sacred texts. So critical was this art of reading for Chu Hsi that compilers of the *Conversations of Master Chu, Arranged Topically* gave over two entire chapters to his comments on the subject.[26] Chu wanted his students to know how to read most effectively, so that they might get at the true meaning of the cherished works of the past, the great Way of the sages.

At the heart of Chu Hsi's highly elaborate *tu-shu fa* was the conviction that in book learning the student had to do more than simply read through the texts—he had to "experience them personally" (e.g., 4.20, 4.21, and 5.25); only if he made the texts his own would they be truly meaningful to him. Chu explained to his students: "Generally speaking, in reading we must first become intimately familiar with the text so that its words seem to come from our own mouths. We should then continue to reflect on it so that its ideas

25. Chu, in the passage cited here, is not only reconciling the various texts in the canonical tradition but also the words of his great master, Ch'eng I, with those canonical texts (cf. *YL* 9.4a/vol. 1, pp. 151–152 [3.12]). Indeed, what made Ch'eng I and the other great Neo-Confucians of the Northern Sung such heroes to Chu Hsi was that their words in the end were one with those of the revered sages of antiquity: principle was readily apparent in all of them. In quality and kind there were no differences between the sacred texts of the past and the words of the more recent sages of the early Sung.

26. *Chüan* 10, 11.

seem to come from our own minds. Only then can there be real understanding" (4.33).[27] The text and the reader had to become one.

To experience the text as he should, there were certain guidelines the reader had to follow. First of all, Chu advised, the reader should delimit his curriculum. With the proliferation of printing, books had become widely available; the Sung literatus now faced a complement of texts that was truly intimidating. Thus there developed among readers, hoping to cover as many texts as possible, a tendency to jump from one to another. Of course, the result was that readers absorbed little or nothing of what they read. This troubled Chu, who wanted his students to learn to cope with the heavy burden that Sung culture had placed on them. He cautioned them: "In reading, the greatest failing is to strive for quantity."[28] Quantity simply could be no substitute for true understanding: "Don't value quantity, value only your familiarity with what you've read" (4.29).[29] Chu Hsi's desire to establish a basic curriculum for his students and, moreover, to have them focus on the Four Books as the central texts in that curriculum would seem, then, to have been entirely consistent with his theory of reading.

The curriculum thus had to be limited; but it also had to be read in sequence, Chu argued. In general, students were to proceed from easier, more accessible texts to the more difficult. This no doubt was one of Chu's major considerations in placing the Four Books at the top of the curriculum, before the Five Classics and well before the histories: "In reading, begin with passages that are easy to understand. For example, principle is brilliantly clear in the *Greater Learning*, the *Doctrine of the Mean*, the *Analects*, and the *Book of Mencius*, these four texts. Men simply do not read them. If these texts

27. This passage is found in *Wen-chi* 74.15b–16a as well. Earlier, Ch'eng I and Ch'eng Hao had suggested this sort of experiential reading, repeatedly calling for students to "get the real taste" of what they read; see Chan, *Reflection*, pp. 101–105, passim.

28. *YL* 104.4b/vol. 7, p. 2614.

29. Elsewhere he entreated his students: "Limit the size of your curriculum" (*YL* 10.5a/vol. 1, p. 165 [4.22]; cf. other comments in *YL* 10.5a–b/vol. 1, pp. 165–166 and also in 10.8b/vol. 1, p. 169 [4.38] and 10.12b–13a/vol. 1, p. 174 [4.52]). "Read little but become intimately familiar with what you read" (*YL* 10.4b/vol. 1, p. 165 [4.20]; cf. other comments in *YL* 10.4b/vol. 1, p. 165).

were understood, any book could be read, any principle could be investigated, any affair could be managed."[30] The Way, in Chu's opinion, was simply most approachable when texts were read in the proper order. Indeed, even among the Four Books themselves there was a proper order according to Chu: "You must start with the *Greater Learning*; next read the *Analects*, next the *Book of Mencius*, next the *Doctrine of the Mean*."[31] This order, which Chu was the first to prescribe—the Ch'eng brothers had never given much thought to a reading sequence for the Four Books—became an inviolable article of faith for him. Repeatedly in his writings and conversations with students he insisted on it. For instance:

I want men first to read the *Greater Learning* to fix upon the pattern of the Confucian Way; next the *Analects* to establish its foundations; next the *Book of Mencius* to observe its development; next the *Doctrine of the Mean* to discover the subtle mysteries of the ancients. The *Greater Learning* provides within its covers a series of steps and a precise order in which they should be followed; it is easy to understand and so should be read first. Although the *Analects* is concrete, its sayings are scattered about in fragments; on first reading, it is difficult. The *Book of Mencius* contains passages that inspire and arouse men's minds. The *Doctrine of the Mean*, too, is difficult to understand; it should be read only after the other three books.[32]

Throughout his writings and conversations, then, Chu was insistent that students follow what he believed was a natural progression in making their way through the Confucian curriculum, from easier texts to more difficult ones.

Chu Hsi feared that even after students had accepted the proper sequence in their reading of the Classics and the histories they might be led astray by their eagerness to get through the curriculum. He complained that they tended to read texts too quickly, often skipping from one passage to another, and thus missing the point of the whole (4.28). He frequently admonished his students to read each text from start to finish, faithfully following the natural order of the argument: "Each section, chapter, and line [of a text] is in its proper order; this order cannot be disturbed. . . . When you don't yet understand what precedes, don't venture to what follows;

30. *YL* 14.1a/vol. 1, p. 249.
31. *YL* 14.1a/vol. 1, p. 249.
32. *YL* 14.1a–b/vol. 1, p. 249. The sequence of the Four Books is discussed at length in Gardner, "Principle and Pedagogy."

when you haven't yet comprehended this, don't venture to set your mind on that."[33] Thus, it was not only the curriculum that had to be read in sequence but each individual text within it.

Chu Hsi also emphasized the need to read slowly, with full concentration, even if this meant that students would cover less ground: "If you are able to read two hundred characters, read only one hundred, but on those one hundred make a truly fierce effort. Understand them in every detail, recite them until you are intimately familiar with them. . . . If you read a great deal, but race through what you read, it will be of no benefit at all" (4.23; cf. 4.24 and 4.27).[34] Chu observed that children had an easier time learning than adults, principally because they were less hasty, less ambitious:

That children remember what they've read and adults frequently don't is simply because children concentrate their focus. If in one day they are given one hundred characters, they keep to one hundred characters; if given two hundred characters, they keep to two hundred characters. Adults sometimes read one hundred pages of characters in one day—they aren't so well focused. Often they read ten separate pieces when it would be best to read one part in ten. (4.22)[35]

Students thus had to learn to be patient in their reading; they had to be content to advance gradually.

Chu, in fact, even called for students to recite each text over and over again until they no longer saw it as "other."[36] For every reading would produce a deeper understanding of it—even fifty or a hundred readings was not too many (4.34 and 5.35).[37] There was no prescribed number of times a book was to be read; Chu simply advised that "when the number's sufficient, stop" (5.36).

Chu Hsi's ideal reader, then, would limit the scope of his curriculum, approach the texts in that curriculum sequentially, and read each text gradually from front to back over and over again, to

33. *Wen-chi* 74.15b; cf. *YL* 11.11b/vol. 1, p. 189 (5.40).

34. See other comments in *YL* 10.4b–7b/vol. 1, pp. 165–168.

35. Cf. *YL* 10.14b/vol. 1, p. 175 (4.54), where Chu advises those beyond middle age to read very little but to turn the little they do read over and over in their minds.

36. Chu revealed that when he was seventeen or eighteen he recited the *Chung-yung* and the *Ta-hsüeh* each ten times every morning; see *YL* 16.4b/vol. 2, p. 319.

37. See other comments in *YL* 10.8a/vol. 1, pp. 168–169.

the point of "intimate familiarity." Still, what guarantee was there
that he would finally understand each text as he should? How could
he be certain to get at the true intentions of the sages and worthies
of the past? The reader, Chu argued, had to have an "open mind"
(*hsü-hsin*). For only an open mind would be faithful to "the true
meaning of the classical text" (5.21; cf. 5.18) and allow the text to
speak for itself. To Chu an "open" mind was a mind "empty" (*hsü*)
of preconceived ideas about what the text should or might say.[38]
The reader who came to the text with preconceived ideas was certain to read those ideas into the text.[39] In the end, the text would
serve merely to prop up his ideas, not to reveal the truth expressed
there by the sages.[40] This sort of subjective reading alarmed Chu:
"Nowadays people usually have an idea in their own minds first,
then take what other men have said [in the texts] to explain their
idea. What doesn't conform to their idea they forcibly make to conform" (5.31).[41] Chu speculated that the intelligent person in particular would have a difficult time reading texts with an open mind
since his mind was already full of ideas, full of convictions.[42] He
therefore admonished his own students: "In reading, don't force
your ideas on the text. You must get rid of your own ideas and read
for the meaning of the ancients" (5.30; cf. 5.59).[43] Effective reading,
then, depended on a willingness to doubt (*i*), and not just the views
of others but one's own as well.[44] Indeed, this willingness was the
starting point, the premise, of Chu's *tu-shu fa* (5.36),[45] for only a
genuinely inquiring mind would have the tenacity to pursue the

38. For example, see comments in *YL* 11.3b–4a/vol. 1, pp. 179–180 and *Wen-chi* 53.7a–b and 74.16a.

39. For example, see comments in *YL* 11.3b–4a/vol. 1, p. 179.

40. See comments in *YL* 11.4a/vol. 1, p. 179.

41. Cf. other comments in *YL* 11.9b/vol. 1, p. 185 and 137.7a–b/vol. 8, p. 3258.

42. *YL* 139.20a/vol. 8, p. 3317.

43. Chu wanted the text to speak for itself: "Depend on the text to read the
text, depend on the object to observe the object. Don't come to the text or the
object with preconceived ideas" (*YL* 11.5b/vol. 1, p. 181 [5.24]; cf. also *YL* 9.10b/
vol. 1, p. 158 [3.37], 9.10b/vol. 1, p. 159 [3.39], 11.10a/vol. 1, pp. 185–186 [5.33],
11.10a/vol. 1, p. 186 [5.34], and 11.15a/vol. 1, p. 191 [5.48]).

44. In *YL* 11.11a/vol. 1, p. 187 (5.37), Chu remarks: "The problem with men is
that they feel the views of others alone may be doubted, not their own."

45. Earlier Ch'eng I had said (*Ho-nan Ch'eng-shih wai-shu* 11.2b): "The student
must first of all know how to doubt."

truth fully, casting aside all preconceived and misguided ideas in the process.

Included in the category of preconceived ideas were traditional views and interpretations of the text that had been passed on and accepted, perhaps even unquestioningly, by the reader (e.g., 5.33 and 5.34). The reader had to learn to treat these received opinions critically. Chu suggested to his students that when they did not understand a passage it might well be that the accepted view of it, which they had made their own, was leading them astray; they should waste no time in questioning it, "washing it away," and seeking a new, open-minded understanding of the passage based on a careful reading of the original text itself (e.g., 5.33, 5.34, and 5.35). Implicit here, it would seem, was a warning to students about the fallibility of the commentary tradition. That tradition could err and hence should not be accepted unconditionally. Chu claimed that even some of the recent commentaries of Yu Tso (1053–1123), Yang Shih, and other disciples of the Ch'eng brothers were riddled with mistakes; these men, according to Chu, had at times shown less interest in analyzing the words of the authors than in presenting their own understanding of principle.[46] As a result their commentaries were not very reliable guides to the ancient texts.

To be sure, Chu never suggested that commentaries be abandoned, for they could provide insight and guidance into the text.[47] He simply wanted to be certain that students did not permit the commentaries to lead them blindly and perhaps obscure the real meaning of the text for them: "The classical texts of the sages are like the master, the commentaries like the slave. Nowadays people are unacquainted with the master and turn to the slave for an introduction to him. Only thus do they become acquainted with the master. In the end it's not like [turning to] the classical texts them-

46. For example, *YL* 62.6b/vol. 4, p. 1485 and 62.7a/vol. 4, p. 1485. Even Ch'eng I's commentaries came in for criticism on occasion; see, for instance, *YL* 19.10b/vol. 2, p. 438 and 11.17a/vol. 1, p. 193 5.57). Chan, *Reflections*, pp. 110–111, quotes additional passages from Chu Hsi on Ch'eng I's *Commentary on the Changes*.

47. Indeed, Chu would have students read and compare the different commentaries on a given text (*YL* 11.16a/vol. 1, p. 192 [5.50, 5.51] and 11.14b/vol. 1, p. 190 [5.46]).

selves" (5.58). Students were to read the commentaries critically (e.g., 5.51),[48] and only after they had struggled with the classical text itself: "If there are passages you don't understand, ponder them deeply, and if you still don't get them, then read the commentaries—only then will the commentaries have any significance" (5.48; cf. 5.47). The commentaries surely had a place in the students' reading, Chu believed, but they were not to supersede the classical texts themselves (5.56 and 5.57), nor were they to be allowed to prejudice the reader's "open-minded" reading of the classical texts.

The successful reading of the texts in the curriculum depended, then, not only on the intelligence of the reader's mind but, as importantly, on its disposition.[49] It had to be "open," free of preconceived ideas. "Opening" the mind, however, required conscious effort. The mind had to be readied to receive the truth in the text. All selfish desires and prejudices had to be thoroughly "cleansed" from the mind so that it could approach the text without impediment. Chu commented: "There is a method to book learning. Simply scrub clean the mind, then read" (5.12). Chu sometimes talked about "settling" the mind as well: "Presently, should you want to engage in book learning, you must first settle the mind so that it becomes like still water or a clear mirror. How can a cloudy mirror reflect anything?" (5.10). To reflect accurately what was contained in the text, the reader's mind, then, had to have achieved a clear, settled state, free from unchecked emotions and desires. To help his students attain his state of mind, Chu urged them to practice *ching-tso*, or "quiet-sitting" (e.g., 5.8 and 6.61),[50] once even suggesting that it would be best to give half a day to quiet-sitting and the other half to reading.[51] Chu's hope here was that in their time off from reading students would sit quietly in meditation, ridding the mind of any personal thoughts or desires that might interfere with a fair and faithful reading of the text when they did turn to it.

48. Cf. also *YL* 11.13b/vol. 1, p. 189.
49. See *YL* 11.21b/vol. 1, p. 189.
50. See also *YL* 11.3a/vol. 1, p. 178 and numerous comments in *YL* 12.17bff./ vol. 1, pp. 216ff. Ch'ien Mu, *Chu-tzu hsin hsüeh-an*, vol. 2, pp. 277–297, discusses Chu's views of *ching* and *ching-tso*.
51. *YL* 116.20a–b/vol. 7, p. 2806.

Quiet-sitting thus played an important role in the reading process for Chu Hsi.

Still, how would this perfectly calm and unobstructed mind come to understand the principle embedded in the text? What enabled the reader, who had worked to settle his mind and keep it unobstructed, to apprehend the message in the canonical writings? The answer to these questions makes clear the close relationship that existed between Chu Hsi's *tu-shu fa* and his system of metaphysics. Chu's *tu-shu fa*, in fact, is not particularly intelligible or meaningful unless we appreciate his ontological views, for the efficacy of his *tu-shu fa* was rooted in his assumptions about principle, human nature, the mind, psychophysical stuff (*ch'i*),[52] and so forth.[53]

According to Chu, all things in the universe possessed principle, which as defined by him and the Ch'eng brothers before him was both the reason why a thing was as it was and the rule to which a thing should conform.[54] In Chu's view principle in the world was one, it simply had many manifestations.[55] So although different things manifested it in different ways, the rule to which those things conformed was ultimately one, as was the reason those things were as they were. Perhaps "principle," a translation that on its own has little meaning, should be understood as something like a blueprint or pattern for the cosmos, a blueprint or pattern that underlies everything and every affair in that cosmos.[56] Man, too, naturally possessed principle. And in man this principle, Chu argued, was identical with the human nature (*hsing*) heaven had endowed in

52. *Ch'i* is a difficult term to define or translate, referring as it does to both the material and the energy that pervade the universe and everything in it. For a discussion of *ch'i* see Schwartz, *World of Thought*, pp. 179–184. "Material force" has become a conventional translation of *ch'i*, but even though I find it less cumbersome than "psychophysical stuff," I also find it less meaningful.

53. Modern scholarship has unfortunately tended to focus on Chu Hsi's metaphysics, suggesting that issues of metaphysics were his primary interest. In fact, learning was at least as important for Chu Hsi; after all, the apprehension of principle was the aim of his philosophical program. Chu's metaphysics sustains but by no means overwhelms his epistemological concerns.

54. This is the definition given by Chu in his *Ta-hsüeh huo-wen* 15a. See also *YL*, *chüan* 1–2, passim.

55. Chu was drawing on Ch'eng I's views; see *Ho-nan Ch'eng-shih i-shu* (hereafter *I-shu*), pp. 214 and 13, and *I-ch'uan I-chuan* 3.3b. Chu's sympathy with Ch'eng I's formula can be found in *YL* 1.2a/vol. 1, p. 2, for example.

56. On principle see the annotation that follows 1.4.

him at birth.[57] As reason here would suggest, this human nature
was in each and every person the same. And in every person it was
morally good, constituted as it was of the four cardinal virtues,
benevolence, righteousness, propriety, and wisdom, as Mencius
earlier had argued.[58]

But every thing—and thus every person—was also born with an
endowment of psychophysical stuff. The quality as well as the
quantity of the psychophysical stuff differed from one thing and one
individual to another. Some psychophysical stuff was clearer than
others, some more refined than others, some less dense than others.
This endowment of psychophysical stuff gave each thing or person
its peculiar form and individual characteristics.[59] As to the relationship between principle and psychophysical stuff, Chu was very
clear: "There has never been any psychophysical stuff without
principle nor any principle without psychophysical stuff."[60] The
two entities simply could not exist independently of each other:
without principle the psychophysical stuff had no ontological
reason for being, and without psychophysical stuff principle had
nothing in which to inhere.

A person's endowment of psychophysical stuff, depending on its
clarity and density, could allow his principle—which was one with
his benevolent human nature—to become manifest, or it could
obscure it, preventing it from becoming manifest.[61] To obscure it
was to cut the person off from the ontological basis of his morality
and thus ensure that he would lose the Way.

Man consequently found himself in a predicament, for he lived

57. Chu was following Ch'eng I here. See his comment praising Ch'eng I's
formulation, cited in Chan, *Reflections*, p. 29: "'The nature is the same as principle.' None since Confucius and Mencius has ever had this insight. None from
ancient times on has ever made such a bold statement."

58. For numerous comments by Chu on human nature see the annotation that
follows 2.3.

59. On *ch'i* see *YL*, *chüan* 1–2, passim.

60. *YL* 1.1b/vol. 1, p. 2.

61. Chu put it quite succinctly in his "Preface to the Greater Learning in
Chapters and Verses" (preface to *Ta-hsüeh chang-chü* 1a): "Since heaven first gave
birth to the people down below, it has granted them all the same nature of benevolence, righteousness, propriety, and wisdom. Yet their psychophysical endow-
ments often prove unequal; so not all are able to know the composition of their
natures and thus to preserve them whole." Translation from Gardner, *Chu Hsi and
the Ta-hsueh*, p. 77.

with the capability of being fully moral yet in most cases found himself falling short of that moral perfection. That is, he was confronted with an innate moral potential, but one that needed consciously and actively to be given realization. To this end his endowment of psychophysical stuff had to be kept refined and clarified, so that principle would be unimpeded and shine forth.

The responsibility that Chu's philosophy placed on the mind was huge, for it was the mind that housed principle (e.g., 3.22, 3.23, and 3.27) and thus the mind that could issue it forth and bring it to realization. But the mind could fail in this task, as it could be led away from realization of principle if excessive emotions or human desires got the better of it. Chu, like Chang Tsai before him, believed that the mind embraced and governed both human nature (or principle) and the emotions (*ch'ing*);[62] thus for him the mind could become the battleground for conflict between the two, the locus of man's struggle to achieve morality. Chu told his students: "As for the mind of man, if heavenly principle is preserved, human desire will disappear. If human desire should overcome it, heavenly principle will be extinguished. Never do heavenly principle and human desire permeate each other" (7.9).

In its original condition the mind was in a state of equilibrium; it was this balance that had to be maintained or regained if the principle in it was not to find itself overwhelmed by emotions or selfish human desires (6.29). Chu spoke frequently of "preserving the mind" and "seeking the lost mind." As he put it: "It's simply because man has let go of his mind that he falls into evil" (6.18); or elsewhere, "If a person is able to preserve his mind so that it is exceptionally clear, he'll naturally be capable of merging with the Way" (6.25). Thus, according to Chu Hsi, the mind, which was constituted of only the most refined and spirited psychophysical stuff,[63] was "the root" (6.1). It served as "master" of the person (e.g., 6.4, 6.5, and 6.13). This mind had to be tended to, had to be kept refined, if man was to behave as he should, if he was to conform to principle (3.31).

The will, *chih*—which Chu described as the intention or inclina-

---

62. See, for example, passages in *YL* 5.9bff/vol. 1, pp. 91ff. and 98.8a–9b/vol. 7, pp. 2513–2515. For Chang's original comment see *Chang Tsai chi*, p. 374.

63. E.g., *YL* 5.3b/vol. 1, p. 85.

tion of the mind or, literally, "where the mind was headed"[64]—
could help guide the mind in the right direction. Man thus had to
strive to keep his will firmly fixed; for if it was strong and determined, it would lead the mind along the right path toward the good
nature and away from insidious human desires. That is, intemper-
ate desires and emotions would not have the opportunity to develop, if man so willed. *Li chih*, "to establish or fix the will," signif-
icantly, was one of Chu's most common refrains in discussions
with disciples.[65] The mind thus functioned as the indeterminate
element in Chu Hsi's philosophical system, the element that made
the moral perfection Chu was seeking a possibility, but not by any
means an inevitability.[66]

Consequently, we find Chu throughout the *Conversations of Master
Chu, Arranged Topically*, particularly in chapter 12, urging his students variously to "control" the mind, "hold on to it," "gather it
in," "possess it," "keep it constantly alert," and so forth. In different ways he was telling them the same thing: ready the mind for its
confrontation with things and affairs in the world. The mind was to
be fully "present" always, fully balanced in its response to matters.
To be present and balanced, the mind first had to be made *ching*, a
state in which it was absolutely attentive to whatever was before it,
without being distracted by anything else.[67] To be *ching* to something was to concentrate all of one's mental energy on it (6.54).
Although *ching* itself referred to a state of mind and was dependent
on rigorous mental discipline, Chu Hsi suggested certain physical
attitudes that would encourage the development of *ching*: "The
head should be upright, the eyes looking straight ahead, the feet
steady, the hands respectful, the mouth quiet and composed, the
bearing solemn—these are all aspects of inner mental attentiveness" (6.46). If a person were to practice *ching*, his mind would
become one, preserved in its whole (6.40).

The person who practiced inner mental attentiveness, then, in
Chu's view possessed a mind that could efficiently and successfully

64. See passages in *YL* 5.14a/vol. 1, p. 96.
65. E.g., *YL* 8.5a–6a/vol. 1, pp. 133–134.
66. This discussion of the mind is based on *YL*, *chüan* 5.
67. Chu's understanding of *ching* derived from Ch'eng I's; see passages in *YL*
12.7bff./vol. 1, pp. 206ff.

"apprehend the principle in things" (*ko wu*).[68] For the mind of man, after all, embraced the myriad manifestations of principle; thus as it confronted things, the mind—if fully attentive, fully concentrated—could through a sort of resonance sense the principle in those things. A natural response occurred between principle in one's mind and in the things before that mind.[69] With effort and over time this process would lead to a clearer and clearer understanding of principle. Learning about principle, then, rested on a dialectical relationship: the mind and its principle would make intelligible the things in the world out there and their principle, but the things out there at the same time would help to illuminate the principle contained in the mind. Or in Chu's words: "The effort to probe principle is naturally subsumed in the nurturing process—one probes the principle being nurtured. The effort to nurture is naturally subsumed in the process of probing principle—one nurtures the principle being probed. These two processes are inseparable" (3.7; cf. 3.11, 3.8, 3.23, and 3.9).[70] Probing principle to the point of complete apprehension was, of course, the crucial step in Chu Hsi's program of self-cultivation; for since the principle in things and the principle in man were the same, and since principle in man was identical with his nature, apprehending principle either in things out there or in oneself was nothing but self-realization.

Reading the classical texts in the manner set forth in Chu's *tu-shu*

68. The term *ko wu* comes from the *Ta-hsüeh*, "Classic of Confucius," para. 4; Ch'eng I had been drawn to the term earlier, arguing that the process of *ko wu* enables men to uncover principle, the source of morality underlying heaven, earth, and all human beings. Chu Hsi, in an elaboration of Ch'eng I's position, made *ko wu* the centerpiece of his program of self-cultivation, systematically developing its philosophical significance; he even replaced the "missing" chapter on it in the *Ta-hsüeh* text. See Gardner, *Chu Hsi and the Ta-hsueh*, pp. 53–57, and the annotation to 3.5 in Part Two. *Ko wu* is often translated "the investigation of things," but "apprehending the principle in things" accords much better with Chu Hsi's understanding of it as it appears in his gloss in his commentary to the "Classic of Confucius," para. 4; see footnote to passage 1.1 in Part Two.

69. In *YL* 12.20b/vol. 1, p. 220, Chu comments: "Principle in things and in our mind are essentially one. Neither is deficient in the slightest. What's necessary is that we respond to things, that's all. Things and the mind share the same principle." See also *YL* 12.20b/vol. 1, p. 220 and 12.11b/vol. 1, p. 210 (6.38) and the annotation that follows the translation in 6.38.

70. In *YL* 126.10a/vol. 8, p. 3016, we read: "According to our Confucian teachings 'maintaining inner mental attentiveness' is the foundation, but 'probing principle' gives that foundation its full development."

fa was just one way to apprehend principle, one way to realize one-self. For Chu it was perhaps the best way, since principle was, to his mind, more accessible, more manifest, in them than anywhere else. Indeed, what should be obvious is that Chu possessed a deep faith in the efficacy of the classical writings, in their ability to reveal principle—fully embodied by the sages and thus by what they wrote—to the reader who really cared (e.g., 4.31). After the tenth or hundredth reading the principle embodied in the texts might illuminate the moral principle in ourselves. And at that point when principle in the text was finally able to awaken fully the principle in the reader's mind, text and reader truly became inseparable; the reader, it might be said, had at that moment "experienced" the text to the fullest, as Chu hoped he would. It was this sort of resonance between the reader and the text that Chu seemed to be describing in the following comment:

In reading, we cannot seek moral principle solely from the text. We must turn the process around and look for it in ourselves. Since the Ch'in-Han period [Ch'in, 221–206 B.C.; Han, 206 B.C.–A.D. 220] no one has spoken about this; people simply have sought it in the text, not in themselves. We have yet to discover for ourselves what the sages previously explained in their texts—only through their words will we find it in ourselves. (5.26)[71]

The dialectical relationship between man's mind and the principle in things was the epistemological premise of Chu's *tu-shu fa* then. The mind was what enabled the reader to grasp the essence, the principle, of the classical texts in the first place, but that essence was what ultimately gave full realization to the potentiality of the mind. In the end, therefore, genuine understanding of the canon was simply self-understanding. Experiencing the text meant experiencing the self.

In developing his rather elaborate *tu-shu fa*, Chu Hsi was launching an all-out attack on the superficial and misguided literati learning he found typical of the day. The student had to approach the Confucian texts with a new, almost religious attitude. The truth was in them, he should assume, but he would have to struggle to uncover it. He would have to burrow through layer after layer of

---

71. Cf. similar comments in *YL* 11.5b/vol. 1, p. 181 and 11.12a/vol. 1, p. 188 (5.41).

meaning to get at the profound intentions of the sages (4.9 and 4.10). The reward of doing so, however, was more than mere advancement in officialdom. It was spiritual enlightenment. For the texts had an affective force, a transforming power:[72] in "experiencing" them, the reader could hope to give fulfillment to the principle in his mind, his moral potential. And having awakened the latent humaneness of his spirit, he might then become interconnected with all other things in the universe (e.g., 3.28).

Reading for Chu Hsi was thus nothing but a method of self-cultivation, a way of realizing one's inner perfection through an investigation of things in the world out there; reading could truly change one's spiritual life. The Ming critics who assailed Chu for an overly scholastic and wooden approach to the Confucian texts, an approach lacking in moral significance, did not particularly understand Chu; they were perhaps fairer critics of the late Sung through Ming followers of the Chu Hsi school than of Chu Hsi himself.[73] After all, it was these later Neo-Confucians, not Chu, who authorized certain interpretations of the Classics as the standard readings for the civil service examinations. Eager to succeed in the examinations, candidates tended to follow these interpretations blindly. It is one of those ironies of history that many of these "standard" readings were Chu's own. As we have seen, Chu Hsi insisted that his students take anything but an uncritical approach to the canon. The interpretations and commentaries of others, even those of illustrious Neo-Confucians, were all open to question. Each student was encouraged to confront the texts directly, without the aid of intermediaries, at least at first; as Chu put it, reading the texts of the sages should be "like speaking with them face to face" (4.6). There was a confidence on Chu's part, then, in the individual's ability to find for himself the truth in the text. To do so, of course, he had to have the right, reverential attitude; that is, if he approached the work with a singleness of mind (*ching*), convinced that the truth was indeed imbedded in the text, he might be fortunate enough to hear that truth.

Chu's *tu-shu fa* thus placed a great deal of value on the autonomy of the individual in the reading process. But we must recog-

---

72. Cf. de Bary, *Liberal Tradition*, pp. 60–62.
73. For example, see Wang Yang-ming's implicit criticism of Chu in Chan, *Instructions*, pp. 275–276.

nize that autonomy in the process did not by any means translate into subjectivity in the final understanding. For according to Chu, the truth in the text was the same for every reader. It was an objective truth, first expressed long ago by the revered sages. Chu may have required the reader to "experience" the text personally, but that was simply so the sages' message would become his own. The message was supposed to transform the reader, not the reader the message. In Chu's *tu-shu fa* the authentic reader, the reader who approached the text in the proper spirit, was guaranteed of reading the classical text objectively, for the principle residing in his mind and that residing in the mind of the sages and expressed in their works were one and the same. Hence, a resonance was certain to occur between the reader's mind and the text, fully awakening the reader to the true intentions of the sages of the past.

Chu Hsi and the
Transformation of the
Confucian Tradition

Any student of the Confucian tradition knows that Chu Hsi's concern for learning was by no means new. Learning had been a central issue from the very beginning, from the time of Confucius himself. In an autobiographical statement made to disciples late in life, Confucius stressed his early commitment to the task of learning: "At age fifteen I set my heart upon learning," and then went on to suggest that it was this early purpose that enabled him eventually "to know the biddings of heaven" and "to follow the dictates of my own heart without overstepping the boundaries of right."[1] No one had a greater passion for learning than he: "In a hamlet of ten houses you may be sure of finding someone quite as loyal and true to his word as I. But I doubt if you would find anyone with such a love of learning."[2] The message was perfectly clear: his followers too were to set their hearts on learning. Learning was the path to sagehood, leading men both "to improve themselves in the Way" and "to devote themselves to the service of the state."[3] Only those born sages—and Confucius did not number even himself among these—could dispense with learning.[4]

1. *Lun-yü* 2/4; translation based on Waley, *Analects*, p. 88.
2. *Lun-yü* 5/28; translation, with slight modification, from Waley, *Analects*, p. 114.
3. E.g., *Lun-yü* 19/7, 19/13; translations based on Waley, *Analects*, pp. 225, 227.
4. *Lun-yü* 7/20.

From this time on, learning would remain a central task for Confucians; so central was it that one could not ignore it completely and still claim to belong to the school. But even though Confucius may have signaled the critical importance of learning for his followers, his discussion of it in the *Analects* allowed considerable leeway in later interpretations of exactly how and what the Confucian was to learn. For Confucius never drew up a precise and systematic curriculum for study: though we can assume, I think, that he expected students to master the *Book of Poetry*, the *Book of History*, and writings on ritual, he did not establish an order in which they were to be mastered, nor did he discuss how they were to be read or analyzed. It was left, then, for later Confucians to work out a structured program of learning. Indeed, the formation of such a program became one of the major points of debate within the later Confucian school.

More serious, however, was the tension engendered by the "polarity" within Confucius's concept of sagehood. To be a sage meant that one had achieved moral perfection *and* succeeded in serving the people. To Confucius's mind these were simply two dimensions—an "inner" dimension of self-cultivation and an "outer" dimension of ordering the polity—of the same goal; inextricably linked, they could not rightly be separated. But as Confucius's own experience demonstrated, these two dimensions were in fact often separated in real life. All too often it seemed that an official career was achieved at the expense of moral perfection or that service to the people was neglected in the pursuit of self-perfection. Later Confucian thinkers, perhaps in response to practical constraints, often emphasized one dimension over the other, in some cases one to the virtual exclusion of the other.[5]

Thus, although Confucians agreed that learning was essential to their task, they could, and often did, disagree about what constituted both the right curriculum and the proper goal of learning. Of course, these two concerns were closely related. Choice of curriculum was dependent on choice of goals: Was moral cultivation of the individual a higher priority than sociopolitical action? Or was sociopolitical reform more pressing than the moral development of

5. On this Confucian "polarity" see Schwartz, "Some Polarities," particularly pp. 52–54.

individuals in society? Or, in fact, were these two dimensions—inner and outer—to be given equal emphasis?

The relative weight Confucians would give to these various possible goals of learning naturally developed out of their sense of the world around them, out of their perception of how it operated and what its problems were. Just as contemporary debates in the United States that rage over the nature of education and the state of the curriculum reflect differing perceptions of the state of American society, politics, economy, and way of life, so too arguments put forward by Confucian literati down through the ages about the content and purpose of education reflected differing outlooks on Chinese society, the problems it faced, and how those problems might be resolved.

During the Sung period, such debates over the nature of learning became a routine part of intellectual life. These debates were sparked by concern among literati over the state of the society, particularly over the weakness of the central government in the face of the "barbarian" threat. In the mid-eleventh century political foes Wang An-shih and Ssu-ma Kuang both agreed that the outer sociopolitical order had to be reformed if the problems of the realm were to be redressed. But they disagreed about where and how to reform that order. Wang, facing what he believed to be a social, military, and fiscal crisis, was convinced that structural overhaul was necessary, that new governmental institutions and regulations fostering greater administrative efficiency and economic strength were called for. In power, he implemented a series of reform measures and established new agencies—often against considerable opposition—that affected all aspects of government.[6] Consequently, Wang was denounced by many of his peers for being legalistic, concerned only with laws and techniques of administration. Systems of government were what really mattered to him, not the morality and integrity of either those who served or those under the influence of those who served, so the argument went.

Ssu-ma Kuang was one of Wang's most vociferous opponents, so

6. For a brief summary of Wang's New Policies see Liu, *Reform in Sung China*, pp. 1–10; cf. Wang's "Ten Thousand Word Memorial," translated in de Bary, *Sources of Chinese Tradition*, vol. 1, pp. 413–419, and Williamson, *Wang An Shih*, vol. 1, pp. 48–84.

vociferous in fact that he was forced into exile in Loyang during the
reform period of Wang An-shih (1069–1085). To his mind government as it had evolved over the centuries did not have to be fundamentally restructured. The institutions and regulations passed
down by the ancient sages had proved durable and sound and were
not in need of major reform. He remarked: "Governing the empire
may be likened to living in a house. If it becomes worn, one repairs
it. Unless there is great ruin, one does not build it anew."[7] For him
"government was at bottom an ethical and moral problem, not a
technical one"; it consisted in employing the "right men," not in
devising regulations, laws, and institutions that would work regardless of the individuals who administered them.[8] That is, the
age-old institutions of state were entirely adequate in administering
the realm; what was necessary now were moral men—beginning of
course with the emperor himself—who would serve those institutions well and, through the agency of government, bring order to
society and prosperity to the people. Simply put, for Ssu-ma good
government would be sure to prevail when good men who knew the
principles of good governance were attracted to public service.

The learning each of these men advocated looked to the past—
but not to the same past. Wang An-shih and his followers turned to
those texts in the Confucian canon that purportedly detailed the
institutions and regulations of the Three Dynasties period: the *Book
of Poetry*, the *Book of History*, and the *Rites of Chou* (*Chou li*). These
Classics, particularly the *Rites of Chou*, offered descriptions of those
systems of government that had made early antiquity a golden age;
for Wang these texts could serve as blueprints for government for
all time. He explained:

In the worthiness of its individual officials to discharge the duties of office,
and in the effectiveness with which its institutions administered the law, no
dynasty has surpassed the early Chou. Likewise, in the suitability of its
laws for perpetuation in later ages, and in the expression given them in
literary form, no book is so perfect as the *Institutes of Chou* (*Chou-kuan*).[9]

7. Huang I-chou, *Hsü Tzu-chih t'ung-chien ch'ang-pien shih-pu* 6.8b; translation
from Sariti, "Monarchy, Bureaucracy, and Absolutism," p. 57.
8. Sariti, "Monarchy, Bureaucracy, and Absolutism," pp. 74–75.
9. I.e., the *Rites of Chou*. *Lin-ch'uan hsien-sheng wen-chi* 84.1b–2a; translation from
de Bary, *Sources of Chinese Tradition*, vol. 1, p. 412.

Wang naturally was not suggesting that the institutions of the Chou be adopted in their exact form in the present but rather that the substance of those institutions could serve as a model, even in the Sung. And, indeed, he routinely appealed to these three ancient texts in citing precedents for his reform program. So devoted was Wang to these Classics that in 1073 he established a commission under his direction to provide official commentaries for them; two years later the commentaries were completed, at which time he had them published and sent to all the government schools in the empire.[10] Henceforth, throughout most of the last half-century of the Northern Sung these three texts and the commentaries on them by Wang served as the basis for the civil service examinations. It was Wang's belief that by studying the model institutions and legislation in his favored Classics, literati of the Sung could come to know the good works of the sages and learn for themselves how to restructure the outer sociopolitical realm into a coherent order.

For Ssu-ma Kuang, more interested in statecraft than in institutions of state, the past offered a long record of the successes and failures of governmental policy and action. Therefore, rather than turning to texts that presented an idealized account of the past—as Wang had—Ssu-ma preferred to study the stream of known history. In his view the premier text in the Confucian tradition, the text to be valued and studied most, was the *Spring and Autumn Annals*—a text Wang had found contemptible and had banished from the examinations. An annalistic account of historical events, the *Spring and Autumn Annals* could be used as a casebook for proper behavior. From it literati could learn why some periods were orderly and some disorderly, why some policies were successful and others had failed, and most important, what course of action would be most appropriate in the situations confronting them in their official capacities. With his unshakeable conviction that history could serve as a guide to the present, that the emperor and his officials could learn from the past how to serve the people effectively and morally, Ssu-ma spent most of his years in exile in Loyang completing his magnum opus, the *Comprehensive Mirror for Aid in Government*, an annalistic account in 294 *chüan* of the history of China from 403

10. Hartwell, "Historical Analogism," p. 712.

B.C. to A.D. 959, the last year of the Five Dynasties period.[11] A
memorial sent by Ssu-ma to Emperor Ying-tsung (r. 1064–1067)
leaves little doubt as to the purpose he himself had in mind for his
work:

Disregarding my inadequacy I have always wanted to write a chronological history roughly in accordance with the form of the *Tso Commentary*
[on the *Spring and Autumn Annals*], starting with the Warring States and
going down to the Five Dynasties, drawing on other books besides the
Official Histories and taking in all that a prince ought to know—
everything pertaining to the rise and fall of dynasties and the good and ill
fortune of the common people, all good and bad examples that can furnish
models and warnings.[12]

The succeeding emperor, Shen-tsung (r. 1068–1085), conferred
upon the book its title, *Comprehensive Mirror for Aid in Government*.[13]

As a "historical analogist" Ssu-ma clearly found great value in
all history, even in recent history.[14] Whereas Wang An-shih viewed
the post–Three Dynasties period as a time of deviation from the
Way and thus unworthy of study, Ssu-ma believed that all history,
down through the T'ang and Five Dynasties, was useful and relevant; for all periods of the past—glorious and bleak—offered lessons for the aspiring official. In his view literati had to know the
causes of failure and corruption as well as the causes of success and
prosperity. Only then would they be prepared to evaluate contemporary policy and respond to the exigencies of governing the state.

In the late eleventh century, literati in the generation after Wang
and Ssu-ma often found themselves out of high political office, largely
as a result of the factionalism generated by Wang's reforms. Not
surprisingly, many of them turned their attention away from the
political order and concentrated more on how they as individuals
could live meaningful lives out of office.[15] The previous generation
had focused on the question, How do we implement the Way in the
governance of the state? This generation shifted the focus, asking

11. On the *Tzu-chih t'ung-chien* see Hervouet, ed., *Sung Bibliography*, pp. 69–70.
12. Li T'ao, *Hsü Tzu-chih t'ung-chien ch'ang-pien* 208.2b; translation, with slight
modification, from Pulleyblank, "Chinese Historical Criticism," pp. 153–154.
13. Pulleyblank, "Chinese Historical Criticism," p. 154.
14. On historical analogism see Hartwell, "Historical Analogism."
15. See Freeman, "Lo-yang."

instead, How do we implement the Way in our own lives? Of course this is not to suggest that men like Ssu-ma had not been interested in the morality of the individual but simply that what had concerned them more was how to bring the outer sociopolitical order in line with the Way. Nor is it to suggest that men of the following generation, such as Su Shih and Ch'eng I, had no interest in seeing the Way prevail in government; it was simply that they were more interested in how individuals might experience the Way in their own lives.

For Su Shih the Way was mysterious and incapable of definition; it was not something that could be analytically studied or fully realized through the accumulation of knowledge. Rather, through spontaneous expression of his human emotions, a person could manifest the Way in his own life—human feeling was the source of the Way for Su. Man's task therefore was to awaken to his own feelings, and to the centrality of feeling in mankind.[16] Su declared his preference for an affective apprehension of the Way in his "Discussion of the *Doctrine of the Mean*":

As for sincerity, what is it? It is what is called "delighting in it" (*lo chih*), for delighting in it one will naturally be faithful, therefore it says, "Sincerity." As for enlightenment, what is it? It is what is called "knowing it" (*chih chih*), for knowing it one reaches the goal, therefore it says, "Enlightenment." Only the sage has not reached knowing while he has already entered into delighting. That which is entered first is the host, and as such awaits the rest; here then delighting is the host. In the case of a worthy, he has not reached delighting while already entering knowing. That which is entered first is the host, and as such awaits the rest; here then knowing is the host. When delighting is the host, there are things that are not known, but knowing is always practiced. When knowing is the host, although nothing is not known, there are things that cannot be practiced. The Master said, "To know it is not as good as to love it, and to love it is not as good as to take delight in it." Knowing it and delighting in it—this is the distinction between the worthy and the sage.[17]

The spontaneous expression of feeling, then, would put one in touch with the source and transform one into a sage, a state of

16. See Murck, "Su Shih's Reading of the *Chung-yung*," p. 286.

17. *Su Tung-p'o ch'uan-chi*, vol. 2, pp. 760–761; translation, with slight modification, from Murck, "Su Shih's Reading of the *Chung-yung*," p. 276.

being in which things "are not known, but knowing is always practiced."

Su Shih described his own behavior as spontaneously coming from within, unself-conscious and unreflective, without consideration for external standards of right and wrong:

Alas! I am the man in the empire most wanting in premeditative thought. When something comes up I speak; there is no time for thought. If I think before I speak, I miss my chance; if I think after I have spoken it is too late. And so all my life I do not know what I think. Words arise in my mind, and rush into my mouth. If I spit them out I offend other people; if I swallow them back I offend myself. And thinking it better to offend others, in the end I spit them out. The gentleman reacts to good just as he loves a lovely color, toward evil just as he hates a hateful smell. How could it be that when confronted with a matter he thinks, calculating and deliberating its good and evil aspects and only then rejects or espouses it?[18]

This is obviously more than a mere confession on Su's part; it is a proposal that his intuitive responsiveness become a model for others.

In suggesting how to cultivate the Way, Su Shih advocated that men cultivate their creativity, that they learn to give expression to their inner feelings, the source of the Way, through literature and art, through the pursuit of culture. There was no prescribed body of texts to be mastered as part of this pursuit; the whole range of earlier literary and cultural accomplishments was available to inspire the creative seed innate in men. As one scholar has observed, Su's "apprehension of the *tao* was aesthetic, not rational. . . . For Su Shih, the function of literature was to intuit the *tao* (*wen yi kuan tao*), a mode of apprehension as well as expression."[19] And that Su felt he had indeed apprehended it, he made very clear:

My writing is like a ten-thousand-gallon spring. It can issue from the ground anywhere at all. On smooth ground it rushes swiftly on and covers a thousand *li* in a single day without difficulty. When it twists and turns among mountains and rocks, it fits its form to things it meets: unknow-

18. *Su Tung-p'o ch'üan-chi*, vol. 1, p. 393; translation from Hatch, "Su Shih," vol. 3, pp. 959–960.
19. Hatch, "Su Shih," vol. 3, p. 960; cf. Hatch, "Thought of Su Hsün," pp. 149–150.

able. What can be known is, it always goes where it must go, always stops where it cannot help stopping—nothing else. More than that even I cannot know.[20]

But not all thinkers of the time agreed with Su. Most notably, Ch'eng I found the preoccupation of Su and his followers with literary pursuits misguided, denouncing it as one of the three "evil practices" among students of the day, one that prevented them from advancing toward the Way.[21] Su, in Ch'eng's eyes, had made literary expression primary and, in the process, had lost sight almost entirely of the more fundamental moral concerns of the Confucian persuasion; in Su's program of learning through culture the Way had become relativistic, something that might be realized or expressed altogether differently by each individual. There were simply no guarantees that the Way practiced by everyone would be the same.

This troubled Ch'eng I, who was seeking moral order and stability in the universe. For Ch'eng the Way was absolute and knowable, a unity residing in heaven, earth, and each and every person. Each person, then, had the potential, indeed the responsibility, to learn to give realization to the Way residing in him:

What is the way to learn? Answer: From the essence of life accumulated in heaven and earth, man receives the five agents in their highest excellence. His original nature is pure and tranquil. Before it is aroused, the five moral principles of his nature, called humanity, righteousness, propriety, wisdom, and faithfulness, are complete. As his physical form appears, it comes into contact with external things and is aroused from within. As it is aroused from within, the seven feelings, called pleasure, anger, sorrow, joy, love, hate, and desire, ensue. As feelings become strong and increasingly reckless, his nature becomes damaged. For this reason the enlightened person controls his feelings so that they will be in accord with the mean. He sets his mind in the right and nourishes his nature. This is therefore called turning the feelings into the [original] nature. . . .

The way to learn is none other than setting one's mind in the right and nourishing one's nature. When one abides by the mean and correctness and becomes true to oneself, one is a sage. In the learning of the superior

20. *Tung-p'o t'i-pa* 1.15b; translation from March, "Self and Landscape," p. 385.
21. *I-shu*, p. 208.

man, the first thing is to be clear in one's mind and to know where to go
and then act vigorously in order that one may arrive at sagehood.[22]

Since in Ch'eng's view heaven and earth participated in the Way
with man, they could serve as guide or model in man's quest for
sagehood, for realization of the Way. In heaven and earth man
could become awakened to the Way in himself, to the principle
embodied in his mind and one with his nature. This is why Ch'eng
I called for *ko wu*:

Someone asked what the first step was in the art of moral cultivation.
There is nothing prior to "setting the mind in the right" and "making the
thoughts true." Making the thoughts true lies in the extension of knowledge, and "the extension of knowledge lies in *ko wu*."[23] *Ko* means *chih*, "to
arrive," as in the phrase *tsu-k'ao lai ko*, "the ancestors arrive."[24] In each
thing there is a manifestation of principle; it is necessary to pursue principle to the utmost.[25]

Man was to apprehend principle in the myriad things of heaven
and earth in order to give expression to his own moral propensities.

What made this process possible philosophically was Ch'eng I's
fundamental belief that moral truth was immanent in all things,
that it was one, absolute, and ultimately knowable—a conviction
clearly not shared by Su Shih: "Things and self are governed by the
same principle. If you understand one, you understand the other,
for the truth within and the truth without are identical. In its mag-
nitude it reaches the height of heaven and earth, but in its refine-
ment it constitutes the reason of being in every single thing. The
student should appreciate both."[26] For Ch'eng, Su Shih's creative
literary expression was not tied to fixed values and moral standards. Hence, Su and his followers were mere libertines ultimately
destructive of the Confucian Way.[27] By the same token, Ch'eng I's
insistence that morals were absolute and values immutable and his
fastidious observance of the rules of decorum led Su to conclude

22. *I-ch'uan wen-chi* 4.1a; translation, with slight modification, from Chan,
Source Book, pp. 547–548.
23. From *Ta-hsüeh*, "Classic of Confucius," para. 4.
24. From *Shang shu* 5.14b; cf. Legge, *Chinese Classics*, vol. 3, p. 87.
25. *I-shu*, p. 209.
26. *I-shu*, p. 214; translation from Chan, *Source Book*, p. 563.
27. See Hatch, "Thought of Su Hsün," pp. 149–150, and *I-shu*, p. 262.

that Ch'eng I was something of a martinet, whose philosophical vision in the end posed a grave threat to the creativity and the responsiveness called for by the Way.[28]

Even though Ch'eng I and Su Shih did not get along, neither of them in turn cared much for Wang An-shih and his New Policies. By the late eleventh century these three men and the "schools" of followers they attracted had come to constitute three rather distinct intellectual orbits. Certainly this is how Ch'eng I at the time viewed it when he observed that in his day there were three schools of learning: the school of literary writing, the school of classical commentaries, and his own school of Ju, the true Confucians who pursued the Way.[29] And not long after, Ch'en Shan (fl. late twelfth century) of the Southern Sung echoed Ch'eng I's classification of learning: "Ching-kung [i.e., Wang An-shih] with classical studies, Tung-p'o with argumentative writing, and Mr. Ch'eng with nature and principle [i.e., morality]—these three men established what were essentially schools, each following a different path."[30] These three schools of learning, then, represented the major intellectual alternatives to literati in the closing decades of the eleventh century.

In the early twelfth century, during the post–reform period (1093–1125) of the late Northern Sung, proponents of Wang's reform program were in control of government. Wang's school of learning thus became ascendant, promoted as it was by the state in matters of policy and in the civil service examinations. Indeed, a sort of literary inquisition was launched at this time against those opposed to Wang, and the works of both Su Shih and Ch'eng I were officially condemned and ordered destroyed. But with the fall of the Northern Sung to the Chin invaders in 1125, Wang's political and educational programs quickly lost most of their favor among literati, who held the reformers responsible, at least in part, for the

28. Their dislike of each other is remarked upon by Chu Hsi in *YL* 130.14b–15a/vol. 8, p. 3109, for example. Chu claimed that Su had little patience with correct and high-principled men; see *YL* 130.16b/vol. 8, p. 3110.

29. *I-shu*, p. 208. See Lo Ken-tse's discussion of these three schools in *Chung-kuo wen-hsüeh p'i-ping shih*, vol. 3, pp. 66–70; cf. Liu's treatment of the intellectual divisions of the late eleventh century in *Reform in Sung China*, pp. 27–29.

30. Ch'en Shan, *Men-shih hsin-hua*, p. 23; cited in Lo, *Chung-kuo wen-hsüeh p'i-p'ing shih*, vol. 3, p. 66, and Goyama, "Shu Ki no Sogaku hihan, josetsu," p. 25.

tragic fate of the north. The writings of the Su and Ch'eng schools
now began to attract much greater interest, aided by the patronage
of prominent government officials. To be sure, the doctrines of the
Ch'eng school were occasionally denounced by peace advocate and
prime minister Ch'in Kuei (served 1138–1155) and others, pre-
sumably because followers of the Ch'eng school found Ch'in and
his peace policy reprehensible, but in the end the attacks did little
to stem the rising tide of Ch'eng learning.[31]

It was into this world of literati learning and discourse that Chu
Hsi was born. Although Wang An-shih's name had become odious
to some, his legacy was nonetheless alive. And the schools of learning of Su Shih and Ch'eng I were growing ever more popular. In
fact, Chu's father, Sung, happened to be among the admirers of
Ch'eng I's learning and himself introduced it to his son. Thus, as
early as age eleven, Chu Hsi was already familiar with the Ch'eng
school's teachings. Yet not entirely satisfied and driven by curios-
ity, Chu would continue for the next thirty years or so to take
various teachers—including Buddhists and Taoists—in search of
true learning, until at the age of thirty-nine he returned to the
teachings of Ch'eng I, never to leave them again. In 1168 he compiled *The Surviving Works of Messrs. Ch'eng of Honan* (*Ho-nan Ch'eng-
shih i-shu*), proclaiming in the preface that only with the Ch'eng
brothers had the learning of the Way, not transmitted for more
than a thousand years since the death of Mencius, finally been
revived.[32] To Chu's mind their learning—particularly that of the
younger brother, I—alone transmitted the true Way and thus had
to be vigorously defended. And defend it he did: in two letters written in the same year, Chu Hsi launched harsh attacks on Wang
An-shih and Su Shih, arguing that both their brands of learning
were destructive of the Way and constituted heterodoxies; the Way
had to be defended against them, he said, just as it once had to be
defended against the heterodoxies of Yang Chu and Mo Ti.[33] Men-

31. On the waxing and waning of these three schools in the late Northern–
early Southern Sung period, see Gōyama, "Shu Ki no Sogaku hihan, josetsu," pp.
25–28; Winston Wan Lo, *Life and Thought of Yeh Shih*, p. 35; and Schirokauer,
"Neo-Confucians under Attack," pp. 164–167.

32. *Wen-chi* 75.16b.

33. *Wen-chi* 30.7a–11b; cited in Ch'ien Mu, *Chu-tzu hsin hsüeh-an*, vol. 3, pp.
602–605, who dates them to 1168. The reference here is to Mencius's defense of
the Way against the heresies of Yang and Mo, *Meng-tzu* 3B/9.

cius had made himself protector of Confucius's teachings; Chu would do the same for Ch'eng I's.

Like many literati of the day, Chu Hsi placed much of the blame for the fall of the north on Wang An-shih's New Policies, claiming rather broadly that they were "the source of the calamities and failures of the age."[34] It was not that Wang had not meant well, but his learning, Chu charged, was misguided: "Ching-kung was virtuous in conduct, but his learning was wrong."[35] His learning, then, was the real source of the calamities of the Sung: "Through errors in his learning Wang An-shih brought defeat to the state and destruction to the people."[36] And the reason Wang's learning was wrong is that "he didn't understand moral principle thoroughly."[37] Although Wang had rightly focused on the Classics—much as Chu himself did—he was looking for the wrong message there. Instead of concentrating on apprehending moral truth in them, which could guide all men in all ages, he studied the Classics for what they disclosed about enriching and strengthening the state. For Chu these were not the true concerns of the sages of antiquity; he could only deduce therefore that Wang was not genuinely interested in the Classics or, for that matter, in antiquity itself:

If he had been truly interested in antiquity, why did he not pay the slightest attention to the fundament of rectifying the ruler, the task of winning over the worthies, the policy of nourishing the people, the way of bettering customs—all of which the ancients regarded as matters of the highest priority and greatest urgency—but instead concern himself only with resources, wealth, the military, and punishments?[38]

Chu Hsi simply concluded that "Chieh-fu's learning is incorrect, incapable of explaining the sages' ideas."[39]

Wang had erred in not understanding that moral cultivation was the primary goal of Confucian learning and that the Classics would serve to guide men toward their realization of moral truth. His learning had separated inner morality from outer sociopolitical

34. *Wen-chi* 70.7a; cf. *Wen-chi* 70.10b.
35. *YL* 130.3b/vol. 8, p. 3097.
36. *Wen-chi* 70.12b.
37. *YL* 130.3b/vol. 8, p. 3097; cf. *Wen-chi* 70.13a.
38. *Wen-chi* 70.10b; cf. Bol, "Literati Learning," p. 169.
39. *YL* (Chung-hua Shu-chü edition), vol. 7, p. 2694 (*chüan* 109, which is missing from my Ch'uan ching t'ang edition).

concerns; if it had not, his reform program might well have been successful.[40]

Wang, in Chu's view then, had rightly made the Classics the core of his curriculum; it was his inability to appreciate the true message of the sages, to uncover the moral principle in them, that had left his learning deficient. But Chu Hsi also criticized Wang for taking no interest in historical texts (5.44). Historical texts would help illuminate how moral principle had operated in actual historical circumstances and thus enhance understanding of moral principle itself. They would also provide lessons that would be of use in administering the realm. Chu Hsi here was something of a historical analogist himself, who could argue:

Simply to read through the histories is not as good as reading through the twists and turns in them with an eye to the present, observing that this is what order and disorder are, this is what victory and defeat are, and that "following the path of orderly government is certain to lead to prosperity, while following the path of disorder is certain to lead to ruin."(5.66; cf. 5.42, 5.65, and 5.67)

He even urged students to study the institutions and laws presented in historical works (5.65). But naturally, for Chu, the study of history had to be informed by a sound understanding of moral principle, which was to be reached by a thorough study of the Classics; only a prior understanding of moral principle would give one the wherewithal to assess the past judiciously and apply its lessons effectively.[41] And Wang An-shih, Chu lamented, had never even reached an understanding of moral principle—that he had not turned to the histories was not his gravest fault.

Chu Hsi was even more anxious about the Su school than he was about the Wang school, for in his day it wielded far greater influence. As indicated earlier, many of Chu's essays, letters, and conversations evince an uneasiness over Su's writings, a fear that

---

40. *Wen-chi* 70.13a. This is why if a man like Ch'eng Hao had effected the policies they would not have ended in disaster; see *YL* 130.3a/vol. 8, p. 3097.

41. Chu Hsi, for example, roundly attacked his contemporaries Lü Tsu-ch'ien and Ch'en Liang (1143–1194) of the Chekiang school for their preoccupation with history and their ignorance of the Classics; because their learning was imbalanced and misguided, their values and goals were wrong. See Tillman, *Utilitarian Confucianism.*

his learning posed a severe and real danger to the Way.[42] Although, to be sure, the learning of the Wang school had enjoyed a resurgence during the prime ministership of Ch'in Kuei, its association with the reform program and the loss of the north limited its appeal among literati. But the elegance of Su Shih's writing and the premium placed on literary style by official examiners and arbiters of culture since the Northern Sung had made the works of the Su school enormously popular in Chu's day. They could be found circulating everywhere and were imitated quite freely by candidates hoping to win examination degrees. The popularity of Su's works received still a further boost during the reign of Emperor Hsiao-tsung (r. 1163–1189), whose admiration for Su led him in 1173 to write a preface to his collected writings and to confer posthumously upon him the prestigious position of grand preceptor (rank 1A).[43]

Chu actually felt that it was dangerous to read Su's works; that is why he found their popularity among twelfth-century literati so alarming. Su's learning, after all, was not correct, for his writing rarely touched upon the Way. Su Shih himself had not first cultivated the Way then produced good writing that manifested it as he should have; rather he had cultivated good writing, without paying much attention to the Way at all. Chu argued that by throwing themselves into Su's works—as they were wont to do—students might well learn a "profound and clever literary style," but at great cost.[44] As he put it, over time Su's "cunning and insolence enter deep into the minds of men."[45] It was not, then, simply that Su's writing did not teach the Way but that it had the power to transform men for the worse, to inculcate in them habits of artifice and cunning. And this would happen without their knowing it; Chu therefore urged them not to turn to Su's works at all, even for mere diversion.[46]

Dangerous too was Su Shih's program of moral cultivation. Men, Su had suggested, could apprehend the Way through literary and artistic pursuits. This, in Chu's view, was to make the Way

42. E.g., *YL* 139.9a–b/vol. 8, pp. 3305–3306.
43. Gōyama, "Shu Ki no Sogaku hihan, josetsu," p. 27.
44. *Wen-chi* 37.20b.
45. *Wen-chi* 37.20a.
46. *Wen-chi* 33.5a–b.

secondary to literary cultivation, to reverse the proper order of things: "If you use literary writing to intuit the Way, this is to make the root the branches and the branches the root—it can't be done."[47] For Chu the Way was not mysterious and unknowable (e.g., 3.36), something to be intuited only through creative expression; both it and moral principle were solid, in all things, and open to direct apprehension and cultivation. Embrace the Way first through investigation, he advised, and good literary writing will flow from it naturally. The Way must guide one's literary expression if that expression is to be true and compelling. If one's literary expression serves as guide to the Way, what ensures that one will arrive at the true Way? What guarantees that all individuals necessarily will arrive at the same fixed Confucian Way? Chu suspected that in fact there were no guarantees and therefore routinely accused Su of being Buddhist or Taoist.[48]

Ch'eng I earlier had condemned both the literary learning of the Su school and the classical learning of the Wang school, referring to them as evils plaguing the world of Sung literati; both compromised the only true learning, the learning of the Way.[49] True learning for Ch'eng I was learning to be moral. And learning to be moral was a lifelong enterprise requiring students to investigate not only what constituted moral behavior but what the very nature and source of morality were. Ch'eng himself assumed that there was a moral order underlying the entire cosmos, both the physical world and the human world. The physical world manifested this moral order naturally and at all times, but the human world had to struggle to manifest it. That is, the human world could be made to reflect the cosmic order but only with effort, only if men resolutely determined to study this order and cultivate it in their own lives. Both Ch'eng's assumption about the cosmos and his hope for humankind were embraced by Chu Hsi, indeed, were what drew him to Ch'eng I's school of learning.

The Ch'eng school for Chu represented a belief in a universe possessed of an embedded moral standard; the Way was absolute, unchanging, inhering in all things, all human beings, heaven and

---

47. *YL* 139.9a/vol. 8, p. 3305.
48. E.g., *Wen-chi* 30.7b and *YL* 139.9a–b/vol. 8, pp. 3305–3306.
49. *I-shu*, p. 208.

earth. There was none of the moral relativism or lassitude Chu had found so threatening in Su Shih's learning. One of Chu's most oft-quoted lines from Ch'eng I was "principle is one, its manifestations many"; he clearly found the moral certitude provided by Ch'eng I comforting. After positing the ultimate oneness of moral principle, the Ch'eng school then urged students to pursue it in all things and affairs—to apprehend it fully, thereby realizing it in themselves. *Ko wu*, arriving at an understanding of principle, of the moral pattern underlying the cosmos and self, was the mission all followers of the Ch'eng school agreed to undertake; consequently, the subject matter of the school was the entire universe and all things in it.

Chu Hsi found Ch'eng I's proposal to investigate principle in the universe enormously compelling and, indeed, made it the very foundation of his philosophical program. He worked hard to fashion Ch'eng I's various remarks on *ko wu*, appearing throughout Ch'eng's works, into a coherent vision, which would give direction to his own students in their pursuit of the Way.[50] But where I think Chu Hsi differed from Ch'eng I, and where I think one of his great original contributions to Neo-Confucianism lay, was in narrowing the field of the study of principle. For Chu, as for Ch'eng, principle could be found everywhere and thus was to be investigated everywhere. But Chu wanted to give more guidance to the inquiry, wishing to make principle as readily accessible to students of the Way as possible. Thus he rooted the study of principle firmly in the study of books, and in particular, the Confucian Classics. In short, what he did was to take Ch'eng I's abstract, discursive discussion of principle and nature and ground it thoroughly in the canonical tradition, in effect to merge what in the Northern Sung had been the study of the Classics and the study of morality. I naturally do not wish to suggest here that Ch'eng I was not interested in the Classics—he was, and he urged his students to turn to them in their study of principle.[51] But Ch'eng I viewed the canon as just a small part of the students' field of investigation,[52] and he himself spent little of his life annotating and commenting on the classical texts, with the notable exception of the *Book of Changes*.

50. See Chan, "Chu Hsi's Completion," p. 87.
51. See, for example, his remark in Chan, *Reflections*, pp. 47–48.
52. For example, *I-shu*, p. 209.

Chu, by contrast, made the canon *the* field of study, *the* place to turn
to apprehend principle. He was completely confident that even
though principle inhered in all things it was most readily revealed
in the works of the sages, men who themselves had fully realized the
Way and principle in their daily lives. This, of course, explains why
Chu Hsi, and not Ch'eng I, gave so much consideration to the
development of a curriculum and hermeneutics.[53] It also explains
why he spent such a large part of his adult life writing and refining
commentaries on the classical canon. For Chu the Classics in a
sense were the microcosm of Ch'eng I's heaven and earth and could
mediate between the human world and the physical universe: it
was in them that principle was most accessible.

It might be noted here that Chu's well-known philosophical
opposition to his contemporary Lu Chiu-yüan was precisely over
this issue of how and where best to locate principle. Arguing that
the original mind of man was identical with principle, and that this
original mind and the universe were one, Lu had little philosophical reason to propose a process of external investigation or any
process of mediation between man and the universe; for him the
apprehension of principle required simply that men turn their gaze
inward to the realization of the perfect mind, the universal mind
with which they were born. No curricular guidance, no field of
study, was necessary. Chu found Lu's program for self-perfection
dangerously subjective, frequently even calling it Buddhistic.
Arguing instead that principle was one with human nature and not
the mind, and that the mind was precarious and prone to error,
Chu Hsi regarded the establishment of a clear, detailed curricular
program that could guide men carefully but surely to an understanding of principle (and hence their nature) a critical part of his
philosophical program and life's mission.

In any event, by grounding the Ch'eng school's discussion of
abstract metaphysics in the Confucian canon, Chu Hsi was able to
bring the learning of Ch'eng I more firmly into the Confucian fold
than had Ch'eng himself: he was able to convince Sung Confucians
that discussion of principle and nature was a truly legitimate Confucian enterprise. By this means Chu was responsible for making
Ch'eng I's school of the Way, which in the Northern Sung period

53. Gardner, "Principle and Pedagogy," pp. 65–67.

had been but a peripheral current, the Confucian mainstream by the dynasty's close.

To speak generally, then, literati of the eleventh century gave most of their attention to the reform of the sociopolitical order. By the late eleventh–early twelfth century, however, a rather dramatic shift had begun to occur: literati now tended to focus more on the reformation of man, on the moral perfectibility of the individual. To be sure, in the eleventh century, literati such as Wang An-shih and Ssu-ma Kuang had expressed an interest in identifying good men and bringing them into government service; but Ch'eng I and Chu Hsi were not nearly so concerned with how to identify good men as they were with how to make good men. This, for them, was the consuming problematic. Social and political harmony would prevail only when individuals in society had first cultivated their moral goodness. The belief that the state of the sociopolitical order was dependent on the moral state of those in that order had its sanction in one of the Confucian Classics, the *Greater Learning*:

> Only after the principle in things is fully apprehended does knowledge become complete; knowledge being complete, thoughts may become true; thoughts being true, the mind may become set in the right; the mind being so set, the person becomes cultivated; the person being cultivated, household harmony is established; household harmony established, the state becomes well governed; the state being well governed, the empire becomes tranquil.[54]

This text, which Chu required his followers to read before all others in the Confucian tradition, provided powerful justification for the Ch'eng-Chu shift in interest toward the inner realm of human morality. For it asserted quite unambiguously that the well-being of family, state, and even empire hinged entirely on the moral rectitude of the individual.

Taking note of the literati shift in focus that occurred in the later years of the Northern Sung period is easier than explaining it. The spirit of political reform so evident since the reign of Emperor Jen-tsung (r. 1023–1063) had run its course and given way to a political pessimism, to a sense that little was to be achieved through political action. After all, reformers since the 1040s had labored hard to

---

54. *Ta-hsüeh*, "Classic of Confucius," para. 5.

bring about political change, to make government strong, efficient, and fair. Yet, as the Northern Sung approached its end, the bureaucracy was embroiled in bitter, paralyzing factionalism, the country's economy was weak and overburdened, and to the north China faced a menacing military threat in the Jurchen. What had gone wrong? Why hadn't reform efforts succeeded? Reflecting on the current state of affairs, men like Ch'eng I were convinced that simply too little attention had been given to the inner sphere. Political and social action without a strong moral foundation would lead nowhere. The results of Wang's bold efforts to reform the polity under Shen-tsung merely served to confirm this conviction. Wang's efforts were well intentioned, they conceded, yet they failed largely because Wang had not attended to the inner sphere; he had made the serious error of separating inner moral concerns from outer sociopolitical ones. Ch'eng and later Chu, feeling that such imbalance had to be redressed, tried to redirect literati attention back to the inner, to questions about man's morality, its source, and how to realize it in daily life. Perhaps once men focused on these questions, once they had learned to manifest their own moral selves, they could then turn their efforts to the larger realm with greater success than Wang had.

The turn inward resulted then partly from the perception that political reform—without attention first to the moral development of the individual—had not been very successful. But the inward shift may be linked, at least indirectly, to another perception of late Northern Sung literati, that holding high office was dangerous. The fierce factionalism encouraged by Wang An-shih's reform attempts had resulted in harsh recriminations against prominent officials who found themselves on the wrong side at the wrong time. Su Shih's banishment to the hot and uncultured far south was just one measure of the risk high office holding held, but it must have cast serious doubts in the minds of many a potential official. "Hawks" and "doves" in bitter disagreement over how to deal with the Chin occupation of the Central Plain continued the acrimonious factionalism into the Southern Sung period; Chu Hsi's own father was forced from office because of his opposition to Ch'in Kuei's "peace party." Fearful, then, that changing political winds in the capital would put them and their families in trouble sooner or later, literati of the late Northern and Southern Sung retreated from the national political scene, directing their attention instead toward their own localities and communities. Indeed, Chu's own involvement in the development of local institutions such as the community compact and academies reflected this trend.[55]

As their practical concerns shifted from the national to the local, so too the focus of their philosophical interests shifted: matters relating to the governance of the empire became less immediate, less compelling, to them, and matters relating to the self and its new predicament became more so. In short, as they became less directly involved in running the empire, their thoughts turned away from questions of statecraft toward questions of how they as individuals could live meaningful, virtuous lives out of high office.

In fact, by the turn of the twelfth century living a meaningful, virtuous life out of office had gained a legitimacy among literati that it surely did not have earlier in the early to mid–Northern Sung period. At that time one could hardly claim membership in the elite unless one served in public office. But with the exile from office to Loyang of Wang An-shih's political opponents—some of them among the most prominent literati of the day—literati themselves had little choice but to begin to attach greater value to life out of office. The life of scholarship and moral cultivation came, almost faute de mieux, to replace life in high office. Speaking of the exile in Loyang, one scholar has recently written:

In such a society it was no longer so overwhelmingly important, as it had been at the time of the first reform in the 1040's, to serve in office. What was important was to be numbered in the fellowship of virtuous men. This Confucian society, the society of the virtuous, could be seen as transcending the state (or rather particular political situations) and sometimes as alienated from political life.[56]

"Transcending the state" may be going too far, but for exiled literati the society of the virtuous certainly was an alternative to the state. Part of the legacy of this exile—and the factionalism that prompted it—then, was to give much greater value and currency to the inner sphere of moral cultivation of the individual. Tending to

55. That there was a retreat from the national toward the local beginning in the late Northern Sung is the main argument put forth in Hymes, *Statesmen and Gentlemen*; see, in particular, pp. 121–122, 132–135.

56. Freeman, "Lo-yang," p. 78.

one's own virtue took on greater importance than tending to the vicissitudes of the state.

This is not to suggest that Confucian literati were simply "pushed" into the shift inward by external social, political, and economic circumstances. For literati were intellectually receptive to this shift in the first place; they were intellectually ready to ask the sorts of questions demanded by the new problematic. Buddhists had long been addressing such concerns as human nature, self-realization, man's relation to the cosmos, and enlightenment. Confucian literati since the T'ang, even while challenging many of the specific philosophical formulations of the Buddhists, had nonetheless come to find some of the general concerns raised by them relevant and meaningful. And by the Sung, dialogue between the Buddhist and Confucian schools was commonplace and quite active: for instance, Ou-yang Hsiu, Wang An-shih, Su Shih, Chou Tun-i, Chang Tsai, the Ch'eng brothers, the Ch'engs' disciples, and Chu Hsi, just to mention a few of the great Confucians, not only numbered prominent Buddhists among their acquaintances but had themselves all studied Buddhism. In other words, Sung literati were already predisposed to confront questions about the nature of man, the source of his morality, and his place in the universe; these were men poised for the turn inward.

The literati shift inward we have been describing was accompanied by and reflected in a dramatic shift in the Confucian curriculum. Beginning in the Northern Sung, men turned their focus away from the venerable Five Classics—the *Book of Changes*, the *Book of Poetry*, the *Book of History*, the *Book of Rites*, and the *Spring and Autumn Annals*—hitherto the central texts in the Confucian tradition, toward texts in the canon that better addressed their new concerns. Reading through the *Analects* and the *Book of Mencius* (two of the Thirteen Classics) and the *Greater Learning* and the *Doctrine of the Mean* (two chapters from another of the Thirteen Classics, the *Book of Rites*), they discovered writings in the Confucian tradition that probed into the nature of man, the springs or inner source of his morality, and his relation to the universe—the very issues most on their minds. These four works, along with the *Book of Changes*, quickly came to be the favored texts of Confucians. In 1190, Chu Hsi formalized their status by publishing them together for the first time in a collection titled the *Four Masters* (*Ssu-tzu*). And by calling, throughout his life, for students of the Way to read and master the Four Books (as the *Four Masters* commonly came to be known) before all other texts in the tradition, including the Five Classics, he heralded a transition in Confucianism from the age of the Five Classics to the age of the Four Books. From the thirteenth century to the eighteenth century—arguably to the early years of the present century—the Four Books would constitute the central texts of the Confucian school, superseding in importance the Five Classics. The Five Classics, of course, would still be seriously studied by all who claimed to be Confucians, but the Four Books—and the issues they raised—would receive much greater attention and, indeed, in the succeeding Yüan period would even be declared the basis of the civil service examinations.[57]

In his own day Chu's call for a curriculum that took as its core the Four Books must have seemed like an appeal to Confucian literati to lead less politically active, more private, contemplative lives. The new texts of choice, after all, would have men focus principally on cultivating their morality, not on serving. In any case, we cannot fail to notice that the curricular shift to the Four Books was contemporaneous with the literati retreat from national politics suggested in the recent work of Hartwell and Hymes.[58] This, of course, is not to argue that the curricular shift necessarily set off the retreat from high office but rather, at the very least, that the curricular and political changes of the period likely encouraged and justified each other.

Chu himself saw his curriculum as providing literati with a training that was explicitly not professional; it was meant by him to be an alternative to examination-oriented learning, for those seeking spiritual advance, not the material advance resulting from success in the examinations. Chu's aim here was an ambitious one, nothing less than the transformation of learning, from professional preparation for public service to a meaningful way of life in itself, a vocation. His rigorous curriculum, together with his *tu-shu fa*, required of students total commitment to the pursuit of the Way; for him

---

57. For a fuller treatment of the literati shift from the Five Classics to the Four Books see Gardner, *Chu Hsi and the Ta-hsueh*, chap. 1. On the importance Chu Hsi attached to the Four Books see Gardner, "Principle and Pedagogy."

58. Hartwell, "Demographic, Political, and Social Transformations of China," and Hymes, *Statesmen and Gentlemen*.

learning was learning to be a sage—it was lifelong, not merely a stage in one's career. Chu Hsi of course never advocated that literati shun office. But by establishing a highly demanding program of learning and *tu-shu fa,* a full tradition of commentaries on the canonical texts, a rather large body of editions and anthologies of the writings of the great Neo-Confucian masters of the Northern Sung, and academic institutions and centers of teaching where they could engage in disinterested study, he did create for them a valued way of life outside of official service. In Chu's efforts to promote true learning, then, perhaps there was something of a realization that a life of official service was no longer open to all literati, or at least that not all literati found such a life desirable.

Moreover, by redefining the aim and content of literati learning, Chu in effect opened up the Confucian tradition beyond the boundaries set for it in the preceding centuries. No longer would the audience for the message of the ancient sages be confined largely to potential bureaucrats, literati intent on taking the examinations and then serving in office. Now, any literatus—including, of course, the potential bureaucrat—with hopes of learning to become a fully moral human being, a sage, was invited to discover the enduring truths of the great Confucian tradition.

Chu Hsi's ideas on learning—its content, its message, and the methodology for it—were guaranteed a large audience among the literate elite long after his death in 1200. Not only did the *Conversations of Master Chu* continue to circulate but other works—both private and offical—appeared that incorporated Chu's most basic ideas on learning. For example, in the fourteenth century the private scholar Ch'eng Tuan-li (1271–1345) adopted Chu's ideas in drawing up a "schedule for learning" for the use of students in his family school; this "Daily Schedule of Study in the Ch'eng Family School,"[59] which included a detailed curriculum and a method of reading through it, proved highly popular and is said to have become a model for study in academies throughout later times.[60] In

59. "Ch'eng-shih chia-shu tu-shu fen-nien jih-ch'eng." This work is partially translated in Meskill, *Academies in Ming China,* pp. 160–164, and Ebrey, *Chinese Civilization,* pp. 113–117.

60. See Meskill, *Academies in Ming China,* p. 61, particularly n. 55.

1415, at Ming imperial command, the *Compendium of Teachings on Nature and Principle* (*Hsing-li ta-ch'üan*), an anthology of the Neo-Confucian teachings of the Ch'eng-Chu school, was compiled and thereafter used as the official basis of the civil service examinations; three centuries later, in 1714, the Ch'ing emperor K'ang-hsi (r. 1661–1722) had passages from the writings and conversations of Chu Hsi gathered together in the *Complete Works of Master Chu* (*Chu-tzu ta-ch'üan*), and a year later he sponsored the compilation of the *Essential Teachings on Nature and Principle* (*Hsing-li ching-i*), which was more or less an abridgment of the earlier *Compendium of Teachings on Nature and Principle*.[61] These three government-sponsored and widely available anthologies all gave considerable space to Chu Hsi's views on learning, the issue dearer to him and more central than any other to his lifelong mission to resuscitate and transmit the great Confucian Way.

61. For a discussion of the *Hsing-li ching-i,* and how it compares to the *Hsing-li ta-ch'üan,* see Chan. "*The Hsing-li ching-i.*"

Part Two

Selections from the *Conversations of Master Chu, Arranged Topically*— The Chapters on Learning

Note on Text and Translation

The *Conversations of Master Chu, Arranged Topically* was published in 1270, seventy years after the death of Chu Hsi. In compiling the text, the editor, Li Ching-te (fl. 1263), drew on four previously published *yü-lu*, "records of conversations," and two previously published *yü-lei*, "conversations, arranged topically," all collections of conversations recorded firsthand by Chu's disciples between 1170 and 1200. From the title of the work it should be clear that Li's arrangement, which followed that of Huang Shih-i's *yü-lei* of 1219–1220, is by topic, without regard to chronological order.[1] Thus a comment made by Chu on *li*, "principle," in 1171 may be followed immediately by one he made in 1196.[2]

As a record of conversations taken down by Chu's students, the *Conversations of Master Chu, Arranged Topically* presents certain problems to the translator. The language, of course, is highly colloquial and idiomatic, riddled with regional expressions not always as intelligible as this translator would have hoped. I have tried to put

---

1. See Li Ching-te's prefaces of 1263 and 1270, which appear immediately after the table of contents in the *Chu-tzu yü-lei*. For more information on the compilation and editions of the *Chu-tzu yü-lei* see Ichikawa, "*Shushi gorui* zakki"; Tomoeda, *Shushi no shisō keisei*, pp. 503–537; Okada, "*Shushi gorui* no seiritsu to sono hampon"; Hu Shih, "*Chu-tzu yü-lei* te li-shih"; and Hervouet, *Sung Bibliography*, pp. 225–226.

2. Since almost every comment in the text closes with the name of the disciple who recorded it, and since the preface to the text includes a list of all the recorders and the years they were with the Master, it is possible to date most of the comments, even if only roughly. I have seen no reason, however, to attach dates to the comments in the selection that follows.

the Sung colloquial of the text into a colloquial English, although I have consciously avoided using slang, principally because Chu does not strike me as the sort of fellow who would have resorted to slang very often. The reader too should keep in mind that the text is not a record of formal lectures or sustained philosophical exposition but rather of conversations, or perhaps more accurately, of bits and pieces of conversations strung together by an editor years after Chu passed away; many comments thus lack the context necessary to make full sense of them, and the referents used in them are not always as clear to the reader as they surely were to the hearer. Moreover, in reading Chu Hsi's remarks to students, we do not see the gestures or hear the inflection in the voice that gave meaning, and sometimes even life, to those remarks.

With a record of conversations we are, of course, at the mercy of the transcribers, who after all can write down wrong characters, omit characters, or in their haste to get all of what they hear on paper use a shorthand that is comprehensible to themselves but not necessarily to others. In the translation presented here, I have only rarely emended the Chinese text, preferring—perhaps not entirely wisely, but at least safely in the absence of evidence to the contrary—to assume that what is recorded is a reasonable transcription of Chu's words. That is, I have tended not to meddle with the text, even when this has meant letting an awkward passage stand. Naturally, I have informed the reader on those few occasions when I have altered the original wording of the text.

As one would expect of a record of informal conversations spanning a thirty-year period, the *Conversations of Master Chu, Arranged Topically* contains comments that appear contradictory. It is my conviction that even though indeed contradictory passages can be found, there are many fewer than at first meet the eye. Rather than pitting one passage in the text against another, the reader would do better perhaps to read widely through it for a sense of the whole and then challenge that sense with those passages that raise questions in his mind. In any case, I have chosen not to try to explain or reconcile the apparent inconsistencies in the *Conversations of Master Chu, Arranged Topically* because I wish the English reader to confront this important work and the philosophical challenges it poses in much the way a Chinese reader after the thirteenth century would have.

After each translated passage from the *Conversations of Master Chu, Arranged Topically*, two sets of numbers appear. The first is a reference to the Ch'uan ching t'ang edition, which in my experience is the clearest, most reliable available, and the second is a reference to the Chung-hua Shu-chü edition, now the most convenient and readily available edition of the text. Taking the example of 7.1a:4/ 124:4, the first set of numbers refers to *chüan* seven, folio leaf one, recto, line four, of the Ch'uan ching t'ang edition (the line being the number of the opening line of the translated passage); the second set of numbers refers to the page number and the number of the opening line of the translated passage in the Chung-hua Shu-chü edition (all references are to volume 1).

The passages in smaller type are my annotations. What appears in quotation marks in the annotations are the words of Chu Hsi, or occasionally, someone else, and what does not appear in quotation marks are my comments. References in smaller type to the Chung-hua Shu-chü edition of the *Conversations of Master Chu* are to page number and line number and, unless otherwise noted, volume 1. References to all other works cited in smaller type are to *chüan* number, folio or page number, and the number of the opening line of the translated passage.

Finally, in translating the following passages from the *Conversations of Master Chu, Arranged Topically*, I have consulted the few translations of them that now exist.[3] When I have directly drawn on these translations in presenting my own, I so notify the reader; when I have not, I am still nonetheless indebted to them for the guidance they have provided.

3. In particular, I have referred to translations found in Chan, *Source Book*; Chan, *Reflections*; Graham, *Two Chinese Philosophers*; and Morohashi and Yasuoka, *Shushi gorui*.

One

Lesser Learning (Chapter 7)

1.1. In antiquity people entered the school for lesser learning at an early age; here they were instructed in matters such as ritual, music, archery, charioteering, calligraphy, and mathematics,[1] as well as in matters of filial piety, fraternal respect, loyalty, and fidelity. At sixteen or seventeen they entered the school for greater learning at which time they were instructed in principle; for example, they would be instructed in the extension of knowledge and the apprehension of the principle in things,[2] as well as in what constituted loyalty, fidelity, filial piety, and fraternal respect. (7.1a:4/124:4)

Chu Hsi provides a fuller description of schooling in antiquity in his "Preface to the *Greater Learning in Chapters and Verses*": "Amidst the glory of the Three Dynasties, regulations were gradually perfected, and thereafter schools were found everywhere, from the Imperial Palace and the state capitals on down to the villages. At the age of eight all the male children, from the sons of kings and dukes to the sons of commoners, entered the schools of lesser learning; there they were instructed in the chores of clean-

---

1. Referred to traditionally as the *liu-i* ("the six arts"). See *Chou li* 19.24b; cf. Biot, *Le Tcheou-li*, vol. 1, chap. 9, pp. 213–214.

2. "Extension of knowledge" (*chih chih*) and "apprehension of the principle in things" (*ko wu*), terms of great importance in Chu's philosophy, are from the *Ta-hsüeh*, "Classic of Confucius," para. 4; see Gardner, *Chu Hsi and the Ta-hsueh*, p. 92. *Ko wu* is sometimes translated "investigation of things," but Chu's gloss of the term in his commentary on the *Ta-hsüeh*, "Classic of Confucius," para. 4, makes it clear precisely how he understands it: "*Ko* is 'to arrive at,' 'to reach'; *wu* is similar to 'affair.' *Ko wu* is 'to reach to the utmost the principle in affairs and things with the desire that the extreme point always be attained.'" For further discussion of *ko wu* see the annotation to 3.5.

ing and sweeping, in the formalities of polite conversation and good manners, and in the refinements of ritual, music, archery, charioteering, calligraphy, and mathematics. At the age of fifteen the Son of Heaven's eldest son and other imperial sons on down to the eldest legitimate sons of dukes, ministers, high officials, and officers of the chief grade, together with the gifted among the populace, all entered the school of greater learning; there they were instructed in the Way of probing principle, setting the mind in the right, cultivating oneself, and governing others. This was the way instruction in the schools was divided into programs of greater and lesser learning" (preface to *Ta-hsüeh chang-chü* 1a:8).[3]

1.2. From the time they entered the school for lesser learning, the ancients were already personally familiar with many matters. Entering the school for greater learning, they merely wished to make the right moral effort on these matters. People today have never understood this. The ancients simply attended to the mind, and this culminated in the good governance of the empire—everything flowed from the mind. People today attend only to the [many] matters. (7. 1a:7/124:6)

1.3. The lesser learning of the ancients fostered truthfulness and inner mental attentiveness in young children. Their germs of goodness[4] would thus become manifest. Still, they were unable to infer from lesser learning the affairs of greater learning, so they entered the school for greater learning, where they would be instructed in them. (7.1b:1/124:10)

In Chu Hsi's vocabulary "truthfulness" (*ch'eng*) means to be true to one's nature; one does this by keeping one's original mind unified, free from deception. "Inner mental attentiveness" (*ching*) refers to a state of mind in which the mind is fully concentrated on what is before it, without any distractions.[5] Chu's understanding of *ch'eng* and *ching* follows that of Ch'eng I, who earlier had explained the two terms: "To concentrate on one thing is what is meant by inner mental attentiveness. Oneness is what is meant by truthfulness."[6]

3. Translation from Gardner, *Chu Hsi and the Ta-hsueh*, pp. 79–81.
4. "Germs of goodness" is derived from Mencius's discussion of the "four germs" (2A/6) and refers to man's innately good nature: "The heart of compassion is the germ of benevolence; the heart of shame, of dutifulness; the heart of courtesy and modesty, of observance of the rites; the heart of right and wrong, of wisdom. Man has these four germs just as he has four limbs." Translation from Lau, *Mencius*, p. 83.
5. Chu discusses inner mental attentiveness at length in 6.33–60.
6. *I-shu*, p. 346.

1.4. Lesser learning is the direct understanding of such-and-such an affair. Greater learning is the investigation of such-and-such a principle—the reason why an affair is as it is. (7.1b:3/124:12)

As there is no one English word that conveys the full sense of Chu Hsi's Neo-Confucian understanding of the term *li*, rendered "principle" here, one is tempted to leave it untranslated.[7] But since over the years "principle" has become the standard translation for *li*, I will acquiesce to convention, trusting that the reader will not be deterred by the English "principle" from gaining an understanding of the Chinese concept as he confronts that concept in Chu's numerous comments.

Principle together with *ch'i*, "psychophysical stuff," constitute the backbone of Chu Hsi's philosophical system. According to Chu, there is one principle that underlies the universe; everything—each object, event, relationship, "matter," "affair"—in the universe has its specific principle, which is but a manifestation of the one supreme principle. Psychophysical stuff is the matter and energy of which the entire universe and all things in it, including functions and activities of the mind, are composed. It is the relative density and purity of each thing's psychophysical stuff that give the thing its peculiar form and individual characteristics.

"As far as the things in the universe go, we can be certain that each has a reason why it is as it is and a rule to which it should conform. This is what is meant by principle" (*Ta-hsüeh huo-wen* 15a:3).

"Someone asked: Do dry and withered things have principle or not? Chu said: As soon as there exists a thing, there exists principle. Heaven has never produced a writing brush; man makes brushes with rabbit's hair. But as soon as there exists a brush, there exists principle" (*YL* 4.6a:12/61:12).[8]

"Someone asked: Principle is something that all men receive from heaven. Do insentient things as well have principle? Chu replied: Indeed they do have principle. For instance, a boat can move only in water, a cart can move only on land" (*YL* 4.6b:3/61:14).

"In the universe there has never been any psychophysical stuff without principle nor any principle without psychophysical stuff" (*YL* 1.1b:11/2:5).

---

7. For an interesting discussion of how to understand and translate *li* see Peterson, "Another Look at *Li*."

8. *YL* in the annotation refers to Chu Hsi, *Chu-tzu yü-lei*.

"Someone asked about principle and psychophysical stuff. Chu replied: I-ch'uan explained it well. He said, 'principle is one, its manifestations many.' When we speak of heaven, earth, and the ten thousand things together, there is just one principle. When we come to man, each has his own principle" (*YL* 1.2a:1/2:7).

"Someone asked: The myriad things are splendid; still are they the same or not? Chu replied: Principle alone is one. Moral principle thus is the same, but its manifestations are not. Underlying the relationship between a sovereign and a minister is the principle for the relationship between a sovereign and a minister; underlying the relationship between a father and a son is the principle for the relationship between a father and a son" (*YL* 6.1b:1/99:11).

"There exists just one moral principle, but its manifestations are not the same. . . . It's like this board: it has just one moral principle, but this grain goes this way and that grain goes that way. Or like this house: it has just one moral principle, but it contains different rooms. Or like plants: they have just one moral principle, but there is the peach tree and there is the plum tree. Or like mankind: it has just one moral principle, but there is the third son of Chang and the fourth son of Li. The fourth son of Li can't become the third son of Chang, and the third son of Chang can't become the fourth son of Li" (*YL* 6.3b:8/102:6).

"Before the existence of heaven and earth, there was simply principle. As there was principle, there was heaven and earth. If there hadn't been principle, there'd be no heaven and earth, no people, no things. There'd be nothing at all to sustain them. When there's principle, there's psychophysical stuff; it circulates everywhere, developing and nourishing the ten thousand things. Someone said: Is it principle that does the developing and nourishing? Chu replied: When there's this principle, there's this psychophysical stuff that circulates everywhere, developing and nourishing things. Principle has no physical form" (*YL* 1.1b:2/1:11).

"Someone asked if principle exists first or psychophysical stuff. Chu replied: Principle has never been separate from psychophysical stuff. But principle is above form and psychophysical stuff is within form. From the point of view of what is above and what is within form, how can there possibly be no sequence? Principle has no form, while the psychophysical stuff is coarse and contains impurities" (*YL* 1.2b:6/3:3).

"Someone asked: What about the statement that there must exist this principle and only then will there exist this psychophysical stuff? Chu said: Fundamentally, one can't speak of them in terms of first and later.

But if we must trace their beginnings, we have to say that there first exists this principle. Still, principle is not a separate entity but exists in the midst of this psychophysical stuff. If there weren't this stuff, this principle would have nothing to adhere to" (*YL* 1.2b:8/3:5).

"Someone asked: Does principle exist first and psychophysical stuff later? Chu said: Fundamentally, one can't speak of principle and psychophysical stuff in terms of first and later. But when we look into it, it seems as if principle exists first and psychophysical stuff later. There was a further inquiry: What evidence is there that principle exists in the psychophysical stuff? Chu replied: For instance, that there is an order to the intermixing of the *yin* and *yang* and five elements is because of principle. If the psychophysical stuff doesn't coalesce, principle has nothing to adhere to" (*YL* 1.2b:12/3:8).

"Someone asked about the statement that first there exists principle and later there exists psychophysical stuff. Chu said: There is no need to speak like this. Now we know that whether basically there first exists principle and later the psychophysical stuff or later the principle and first the psychophysical stuff, it's not open to investigation. But if we were to speculate about it, I suspect that this psychophysical stuff, in operating, depends on this principle. When this psychophysical stuff coalesces, principle too is in it. It seems that psychophysical stuff is able to congeal and create. Principle by contrast, does not feel, reckon, or create. It's just that where this psychophysical stuff coalesces, principle is present in it" (*YL* 1.3a:6/3:12).

"Someone asked about the statement, 'There exists this principle and then there exists this psychophysical stuff.' It seems as if we can't divide them into a first and a later. Chu replied: In essence, first there exists principle. It's simply that we cannot say that today there exists this principle and tomorrow there exists this psychophysical stuff. Still, there must be a first and a later" (*YL* 1.3b:2/4:1).

"Man is produced simply by the coming together of principle and psychophysical stuff. Heavenly principle is vast, limitless. And so, if there isn't this psychophysical stuff, then though there exists this principle, it has nothing to attach itself to. Therefore, the *yin* psychophysical stuff and the *yang* psychophysical stuff interact, coalescing and pooling together. Afterward this principle has something to adhere to" (*YL* 4.10a:9/65:12).

1.5. Lesser learning is the study of affairs. Greater learning is the study of the reasons behind the affairs studied in lesser learning. (7.1b:4/124:13)

1.6. Lesser learning is the study of affairs—such as serving one's ruler, serving one's father, serving one's brother, and dealing with one's friends. It teaches one to behave according to certain rules. Greater learning illuminates the principle behind these affairs. (7.1b:5/125:1)

1.7. In antiquity lesser learning nurtured people without their even knowing it. So that as they got older, they naturally were possessed of the standard for a sage and worthy—they'd simply add some finishing touches. Nowadays people completely fail to make an effort at lesser learning. Only if they're taught to regard inner mental attentiveness as central and to discipline their bodies and minds will they be capable of making the proper effort. Chu also said: The lesser learning of the ancients instructed people in affairs and thereby nutured their minds naturally; without even being aware of it, they became good. They gradually matured, becoming more experienced and more understanding of affairs and things, until there was nothing they were unable to do. Nowadays people have no foundation and give their attention to useless matters, managing and thinking about this and that. In contrast to the ancients, they do injury to their minds. (7.2a:2/125:7)

1.8. The other night Ch'i-yüan[9] said that inner mental attentiveness is no match for lesser learning. In my view it is lesser learning that is no match for inner mental attentiveness, for inner mental attentiveness already embraces lesser learning. Inner mental attentiveness means to make the proper effort in all matters everywhere. Even if one has entered the realm of the sages, such attentiveness cannot be dispensed with. For example, Yao and Shun were attentive from beginning to end: the four words celebrating Yao's virtue—"reverential, intelligent, accomplished, thoughtful"[10]—take inner mental attentiveness as the foremost of the virtues. The sayings, "[Shun] merely placed himself gravely and reverently with his face due south"[11] and "[the superior man] being sincere and

9. Ts'ao Shu-yüan (*chin-shih* 1190), a disciple of the influential Yung-chia thinker, Ch'en Fu-liang (1137–1203). See *SJCC*, vol. 3, pp. 2210–2211, and Ch'en Jung-chieh, *Chu-tzu men-jen*, p. 194.

10. From the *Shang shu*; see Legge, *Chinese Classics*, vol. 3, p. 15.

11. From *Lun-yü* 15/5; see Waley, *Analects*, p. 193. The seat of the ruler faces south.

reverent, the world will be at peace"[12] do the same.[13] (*YL* 7.2b: 7/ 126: 2)

1.9. Lu Tzu-shou[14] said: "In antiquity young children were taught as soon as they were able to talk and eat. What they studied included cleaning and sweeping and polite conversation. Thus when they grew up, they could easily discuss matters [with others and learn from them]. Nowadays, beginning in their early youth, people are taught to compose couplets. As they get somewhat older, they are taught to compose showy prose. Both [these practices] spoil their originally good natures. I have thought about developing a set of regulations for lesser learning so that beginning in their early youth people might be educated according to a plan. This would surely be of some benefit." The Master said: Just design something in the style of the *Ch'an-yüan Code* [*Ch'an-yüan ch'ing-kuei*].[15] That would do. (7.2b: 12/126: 5)

1.10. In teaching children to read the *Book of Poetry*, don't break a stanza up into parts.[16] (7.3a: 9/126: 11)

1.11. At the outset of their studies youths should read the texts of lesser learning, as they contain the pattern for how a man should behave.[17] (7.4a: 1/127: 7)

---

12. From *Chung-yung* 33/5; see Legge, *Chinese Classics*, vol. 1, p. 433.

13. Chu here is taking *ch'in* ("reverential") and *kung* ("reverently" and "reverent") to be roughly synonymous with *ching* ("inner mental attentiveness").

14. Lu Chiu-yüan's older brother; he lived from 1132 to 1180. The following exchange took place when Lu was visiting Chu Hsi in 1179; see *Nien-p'u*, pp. 75–76.

15. A book of monastic regulations in ten chapters compiled in the Sung dynasty (1103). Its eighty-nine articles were traditionally thought to have been based on regulations established by Ch'an master Huai-hai of Pai-chang Mountain (d. 814) in the ninth century and deal with all matters of the monastery: dress, ritual, food, training and studying, the administrative tasks, and so forth. For a discussion of the *Ch'an-yüan ch'ing-kuei* and a summary of the areas covered by the code see Collcutt, *Five Mountains*, pp. 135–145.

16. I.e., be sure to have them read all the way through it regardless of its length, as it is a coherent whole; cf. the following passage in *YL* 7.3a/vol. 1, p. 126.

17. Chu Hsi believed that in antiquity there had existed a text concerning lesser learning but that it had become fragmented with the passage of time; see "T'i hsiao-hsüeh" in *Wen-chi* 76.21a3–10. With the help of his disciple Liu Ch'ing-chih (1134–1190) (see *SJCC*, vol. 5, pp. 3975–3976, and Ch'en Jung-chieh *Chu-tzu men-jen*, p. 311), Chu complied an anthology of passages from the Classics, the

1.12. If the "Duties of Pupils" [Ti-tzu chih] chapter had not been included in the *Book of Master Kuan* [*Kuan-tzu*], it too would have been lost.[18] It may be that Kuan Chung preserved the writing of some ancient, or it may be that he himself wrote the chapter.[19] There's no way to know. I suspect that when he was serving in government the sons of administrators [*shih*][20] as a rule became administrators and that he wrote the "Duties of Pupils" to teach them. I would think that generally he understood the sorts of things treated in the chapter, though in his own life he went beyond accepted custom and good conduct. (7.5a:4/128:12)

---

histories, the philosophers, and literary collections and published it in 1187 under the title *Hsiao-hsüeh*.

18. The "Ti-tzu chih" outlines the regulations that were to govern the behavior of pupils in school. Passages from this chapter are included in Chu's *Hsiao-hsüeh* anthology.

19. Kuan Chung (d. 645 B.C.), the purported author of the *Kuan-tzu* text, served as prime minister of Ch'i and is usually considered the forerunner of the Legalist school.

20. *Shih* is a difficult term to translate. During Kuan Chung's time, *shih* were those trained in both the martial and literary arts; they therefore tended to serve as military officers and government officials. From the context here it is clear that Chu understands the term to mean administrators, officials, or the like.

Two

The Method of Learning,
General Discussion
(Chapter 8)

2.1. The substance of the Way is infinite. (8.1a:4/129:4)

"Someone asked how the Way and principle are to be distinguished. Chu said: The Way is the path. Principle is the pattern. Like the grain in wood? the questioner asked. Yes, Chu replied. In that case, the questioner said, they seem to be alike. Chu said: The word Way is all-embracing. Principle refers to the many veins within the Way. He also said: The word Way refers to the whole, principle to the details" (*YL* 6.1a:10/99:9).

2.2. The substance and function of the Way may be extremely subtle, but the explanations of them by the sages and worthies are very clear. (8.1a:5/129:5)

To know the Way, one should study the Confucian Classics: "The sages wrote the Classics in order to teach later generations. These texts enable the reader to reflect on the ideas of the sages while reciting their words and hence to understand what is in accordance with the principle of things. Understanding the whole substance of the proper Way, he will practice the Way with all his strength, and so enter into the realm of the sages and worthies" (*Hui-an hsien-sheng Chu Wen-kung wen-chi* 82.26a:4).

Chu Hsi never precisely defines the terms substance and function. But he uses them rather frequently. For example: "Someone asked about the substance and function of the Way. Chu said: If the ear is substance, to hear is function. If the eye is substance, to see is function" (*YL* 1.3a:4/3:10).

"Substance is moral principle. Function is its application. That the ears hear and the eyes see is natural; it's principle. To open the eyes and see something, to prick up the ears and hear something, are function" (*YL* 6.3a:8/101:14).

"What is manifest is substance; what is produced later is function. This body is substance; its movements are function" (*YL* 6.3a:4/101:11).

"Water sometimes flows, sometimes stops, and sometimes makes great waves; this is function. The water's capacity, that it can flow, stop, and make great waves, is substance. This body is substance; the eyes seeing, the ears hearing, the hands and feet moving are function" (*YL* 6.2b:10/ 101:8).

"What people simply should do is substance; what people do is function. It's similar to a fan. There's a frame, there's a handle, and it uses paper and paste; this is substance. A person's waving it is function. It's [also] like a measuring device: that there are markings on it is substance; that one measures things with it is function" (*YL* 6.3b:5/102:4).[1]

2.3. The teachings of the sages are generally concerned simply with everyday, routine behavior, such as filial piety, fraternal respect, loyalty, and fidelity. If men are able to practice such behavior, their "lost minds" will naturally be retrieved,[2] and their beclouded natures will naturally become manifest. Words like mind and nature were discussed in detail for the first time with Tzu-ssu[3] and Mencius. (8.1a:10/129:10)

Chu Hsi bases his understanding of human nature on Mencius. Hence, he argues: "Nature is purely the good" (*YL* 5.1b:8/83:3).

"Nature is how we should be" (*YL* 5.1b:7/83:2).

But Chu, following Ch'eng I, gives Mencius's theory an ontological basis: it is because human nature is identical with principle that it is naturally good. "Nature is simply this principle" (*YL* 5.1b:6/83:1).

---

1. For a discussion of Chu's understanding of substance and function see Chan, "Patterns for Neo-Confucianism," pp. 111–120.

2. This is a reference to *Meng-tzu* 6A/11, where we read: "Mencius said, 'Benevolence is man's mind, and righteousness is man's path. How lamentable is it to neglect the path and not pursue it, to lose this mind and not know to seek it again! When men's fowls and dogs are lost, they know to seek for them again, but they lose their mind, and do not know to seek for it. The great end of learning is nothing else but to seek for the lost mind.'" Translation from Legge, *Chinese Classics*, vol. 2, p. 414.

3. Confucius's grandson, who, Chu believed, wrote the *Chung-yung*.

"Nature is simply how we should be. It is simply principle; it isn't that there exists some *thing*" (*YL* 5.11b:9/93:11).[4]

"Nature is concrete principle. Benevolence, righteousness, propriety, and wisdom are all contained therein" (*YL* 5.2a:1/83:7).

Human nature, Chu would argue then, is principle and so always the same and always good. But one's particular endowment of pyschophysical stuff can "becloud" one's nature. "Human nature is always good. But there are those who at birth are good and those who at birth are evil. This is because their psychophysical stuff is different" (*YL* 4.13b:7/69:4).

"In the universe there is but one moral principle. Human nature is principle. The reason that there are good and bad men is simply that each allotment of psychophysical stuff has its clarity and turbidity" (*YL* 4.12b:5/68:2).

"'Nature is principle.' Principle as it ought to be has nothing that isn't good. Thus in his discussion of nature Mencius was speaking of the original essence of nature. Yet it must have something to cleave to in order to establish itself. Hence the endowment of psychophysical stuff, which cannot but have differences in quality and quantity" (*YL* 4.12b:2/67:16).

"Nature is similar to water. If it flows through a clear channel, it remains clear; if it flows through a filthy channel, it becomes turbid. [Nature] that acquires clear and balanced psychophysical stuff will remain whole—this is what happens to man. [Nature] that acquires turbid and unbalanced psychophysical stuff will become obscured. This is what happens to beasts. Psychophysical stuff is both clear and turbid. Men acquire the clear stuff, beasts acquire the turbid stuff. Men, for the most part, are fundamentally clear and thus different from beasts. But there are also those who are turbid and so not very different from beasts" (*YL* 4.17b:4/73:1).

"Once there exists this principle, there exists this psychophysical stuff. Once there exists this psychophysical stuff, there is certain to exist this principle. It's simply that he who receives clear psychophysical stuff is a sage or worthy—he is like a precious pearl lying in crystal clear water. And he who receives turbid psychophysical stuff is an idiot or degenerate—he is like a pearl lying in turbid water. What is called 'keeping the inborn luminous Virtue unobscured'[5] is the process of reaching into the turbid water and wiping clean this pearl" (*YL* 4.17b:8/73:4).

---

4. Based on translation in Graham, *Two Chinese Philosophers*, p. 48.
5. From the *Ta-hsüeh*, "Classic of Confucius," para. 1.

Human nature and the mind, although distinct entities, are intimately related in Chu's thought: "Nature is the principle contained in the mind. The mind is where principle gathers" (*YL* 5.7a:3/88:13).

"'Nature is principle.'[6] In the mind it's called nature, in affairs it's called principle" (*YL* 5.1b:4/82:12).

"Nature is principle. The mind is what embraces and sustains it, issuing it forth into operation" (*YL* 5.7a:4/88:14).[7]

2.4. The everyday effort required by the Confucian school appears to be extremely simple, but the principle one derives from it will embrace and penetrate everything. Extend it and you can share its vastness with heaven and earth. Thus to be a sage or a worthy and to put heaven and earth in their proper order and nourish the myriad things[8] are a matter of this one principle and nothing more. (8.1b:4/130:1)

2.5. The effort that the sages and worthies talk about is always of the same type: it is simply to "choose what is good and firmly hold fast to it."[9] The *Analects* says "to learn and at due times to repeat what one has learnt,"[10] and the *Book of Mencius* says to "understand goodness and make oneself true."[11] It is just because each speaks from its own point of view that what they [literally] say is different. The writing in each, of course, gets down to extremely fine points. But, in fact, the effort that they talk about is of the same general type. It is necessary to understand fully the reason for the differences in the texts, for only then might one understand the similarity of what they express. (8.1b:9/130:5)

2.6. As for moral principle, each [manifestation of it] has its own spot. You can't talk about it from one perspective only. When it's here, you should talk about it this way; when it's there, you should

6. This remark was made by Ch'eng I and often cited by Chu Hsi and other followers of the Ch'eng-Chu school; see *I-shu*, p. 318.

7. For much more on Chu's views of the mind and its relationship to nature, see below, Part Two, chapter 6, "Holding On to It."

8. This line derives from *Chung-yung* 1/5; cf. Legge, *Chinese Classics*, vol. 1, p. 385.

9. From *Chung-yung* 20/18; translation based on Legge, *Chinese Classics*, vol. 1, p. 413.

10. *Lun-yü* 1/1; translation from Waley, *Analects*, p. 83.

11. From *Meng-tzu* 4A/13.

talk about it that way. Its relative circumstances are different in every case. (8.2a:1/130:8)

2.7. In their efforts students should be worried lest they not get the essentials. If they investigate moral principle, everything will naturally fall into place and interconnect with everything else; each thing will have its order. But if they don't, they'll run into difficulties everywhere. Students talk nonstop, speaking frequently of "holding on to it"; but if they haven't yet understood the essentials, they don't know what "to hold on to." They speak of "extending it," or "personally experiencing it," or "nurturing it"—all are instances of choosing the right words for conversational purposes. Only if they are really capable of these things will they succeed. When it is said "we have to pay attention to the essentials," it's probably for this reason. (8.2a:3/130:10)

2.8. In learning, we must first establish the framework, then turn to the interior to put up the walls and corners; in this way the edifice will be well constructed. People nowadays often proceed directly to the building of a room or so even before they're familiar with the general plan. What they do as a result is of little use. (8.2a:8/130:13)

2.9. To understand the essence of moral principle is the foundation. It may be compared to a person who wants to build a house: he must first ram the earth hard so that the foundation is solid, and only then can he stand the house on top of it. If he doesn't have a good foundation for it himself, it's foolish for him to buy wood today to build the house. For soon he'll just have to build it on someone else's land—and he himself won't have a place to settle. (8.2a:11/130:15)

2.10. You must go to the source to gain a full understanding of the big moral principle. Enlarge your foundation, broaden your boundaries: if you want to build a hundred rooms, you have to have the foundation for a hundred rooms; if you want to build ten rooms, you have to have the foundation for ten rooms. Since principle is essentially the same everywhere, persons A, B, and C will have foundations of the same size.[12] (8.2b:2/131:1)

---

12. The meaning of this last sentence is somewhat unclear.

2.11. In learning, you must first understand the big. When you've understood the big, you'll naturally thoroughly grasp the small within. People nowadays, however, without understanding the big, merely seek out the tiny details within. (8.2b:5/131:3)

2.12. In learning, you'll benefit only if you make the one great advance. If you're able to ascertain the one point, the big point (i.e., moral principle), you'll see that the many small fragments are nothing but this one moral principle—and you'll feel pleased. Still, it isn't that you should ignore the fragments; but if you don't ascertain the critical point, even though you might understand the fragments somewhat, in the end you won't be pleased. Tseng Tien and Ch'i-tiao K'ai[13] knew what their great wishes were only because they already clearly understood the critical point. Now, we should talk about what that critical point is: under heaven there is only one moral principle. In learning, you should desire nothing more than to understand this moral principle. Once you appreciate this, you will completely appreciate the distinctions between heavenly principle and human desires, righteousness and profit, impartiality and partiality, good and evil. (8.2b:7/131:5)

2.13. Someone asked about how to rescue the psychophysical stuff from an imbalance. Chu replied: Just now you've spoken of an imbalance; but if in meeting up with some thing or affair you seek to rescue it from its imbalance, the more you'll focus on the unevenness of the stuff, and the less, in your investigation, you'll focus on what's important. Just recognize clearly the big moral principle, and the imbalance will become apparent of itself. It's like looking for something in a dark room—hold a light to illuminate the way. If you just grope around for it, it'll be a waste of psychic energy. You'll simply grope for it without finding it. Once you understand the big moral principle clearly, when imperfections exist, you'll be able to transform them naturally, without even being aware of it. You won't have to make any effort. (8.3a:1/131:9)

2.14. Complete yourself and only then will you be able to complete other things—the completion of things lies in the completion of the

---

13. Disciples of Confucius. The references here are to *Lun-yü* 11/24 and 5/6; cf. Legge, *Chinese Classics*, vol. 1, pp. 246–249, 174.

self. Only if you push outward [from the self] in this manner will
you be able to accord with moral principle. The myriad words of
the sages and worthies teach man to proceed from what's near
at hand. For instance, sprinkling and sweeping the main hall and
the main corridors is just like sprinkling and sweeping a small
room. Once you've swept a small place clean, a large place is no
different. If you're unable to bring a large place under cultivation,
you haven't fully exerted yourself on the small places. Students are
fond of the lofty and long for the remote; they're unwilling to proceed from what's near at hand. How will they understand the large
things? Today there are those who don't proceed from within, but
without perform quite well. This is simply because they are extremely talented, and their intelligence overcomes all else. The *Doctrine of the Mean* says of the minute: Just be watchful in your soli-
tude, watchful in your words, watchful in your actions.[14] And of the
large [it says]: King Wen and the Duke of Chou were far-extending
in their filial piety[15]; they adjusted everything under heaven without exception.[16] The small leads to the fulfillment of the large. You
must wish to be watchful in your actions and watchful in your
words—proceeding from the minute—and only then will you be
capable of bringing the large to completion in this way. He also
said: Learning today is extremely difficult because no one practices
lesser learning. Today they begin at the very top. In the lesser matters of lesser learning the ancients preserved the moral principle
found in the greater matters of greater learning. Greater learning
was simply the extension and broadening [of lesser learning]. The
moral principle that they practiced when they were small was preserved in greater learning. Moral principle is just like a mold for
making bricks. (8.3a:6/131:12)

2.15. In making the effort, a student mustn't say that he's waiting
to make one big effort. He should accumulate fragments [of effort]
little by little starting immediately. Waiting just to make the big
effort is to waste the opportunities before him at the moment. A
student must begin his efforts now, forcefully and without hesita-

----

14. For example, *Chung-yung* 1, 13, and 20.
15. *Chung-yung* 19; cf. Legge, *Chinese Classicis*, vol. 1, p. 402.
16. *Chung-yung* 32/1; cf. Legge, *Chinese Classics*, vol. 1, pp. 429–430.

tion, and even ghosts and spirits will flee from him. "Procrastination is the thief of time."[17] (8.3b:6/132:3)

2.16. In learning, they don't know where to begin these days. Thus they naturally do things in a confused manner without being aware of it. If they knew where to begin, they'd be certain to pay due attention to each and every matter—and let me just say that there are many, many matters in the world. Chiang Wen-ch'ing[18] said: You, master, hope that every word you say will become a model for the world. Therefore, you necessarily proceed in this way [i.e., paying attention to each and every matter]. Chu replied: It isn't that I want my words to become a model for the world. It's that because I know where to begin, it's natural that I should give due attention to the many matters. I can't but proceed in this way. From the beginning such has been the principle of heaven. (8.3b:10/132:5)

2.17. If you don't know where to begin, whether you proceed in haste or only slowly, you won't get it. And if you know the path just slightly, it's essential that you not give up. If you do, you won't succeed, for getting back on the right track is difficult. This can be compared to a hen sitting on her eggs. Seemingly only little warmth is produced by sitting on them; but if it's done for a long while, the eggs will hatch. Were the hen to boil the eggs in hot water, they'd die. And were she to sit on them, then stop, they'd become cold. But truly knowing where to begin, she naturally doesn't stop. She naturally insists on doing it, and she naturally derives some satisfaction from it. It's like eating a piece of fruit. When you don't yet know its taste, it doesn't matter to you whether you eat it or not. But once you know its taste, though you may want to stop, you naturally can't. (8.4a:3/132:8)

2.18. The common person will prosper only when there's a King Wen.[19] The outstanding person will prosper even when there's no

17. This line is from *Tso chuan*, Duke Ai, fourteenth year; Legge, *Chinese Classics*, vol. 5, p. 836. Translation from Giles, *Chinese-English Dictionary*, p. 590.

18. Chiang was one of Chu Hsi's companions after Chu retired to Chien-yang, Fukien, in late 1194. See *SJCC*, vol. 1, p. 530, and Ch'en Jung-chieh, *Chu-tzu men-jen*, pp. 80–81.

19. King Wen, the architect of the Chou conquest of the Shang, appears in the early records as a paragon of benevolence and wisdom.

King Wen. His stuff is perfect. When he's born, he understands moral principle, without expending any effort. People nowadays are mired in confusion; only when the sages have spoken to them repeatedly [through their texts] are they willing to take leave of it. But if they're already totally stupified and, moreover, don't even know to pursue moral principle, in the end they'll become mere beasts. It seems that man, as the most intellectual of the ten thousand things, is naturally different from them; but if he deludes and confuses his intellect, what difference is there between him and beasts? (8.4a:9/132:12)

2.19. Learning is something we have to do. If we don't know to learn, we make ourselves deficient. Only if we know to learn, will we have no deficiencies. People today think learning is something from the outside added on to them. (8.4b:2/132:15)

2.20. Sages and worthies simply do to the fullest the things a man ought to do. Now to be a sage or a worthy, stop at just the right place and go no further. (8.4b:4/133:1)

2.21. Students must firmly establish their wills. What is meant by "will" isn't to overwhelm other people with one's bearing. It's just simply the desire to study Yao and Shun.[20] "Mencius talked to [Duke Wen of T'eng when he was still crown prince] about the goodness of human nature, always citing Yao and Shun as his authorities." What he said was true. "Returning from Ch'u, the prince again visited Mencius. Mencius said, 'Does Your Highness doubt my words? There is one Way and one only!'"[21] With this moral principle one will not go wrong; it's simply that the goodness of human nature was able to find completion in Yao and Shun and nowhere else. Afterward the text cites Ch'eng Chien, Yen-tzu, and Kung-ming I,[22] who thought that all men were capable of becoming a Yao or Shun.[23] To establish their wills, students must make

---

20. Legendary sage-emperors whose goodness was such that they made the welfare of those whom they governed their sole concern.

21. From *Meng-tzu* 3A/1; translation from Lau, *Mencius*, p. 95, with modification.

22. A brave warrior of Ch'i, Confucius's most illustrious disciple, and a disciple of Tseng Tzu, respectively.

23. From *Meng-tzu* 3A/1; see Lau, *Mencius*, p. 95.

themselves resolute, then as a matter of course they should make progress. The students' great failing is that their wills are incapable of pressing on. (8.5a:7/133:10)

Following Ch'eng Hao, Chu describes the will: "Where the mind is headed is what is meant by 'will'"[24] (*YL* 5.14a:8/96:10). Chu Hsi states repeatedly that the mind must have the will to learn if the student is ever to advance. The will thus becomes a central feature in his philosophical system.

2.22. The reason why the ordinary sort of learning and that of the sages and worthies are different is not difficult to see. Sages and worthies simply do things in earnest. When they say, "Set the mind in the right," they fervently desire to set the mind in the right; when they say, "Make the thoughts true," they fervently desire to make the thoughts true. Nor are "cultivation of the self" and "bringing harmony to the household" just empty words for them.[25] When students today speak of setting the mind in the right, they briefly mouth the words "setting the mind in the right." When they speak of making the thoughts true, they briefly mouth the words "making the thoughts true." And when they talk about self-cultivation, they do nothing more than recite the sages' and worthies' many utterances about self-cultivation. Sometimes they gather together the words of the sages and worthies and compose an examination essay. Engaging in this sort of learning has little effect on one's own person. It's essential that you fully understand this matter. Our friends, of course, take much pleasure in hearing about the learning of the sages and worthies, but in the end they're unable to break away from the ordinary practices of the day—this is simply because their wills are not fixed, and that is all. Fixing the will is of the greatest importance for students. As they study, they should be determined to become sages. (8.5b:1/133:14)

2.23. Students must establish their wills. That people nowadays are aimless is simply because they've never taken learning seriously. In dealing with things, they're reckless simply because their wills aren't firmly established. (8.5b:9/134:3)

---

24. See *Ho-nan Ch'eng-shih wai-shu* 2.2b; cited in Graham, *Two Chinese Philosophers*, p. 61.

25. These four terms are from the *Ta-hsüeh*, "Classic of Confucius," para. 4.

2.24. Someone asked: Does it make any difference to one's learning if one is weak in strength? Chu replied: Learning depends upon firmly establishing the will and isn't related to the strength or weakness of one's psychophysical allotment. He also said: In learning, there's no use being anxious. Simply put yourself at ease so that you're free from anxiety. [I], Yü,[26] raised the matter of Confucius's disciples. [Confucius] praised Yen-tzu alone for his love of learning; next, and only then, would he talk about Tseng Tzu. From this we know the great difficulty in learning. Chu said: It's indeed as you say. I feel that it's sometimes extremely difficult, sometimes extremely easy. If one simply establishes the will firmly and follows moral principle, nothing will go wrong. (8.5b:11/134:5)

2.25. In making the effort, students should forget about eating and sleeping and give it their all; in this way they'll make a successful start. And from then on they'll take pleasure in continuing the effort. To start and stop, making only half an effort and then giving up, is of no use. (8.6a:10/134:14)

2.26. What's important now is to see what a sage is like and what an ordinary person is like, why we are not like sages and why we are mere ordinary people. When we fully understand these matters we may naturally transcend the common and enter sagehood. (8.6a:12/134:16)

2.27. Students today aren't the least bit excited [about learning]. (8.6b:5/135:4)

2.28. If in your learning you do not make progress, it's simply because you're not bold. (8.6b:6/135:5)

2.29. Don't depend on teachers or friends. (8.6b:7/135:6)

2.30. Don't wait. (8.6b:8/135:7)

2.31. People nowadays are unwilling to get started in making an effort—they all want to wait. For instance, if they're busy this morning but not this afternoon, they could get started this afternoon. If they're busy this afternoon, they could get started this evening. Nonetheless, they're sure to wait until tomorrow. And if

---

26. Chu's disciple Hsü Yü; see *SJCC*, vol. 3, p. 1997, and Ch'en Jung-chieh, *Chu-tzu men-jen*, p. 180.

there are still a few days left in the month, they're certain to wait until next month. And if there are still a few months left in the year, they make no effort and are bound to say, "There isn't much time left in the year, we must wait until next year." How are they going to make any progress like this? (8.6b:9/135:8)

2.32. Students must endure trouble and hardship. (8.7a:3/135:12)

2.33. Generally, in learning, though a person might have the natural gift of intelligence, only if he makes the effort of a dullard will he get it. A person who has the natural gift of a dullard, yet makes the effort of an intelligent person, how can he get it? (8.7a:11/136:2)

2.34. In learning, do not claim that there's no one to analyze it for you. You need to go to the core of it yourself, making the most careful effort. You must understand it for yourself. (8.7b:3/136:6)

2.35. Set up a limited curriculum, but exert great effort on it.[27] (8.7b:5/136:7)

2.36. Give your attention to it. You needn't calculate what you'll gain from it. (8.7b:7/136:9)

2.37. Once you begin to calculate the gains to be had from learning, your mind will become divided and your head will hang down in shame. (8.7b:8/136:10)

2.38. ... a strict work schedule, relax your thoughts, and, after a long time, you naturally should find meaning in it. You can't look for quick results. (8.7b:9/136:11)

2.39. People often say that they're busy with things and that this hinders their study. This is unconvincing.[28] When meeting with wealth and high station, make the effort appropriate to wealth and high station. When meeting with impoverishment and lowly status, make the effort appropriate to impoverishment and lowly status. A line from *The Art of War*[29] puts it quite well: "Take circumstance

27. For Chu's more detailed views of the curriculum see below, Part Two, chapter 4, "On Reading, Part 1," and chapter 5, "On Reading, Part 2."

28. Literally, "This is something incapable of making a boat dislike a winding stream."

29. I.e., the *Ping-fa*, which according to tradition was written by Sun Tzu. Griffith, *Sun Tzu*, p. 11, dates the authorship of the text to the period c. 400–320 B.C.

into account and plan your strategy to profit from it."[30] People considered the men of Ch'i to be weak. T'ien Chi[31] taking their [reputation for] weakness into account secured a victory. The first day [he lit] thirty thousand campfires, the second day twenty thousand, and the third day ten thousand.[32] Similarly, Han Hsin[33] purposely placed many of his men in do-or-die circumstances; only then did they obtain a victory.[34] If students have even a shred of strength left in them, they must carry on; only if they're completely out of strength and their mouths can no longer speak may they stop. [Chu] then cited a Buddhist saying: Even if an iron wheel goes round and round on your head, your concentration, wisdom, and perfect brightness should never be lost. (8.7b: 11/136: 13)

2.40. Tsung-kao[35] said: "For instance, to have a cart full of weapons and take them out one by one, tinkering first with this one then with that one, is not the way to kill others. If I had nothing but a short dagger, I could kill others." (8.8a: 11/137:6)

2.41. In learning, it's essential to hold on to the boat-pole with all your strength. As you feel your effort beginning to flag, apply still more effort. Exert yourself fully, without any letup; only then will there be progress. Learning is just like punting a boat upstream.

---

30. This line does not seem to appear in the *Ping-fa* text, but it does appear in the *Shih chi* biography of Sun Tzu (vol. 7, 65.2164); translation based on Griffith, *Sun Tzu*, p. 61.

31. A general of Ch'i who lived in the fourth century B.C.

32. The enemy thus became convinced that the men of Ch'i, who after all were renowned for their weakness and cowardice, had deserted. Thereupon the enemy advanced with only lightly armed troops and suffered a devastating defeat at the hands of Ch'i. Chu's comments here are loosely based on, but not altogether consistent with, the account of the incident found in Sun Tzu's *Shih chi* biography (vol. 7, 65.2164). See Griffith, *Sun Tzu*, pp. 61–62, for a translation.

33. A general from the state of Han who lived during the end of the third century B.C.

34. Han Hsin placed Han troops in a disadvantageous position in order to fool the Chao forces and gain a victory. See *Shih chi*, vol. 8, 92.2613–2617; a translation may be found in Watson, *Grand Historian of China*, vol. 1, pp. 213–217. Han comments that he learned this strategy from the *Ping-fa*. Such strategy is suggested in *Sun-tzu chi-chu* 11.42b–45a; cf. translation in Griffith, *Sun Tzu*, p. 139.

35. I.e., the renowned Ch'an master, Ta-hui Tsung-kao (1089–1163). According to Levering, "Ch'an Enlightenment," p. 318, Chu Hsi was thoroughly acquainted with Ta-hui's *Yü-lu* and may have even studied Ch'an with one of Ta-hui's Dharma-heirs.

Only in the calm spots does the boat move along without problems. As it enters the rapids, the boatman takes up the pole and won't let go of it. He has to punt the boat upstream with all his strength—he can't relax for even a moment. If he lets up for a moment, the boat won't make it upstream. (8.8b:4/137:11)

2.42. Learning for students may be compared to preparing the elixir of life. It's necessary to smelt [the ingredients] for a short time with a hundred-catty charcoal fire, and then with a tiny flame slowly bring [the elixir] to completion. Nowadays people don't smelt [the ingredients] with a hundred-catty charcoal fire but want to bring [the elixir] to completion with a tiny flame. How are they going to succeed? (8.8b:8/137:14)

2.43. You must train your mental energy if you are to understand. The affairs under heaven cannot be carried out successfully in leisure and relaxation. (8.9a:5/138:4)

2.44. You'll be able to do the myriad things only when you have the mental energy. (8.9a:6/138:5)

2.45. When one's *yang* psychophysical stuff issues forth, even metal and stone may be penetrated. When one has the mental energy, there is nothing one can't accomplish. (8.9a:7/138:6)

2.46. Only if man's psychophysical stuff is hard will he be able to accomplish things. For example, the psychophysical stuff of heaven and earth is hard and thus penetrates everything, no matter what it may be. By nature, man's psychophysical stuff is similarly hard. But if in encountering some matter, important or trivial, a man turns his back on it, how will he succeed at it? (8.9a:10/138:8)

2.47. A person without determination can't become a Buddhist priest or practice Taoism. (8.9b:4/138:14)

2.48. Students simply do not do it for their own sake.[36] Thus in the course of a day their minds fix on moral principle very little and on trivial matters a great deal—they remain unacquainted with moral

---

36. This is an allusion to *Lun-yü* 14/24: "The Master said, 'In antiquity men studied for their own sake; nowadays men study for the sake of others'" (Waley, *Analects*, p. 187).

principle and become thoroughly familiar with trivial matters. (8.9b:9/139:2)

2.49. The important thing for students today is to distinguish between the paths. What's important is the boundary between "doing it for one's own sake" and "doing it for the sake of others."[37] "To do it for one's own sake" is to grasp the essence of things and affairs firsthand in reaching an understanding of them—you want to understand them for yourself. It isn't to understand them recklessly, nor is it to understand them in a way that makes you look good, so that people will say yes, you have indeed understood; if this is how you were to go about it, even supposing you did understand them 100 percent accurately, they'd still have no effect on you at all. You must first come to understand these paths; for only if you distinguish clearly between them can you understand the texts. (8.9b:11/139:4)

2.50. In recent times scholarly discussion hasn't been very genuine. Mostly, people are intent on showing off. This situation is like our having food but, rather than eating it ourselves, simply placing it outside the door so that others know our household has it. Only if people readjust their ambitions will they advance in learning. (8.10a:11/139:12)

2.51. Contemporary scholars are quite different from the ancients. Nowadays people tirelessly explore the lofty. The ancients, they took concrete step after concrete step. (8.10b:3/139:15)

2.52. Simply make a concrete effort. Arguing about it a lot just creates a ruckus. (8.10b:5/139:16)

2.53. Learning must genuinely be for the sake of oneself; if it is, one will become tranquil and true and embody the many manifestations of moral principle. If a person touches only slightly on learning, how will he get at moral principle? And even if he does get at it and talk about it, he still won't embody it. (8.10b:7/140:2)

2.54. The first step to entering into the Way is to place yourself in the midst of moral principle; gradually you will become intimate

---

37. The distinction made by Confucius in *Lun-yü* 14/24.

with it. After a while you and it will become one. With people to-day, however, moral principle is here, and they are external to it—moral principle and people have absolutely nothing to do with each other. (8.10b:9/140:4)

2.55. In learning, it is necessary to concentrate. If we Confucians were to concentrate only on moral principle, we'd naturally profit. (8.12b:10/142:4)

2.56. It's best if what you see in yourself is simply the shortcomings but when others see you they see progress. (8.12b:12/142:6)

2.57. As for the way to learn: you must first preserve moral principle, and only then can you examine into particular matters. (8.13a:2/142:8)

2.58. "Extensive learning"[38] refers to all that one ought to learn: the principle of heaven, of earth, and of the myriad things and the way of cultivating the self and of governing others. But there is an order to all that you learn: you must place what is important and urgent first—learning can't be unsystematic and disunified. (8.13a:7/142:12)

2.59. It's like climbing a mountain. Men often want to reach the highest point and don't realize that in the end there is no way to do so unless they're familiar with the low points. (8.13a:11/142:15)

2.60. In your understanding of obvious or easy passages lies an understanding of abstruse ones.[39] (8.13b:1/142:16)

2.61. A student must be intimate with it. When he's intimate with it, as soon as he summons it, it'll be right there in front of him. When he's not intimate with it, he must ruminate about it; but if he gets it only with rumination, the meaning will not be as clear as it would have been had he got it at the very outset. (8.13b:10/143:7)

2.62. To understand it, you must understand it with certainty. (8.14a:1/143:9)

---

38. A term appearing often in the *Lun-yü*; see 6/27, 9/2, 12/15, and 19/6.
39. I.e., understanding of the abstruse begins with an understanding of the easy.

2.63. It's essential that the mind be vast, like this. Only then will it envelop everything and move around freely. (8.14a:2/143:10)

2.64. What I fear most is reading carelessly, then readily entering into no good. (8.14a:6/143:14)

2.65. "There's never been a person whose ears and eyes are narrow yet whose mind is broad." This says it extremely well. (8.14a:9/144:1)

2.66. For the most part students have no shortcuts to understanding. Only if they're broad in learning and vast in experience will they understand. (8.14a:11/144:3)

2.67. If a student is possessed of the foundation, all the many details will congregate there one by one. In reading, he'll be sure to find it easy to understand; and in studying, he'll be sure to find it easy to remember. (8.14b:3/144:6)

2.68. If the great foundation is not established, the norms of conduct will not be right. (8.14b:5/144:7)

2.69. Prune back the branches and leaves, and tend to the root. (8.14b:6/144:8)

2.70. In your expansiveness also be meticulous. In your leniency also be rigorous. (8.14b:10/144:12)

2.71. It's best always to keep moments of decisiveness and strict discipline many and those of utter confusion and turmoil few. (8.15a:1/144:15)

2.72. If you just hold a piece of fruit in your hand, you don't know if its inside is acidic or salty, bitter or harsh. You must chew it, then you'll appreciate its flavor. (8.15a:7/145:5)

2.73. The *Changes* says: "[The superior man] learns and accumulates the results of his learning; puts questions, and discriminates among those results; dwells magnanimously and unambitiously in what he has attained to; and carries it into practice with benevolence."[40] The *Analects* says: "He who sides with moral force

---

40. *Chou i*, pp. 2–3; translation from Sung, *Text of Yi King*, p. 13.

but only to a limited extent, who believes in the Way but without conviction—how can he be said either to have anything or not to have anything."[41] If a person is to continue, after learning, to dwell magnanimously and unambitiously in what he has attained to, and to believe in the Way with conviction, hoping also to side unlimitedly with moral force—he must not hurry his mind. A person's mind must be allowed to acquire one bit of goodness, then another. It's best if goodness presents itself endlessly, and the mind takes it all in with room to spare; if it simply acquires one bit of goodness but can't accommodate the second one when it presents itself, there is no way for it to become broadened and the Way to accumulate there. (8.15a:9/145:6)

2.74. If we ourselves are unable to be pleased with our own thoughts, how can others be completely pleased with them? It's essential to open our minds[42] and follow goodness. (8.15b:2/145:10)

2.75. "Open your mind and conform to principle." Students ought to abide by this phrase. (8.15b:4/145:11)

2.76. People nowadays say that in talking about moral principle they wish to be simple; but they don't understand that reaching the point of simplicity is extremely difficult. Entangled in former practices, how are they going to free themselves? It's like writing: the novel and artful are simple to achieve, but if one wishes to be simple and plain it's difficult. One must repudiate the novel and artful and move on to the simple and plain. He also said: To move from a high and dangerous spot down to a more level and comfortable one is very difficult. (8.15b:7/145:13)

2.77. I have heard only the phrase, "my studies lie low, my penetration rises high."[43] Never have I heard the phrase, "my penetration rises high, my studies lie low." (8.16a:2/146:3)

---

41. *Lun-yü* 19/2; translation based on Waley, *Analects*, p. 224, and Lau, *Confucius: The Analects*, p. 153.

42. Chu explains what he means by *hsü hsin*, "open our minds," at some length below; see Part Two, chapter 5, "On Reading, Part 2."

43. *Lun-yü* 14/35; translation from Legge, *Chinese Classics*, vol. 1, p. 289.

2.78. Students today proceed toward the great Way: the ones who have yet to reach it, though they may be slow-witted, will be sure to get there in the end; it's just that those who have gone too far are unwilling to come back again. (8.16a:3/146:4)

2.79. In discussing the effort required [in learning], students should take into account with whom they're speaking and provide specific instructions. They needn't waste words. For if a person knows in which direction to head and enters upon simple and clear ground, he'll be fine. Giving a lot of vague clues that another feels compelled to pursue for himself will only add to a student's problems, I fear. (8.16a:7/146:6)

2.80. The usefulness of teachers and friends lies simply in their ability to make it known to you at the beginning and to correct it at the end. You have to struggle to do the middle 30 percent of the work on your own. Once you've been instructed in it at the beginning, worked diligently on it yourself in the middle, and deliberated with others to correct it at the end, the benefits will be great. If you don't proceed like this, what good will it do? (8.16a:10/146:8)

2.81. Someone was saying that man's natural disposition will sometimes excel in one regard and fall short in another. Chu said: One must simply improve one's good points and remedy one's failings. Someone else said: Improving the good points and remedying the failings—it's not just the teacher that ought to do this [for the student]. The person doing the learning himself ought to be doing this too. Chu said: That's right. (8.16b:1/146:10)

2.82. You absolutely must get rid of the mind that's attached to externals. (8.17a:2/147:5)

2.83. One part mental concentration yields one part strength. Two parts mental concentration yields two parts strength. (8.17a:3/147:6)

2.84. After you become intimately familar with moral principle, it alone will be your true standard. You'll view the myriad affairs of the world as confusing, enticing, and all part of a staged play— you'll find it truly unbearable to keep your eyes on them. He also said in response to a letter: The myriad affairs of the world might be transformed or extinguished in a split second. They should not become dear to us. Probing principle and cultivating the self alone constitute the perfect way. (8.17a:5/147:8)

The point here, that man must not value things or affairs but rather the one true standard, bears a similarity to the contemporary Buddhist notion that things are illusory and the only true reality is the Buddha-nature.

Three

A Discussion of
Knowledge and Action
(Chapter 9)

3.1 Knowledge and action are normally mutually dependent. It's like this: if a person has eyes but no legs, he cannot walk; if he has legs but no eyes, he cannot see. As for their order, knowledge comes first. As for their importance, action is more significant. (9.1a:4/148:4)

3.2. There was a discussion of knowledge and action. The Master said: When you know something but don't act on it, your knowledge of it is still superficial. After you've personally experienced it, your knowledge of it will be much clearer and its significance will be different from what it used to be. (9.1a:6/148:5)

3.3. Sages and worthies discussed knowledge, then action. The *Greater Learning* first says, "'As if cutting and filing' speaks to the process of learning," and then says, "'As if chiseling and polishing' [speaks] to the process of self-cultivation."[1] The *Doctrine of the Mean* first speaks of study, inquiry, reflection, and discrimination and

---

1. *Ta-hsüeh*, "Commentary of Tseng Tzu," 3.4, makes these remarks as commentary on a poem it cites from the *Shih ching*. The poem reads: "Look to the coves in the banks of the Ch'i / With green bamboo, so lush and fine; / There is our elegant and accomplished prince,— / As if cutting and filing, / As if chiselling and polishing, / [So he cultivates himself!] / How grave is he and resolute! / How commanding and distinguished! / Our elegant and accomplished prince,— / Never can he be forgotten!" Translation from Gardner, *Chu Hsi and the Ta-hsueh*, p. 100.

then speaks of earnest practice.[2] Yen-tzu[3] first speaks of "enlarging one's mind with learning,"[4] which means to "extend knowledge to the utmost" and "apprehend the principle in things," and then of "restraining oneself with ritual,"[5] which refers to "subduing one's self and returning to propriety."[6] (9.1a:8/148:7)

3.4. In your efforts to "extend knowledge to the utmost" and "to act with vigor,"[7] don't be partial toward one or the other. If you lean too much toward one, the other will suffer. As Master Ch'eng has said: "Nurturing requires inner mental attentiveness; the pursuit of learning depends upon the extension of knowledge."[8] It's clear that his was a two-pronged theory. But we must sort out the order and relative importance of the prongs. As to order, we should place "the extension of knowledge to the utmost" first. As to importance, we should consider "vigorous action" the more significant. (9.1a:11/148:9)

3.5. What is called "probing principle" is this: The big must be probed, the small must be probed, and soon everything will become one. What is called "keeping a hold on ourselves" is this: People can't avoid being lured by creaturely desires, but only when they realize this is the case do they rein themselves in. After a while they naturally get good at it—it isn't that today they can right away begin to be good at it. (9.2a:8/149:11)

Ch'iung li, or "probing principle," is Chu's gloss, borrowed from Ch'eng I,[9] for *ko wu* ("apprehending the principle in things"), which according to the *Greater Learning* is the first step in the Confucian self-cultivation process.[10] Chu explains how he understands *ch'iung li* and *ko wu* in his so-called supplementary chapter to the *Greater Learning*. Convinced that the original *ko wu* chapter of the *Greater Learning* had been lost, he supplies

---

2. From *Chung-yung* 20/19; translation based on Legge, *Chinese Classics*, vol. 1, p. 413.
3. Yen Hui, Confucius's most brilliant disciple.
4. *Lun-yü* 9/11; translation based on Legge, *Chinese Classics*, vol. 1, p. 220.
5. *Lun-yü* 9/11.
6. *Lun-yü* 12/1; translation based on Legge, *Chinese Classics*, vol. 1, p. 250.
7. This term, *li-hsing*, is from *Chung-yung* 20; cf. Legge, *Chinese Classics*, vol. 1, p. 407.
8. *I-shu*, p. 209. Cf. Chan, *Source Book*, p. 562.
9. See *I-shu*, p. 209.
10. For a discussion of the translation of the term *ko wu*, see note 2 to 1.1 above.

his own version, which since his time has commonly circulated as part of the Classic itself. It reads: "What is meant by 'the extension of knowledge lies in fully apprehending the principle in things' is, that if we wish to extend our knowledge to the utmost we must probe thoroughly the principle in those things that we encounter. It would seem that every man's intellect is possessed of the capacity for knowing and that everything in the world is possessed of principle. But, to the extent that principle is not yet thoroughly probed, man's knowledge is not yet fully realized. Hence, the first step of the instruction in greater learning is to teach the student, whenever he encounters anything at all in the world, to build upon what is already known to him of principle and to probe still further, so that he seeks to reach the limit. After exerting himself in this way for a long time, he will one day become enlightened and thoroughly understand [principle]; then, the manifest and the hidden, and the subtle and the obvious qualities of all things will all be known, and the mind, in its whole substance and vast operations, will be completely illuminated. This is called 'fully apprehending the principle in things.' This is called 'the completion of knowledge'" (*Ta-hsüeh*, "Commentary of Tseng Tzu," 5; translation from Gardner, *Chu Hsi and the Ta-hsueh*, pp. 104–105).

3.6. Think about moral principle; nurture the source. (9.2b:1/ 149:15)

3.7. The effort to probe principle is naturally subsumed in the nurturing process—one probes the principle being nurtured. The effort to nurture is naturally subsumed in the process of probing principle—one nurtures the principle being probed. These two processes are inseparable. As soon as one sees them as two different endeavors, nothing will be achieved. (9.2b:2/149:16)

3.8. Tse-chih[11] asked whether if one nurtured oneself one would naturally become enlightened after a while. The Master said: One must also probe principle. Nurturing and probing are both indispensable, like two wheels of a cart or two wings of a bird. As for Wen-kung,[12] he simply acted, ignoring the extension of knowledge. (9.2b:4/150:2)

11. Lin Yung-chung, a follower of Chu's. See *SJCC*, vol. 2, pp. 1378–1379, and Ch'en Jung-chieh, *Chu-tzu men-jen*, pp. 145–146.
12. Ssu-ma Kuang. See above, Part One, "Chu Hsi and the Transformation of the Confucian Tradition."

3.9. The student's efforts consist solely in practicing inner mental attentiveness and probing principle, these two matters. These matters are mutually dependent. If one is able to probe principle, one's efforts at practicing inner mental attentiveness will improve daily. If one is able to practice inner mental attentiveness, one's efforts at probing principle will become more intense daily. The relationship here may be compared to a person's two feet: if the left moves, the right stops; if the right moves, the left stops. Or it may be compared to an object suspended in air: if the right side is tugged, the left side shoots up; if the left side is tugged, the right side shoots up. In actual fact, these cases are simply one matter, not two. (9.3a:3/150:9)

3.10. As soon as a person makes the effort, he'll discover the obstacles.[13] When he begins making the effort, he'll be intent on doing one thing, but some other thing will get in his way, and he'll understand neither. It's just like when we practice inner mental attentiveness and probe principle—these two things get in each other's way: practicing inner mental attentiveness refers to the way of controlling and restraining oneself; probing principle refers to the way of investigating the ultimate. These two things simply hinder each other. But when we get good at them, naturally they no longer get in each other's way. (9.3a:7/150:12)

3.11. Adhering to inner mental attentiveness is the basis of probing principle. Probing principle until it is clear is an aid to nurturing the mind. (9.3a:12/150:16)

This is true, since principle out there is the same as principle in the mind.

3.12. If we liken the "extension of knowledge," "inner mental attentiveness," and "subduing the self,"[14] these three matters, to a house, "inner attentiveness" corresponds to the man who guards the door, "subduing the self" corresponds to warding off the robber, and the "extension of knowledge" corresponds to investigating the external affairs that affect one's home. I-ch'uan said, "nurturing

13. Reading *i* as a scribal error for *ai*, which appears three other times in this passage and certainly makes better sense here.
14. This term is from *Lun-yü* 12/1.

requires inner mental attentiveness; the pursuit of learning depends
upon the extension of knowledge."[15] He did not speak of "subduing
the self." It would seem that because inner mental attentiveness
overcomes the hundred depravities, it naturally contains the sense
of "subdue." And if one is true to oneself [*ch'eng*] [by being atten-
tive], there is no need to speak of keeping out depravities. Similarly,
to guard the door well is the same as warding off robbers, so there is
no need to speak separately of warding off robbers. We can if you
wish speak of "nurturing" in contrast to "subduing the self," re-
garding each as a separate matter. Nurturing, then, is like resting,
and subduing the self, then, is like taking medicine to cure oneself;
if the resting is insufficient, you take the medicine. But if you have
rested fully, restoring your strength, you will be free of illness.
What need is there for medicine? If you are able to be perfectly
attentive, naturally you will have no depravities. What use will you
have for "subduing yourself"? Should you have depravities, it is
simply because you practice inner mental attentiveness imperfect-
ly. Blame your inner mental attentiveness alone. Thus, if you are
mentally attentive, there is no self to be subdued—this is what results from inner mental attentiveness. It's essential that beginning
learners exert effort everywhere and do their utmost in everything.
(9.4a:3/151:12)

3.13. Somebody asked about the order of the extension of knowledge and nurturing the self. The Master said: You must first extend
knowledge; afterward nurture the self. Someone then asked what
I-ch'uan meant when he said that it was impossible to extend
knowledge without first practicing inner mental attentiveness. The
Master replied: He was speaking generally. If you wish to probe
principle, you must give your entire attention to it. If you don't,
how will you ever understand clearly? (9.4b:5/152:6)

3.14. The myriad affairs will all [be clear] after you probe principle. If there is no order to affairs and principle is unclear to you, no
matter what you do to keep a hold on yourself it'll merely be in
vain. (9.4b:10/152:10)

15. *I-shu*, p. 209.

3.15. There are people who wish to focus solely on personal experience. This is to neglect other matters. (9.5a:1/152:13)

3.16. Wang Tzu-ch'ung[16] inquired: When I was in Hunan, I visited a master[17] who instructed people simply to act. Master Chu said: If moral principle isn't clear, how can one act? Wang said: He said that if you act, you will then understand. Chu replied: This is like someone walking along a road. If he doesn't see, how can he walk? Nowadays people often instruct others to act—they establish this standard for themselves, then teach it to others. Of course, there is the type of person whose natural disposition is good and doesn't need to probe principle, apprehend the principle in things, or extend knowledge. But the Sage wrote the *Greater Learning*[18] so that all men could enter the realm of sages and worthies. Once men understand moral principle clearly, naturally they cannot but be filial in serving their parents, fraternal in serving their brothers, faithful in intercourse with their friends. (9.5a:2/152:14)

3.17. People today talk only about "governing the mind" and "cultivating the self." But if one doesn't understand principle, how can one's mind be governed, how can one's self be cultivated? If people continue to talk as they have, those with naturally good dispositions will be able to nurture themselves, but those without ability, those whose natural dispositions are not good, won't learn to restrain themselves. Fu Yüeh said: "Learn the lessons of the ancients and you will benefit. That the affairs of one who does not take the ancients as his teachers can be perpetuated for generations is something I have never heard." Why bother to read the lessons of the ancients? It seems that the principle the sages and worthies talked about is found complete in them. We must study them, then we will have learned something. [Fu Yüeh] also said: "In learning, there

16. Little is known about Wang; see Ch'en Jung-chieh, *Chu-tzu men-jen*, pp. 59–60.

17. Probably Chang Shih, a resident of Hunan, or one of his students. On the "Hunan School" see Schirokauer, "Chu Hsi and Hu Hung," pp. 480–491.

18. Chu Hsi was one of the first to deal with the question of the *Ta-hsüeh's* authorship, arguing that Confucius was responsible for what Chu called the Classic portion of the text and Tseng Tzu and his disciples responsible for the ten chapters of commentary. See Gardner, *Chu Hsi and the Ta-hsueh*, chap. 3.

should be a humble will and a striving to maintain a constant earnestness. In which case one's cultivation will be successful. If one sincerely cherishes these things [a humble will and constant earnestness], one will find the Way accumulating in one's person. To teach is one-half of learning. When one's thoughts, from first to last, are constantly fixed on learning, one's virtue becomes cultivated imperceptibly."[19] In antiquity no one discussed the word *hsüeh*, "learning." With Fu Yüeh it was discussed for the first time, and so tightly argued were his few comments that sprinkled water couldn't penetrate them. If from beginning to end one is constantly fixed on learning, one's virtue will improve as a matter of course, without one ever being conscious of it. (9.5a:8/153:2)

3.18. In learning, you must want to know with absolute certainty what is right. Once you come to know that this is completely right and that is completely wrong, your understanding will be thorough. For once you understand what's right, your mind will have that which acts as ruler. It's like studying archery. If your will fixes on the bull's-eye, soon you will occasionally hit the target. If your will fixes on the target, soon you will occasionally hit the target mound. If your will fixes on the target mound, soon you will always hit some other spot altogether. (9.6a:10/154:5)

3.19. It's simply a struggle between knowing it and not knowing it, between knowing it well and not so well. Take, for instance, the man who is determined to do good but upon spotting something bad seems capable of doing it as well; just as he's about to do the good thing, he seems to have a mind to do the bad, a mind that comes from behind to lead him astray. This is just a matter of not knowing it so well. (9.6b:2/154:8)

3.20. Moral principle is engendered with all life. But nowadays people neatly put it aside, in some idle place, and pay it no attention. Their lives are directionless and wasted. It's truly pitiful! Essentially, to understand principle is no big thing. I don't know why people give it so little attention; it seems that they are content

19. These remarks by Fu Yüeh, the worthy and virtuous prime minister under Wu Ting of the Shang dynasty, are found in the *Shang shu*; see Legge, *Chinese Classics*, vol. 3, pp. 260–261. The translations here are based on Legge's.

in their ignorance. Once they become set on understanding it, they should seek to understand it fully. Their understanding mustn't be half-baked, for in the end it'd be of no benefit. (9.6b:8/154:12)

3.21. Man, heaven, and earth are all possessed of the many manifestations of moral principle. It isn't that one forcibly puts them there, nor is it that one cuts into the bowels of things, vainly placing them on the inside. (9.6b:12/154:15)

3.22. The one mind embodies the myriad manifestations of principle. If you are able to preserve the mind, you may then probe principle.[20] (9.7a:2/154:16)

Principle embodied in the mind allows for a resonance to occur between the mind and the principle in things in the world out there. That principle is shared by man and things is the premise of Chu Hsi's epistemology.

3.23. The mind embraces the myriad manifestations of principle. The myriad manifestations of principle are embodied in the one mind. Unable to preserve the mind, one is unable to probe principle. Unable to probe principle, one is unable to give full realization to the mind. (9.7a:3/155:1)

3.24. In probing principle, an open mind[21] and quiet reflection are essential. (9.7a:5/155:2)

3.25. Open the mind to observe principle. (9.7a:6/155:3)

3.26. Now if you can't see moral principle clearly, it isn't that you don't know what it is but rather that it is obstructed by things. Now the ordinary means [of dealing with this problem] is to rectify the many evil distractions in the mind. Only then can [moral principle be seen]. Master Chang said: "If moral principle is obstructed, wash away your old understanding and bring forth new ideas."[22] The big problem is that men frequently are unwilling to give up their old understanding. If intelligent, they will see what isn't right and change it. (9.7a:9/155:6)

20. Cf. above, 3.11.
21. For a discussion of "open mind" see below, Part Two, chapter 5, "On Reading, Part 2."
22. See Chang Tsai's remark in *Chang Tsai chi*, p. 321; I follow the *Chang Tsai chi* passage and read *i* in the *YL* comment here as a simple scribal error for *ai* ("obstructed"). *Ai* certainly makes better contextual sense.

3.27. Principle is not some separate thing in front of us; rather it's in our minds. People must discover for themselves that this thing is truly within them, then everything will be okay. Principle can be compared to what the school of inner cultivation[23] calls "lead and mercury, dragon and tiger"[24]—all are present in our own bodies, not external to them. (9.7b:1/155:9)

3.28. Ch'i-yüan[25] asked whether in probing the principle of affairs and things one ought to probe thoroughly the spot where all things and affairs converge into one. Chu replied: There is no need to talk of convergence. All that appears before one's eyes are affairs and things. Just probe them one by one to their limit and gradually the many, of themselves, will become interconnected. The point of convergence is the mind. (9.7b:8/155:14)

3.29. In general, to appreciate moral principle one must understand the great foundation clearly. The subordinate parts are simply this principle dispersed into myriad manifestations. In teaching others, Confucius spoke of moral principle in matter after matter—never did he speak directly about the great foundation. But gather together all the disparate matters he dealt with and you'll see the great foundation. As for Mencius, he already referred to it in his teaching. Master Chou[26] spoke about the great ultimate and was exceedingly clear. Inferring from [Mencius's] "germ of compassion,"[27] you'll arrive at the benevolence of this mind. Benevolence is what is called "the beginning of heavenly virtue"; and "the beginning" is the *yang* movement of the great ultimate. If you proceed like this, part by part, you'll naturally reach an understanding of the great foundation. And once you understand the great ultimate clearly, you will surely understand that the many manifestations of moral principle in the universe come from it. All affairs and things

23. "The school of inner cultivation" refers to the inner alchemical Taoists who sought to "prepare" within their bodies an "interior elixir" composed of ingredients found in their bodies. See, for example, Welch, *Taoism*, pp. 130–132.

24. Lead and dragon refer to the *yang-ch'i* and mercury and tiger to the *yin-ch'i* within one's body.

25. See 1.8.

26. Chou Tun-i. Chu regarded Chou as one of the four great Neo-Confucians of the Northern Sung and drew heavily on his ideas in developing his own philosophical system.

27. *Meng-tzu* 2A/6.

have moral principle—absolutely nothing is without it. (9.7b:11/ 155:16)

3.30. Today's scholars have never understood the main point of learning. One should simply probe moral principle; moral principle is the same as heavenly principle [*t'ien-li*]. Even if sages don't appear, this heavenly principle exists of its own. In the realm of heaven and earth, "heaven is high, earth is low, and the ten thousand things, distinct and different, flow on without stop, conjoining with one another and metamorphosing."[28] In the realm of heaven and earth it is this moral principle alone that flows everywhere. We mustn't think that if the sages don't talk about it moral principle doesn't exist. Moral principle exists of itself eternally in the realm of heaven and earth. It simply avails itself of the sages to explain it to people. For example, the *Changes* treats nothing but the one principle of *yin* and *yang*. When Fu Hsi first drew [the eight trigrams], he was simply drawing this principle. King Wen and Confucius [in their work on the *Changes*] were both elucidating this principle.[29] [The judgments of] "good fortune," "bad fortune," "remorse," and "humiliation" were all inferred from this principle. When Confucius spoke about it, he said: "The superior man abides in his room. If his words are well spoken, he meets with assent at a distance of more than a thousand miles. If his words are not well spoken, he meets with opposition at a distance of more than a thousand miles. Words and deeds are the hinge and bowspring of the superior man. As hinge and bowspring move, they bring honor or disgrace. Through words and deeds the superior man moves heaven and earth. Must one not, then, be cautious?"[30] The Sage hoped men would be like this. The *Book of History* records the many affairs of Yao, Shun, and Yü[31] as well as those words "Oh!" "Oh,

28. From the "Yüeh-chi" chapter of the *Li chi*. See *Li chi* 37.19a; cf. Legge, *The Li Ki*, vol. 28, p. 102.

29. Fu Hsi is one of China's great legendary cultural heroes, who traditionally is credited with having invented the trigrams and hexagrams found in the *I ching*. Tradition further has it that King Wen wrote the explanations of the hexagrams and Confucius the "Appendixes" to the *I ching*.

30. This passage is from *Chou i*, p. 41. Translation from Wilhelm, *I ching*, p. 305 (with modification).

31. Yü, like Yao and Shun, was a legendary sage-emperor devoted totally to the welfare of the people; according to tradition, he was the founder of the Hsia dynasty.

yes," "Alas!" "No, by no means."[32] All are principle in perfection.[33] (9.8a:7/156:5)

3.31. When the mind is cultivated, naturally it'll understand principle. Cultivated, the mind is subtle. If it doesn't understand principle, it's simply because it's unrefined. (9.9a:4/157:3)

3.32. Moral principle is infinite. What our predecessors have said doesn't necessarily exhaust it [moral principle]. We must pick it up ourselves and look at it from every angle, penetrating it deeply and exploring it fully. (9.9a:8/157:6)

3.33. Moral principle is the moral principle right in front of your face. When you talk about it easily and effortlessly, you've got it; when it's awkward to talk about it, you don't actually understand it. (9.10a:5/158:7)

3.34. For today let's take what we ourselves are able to write and say and probe it fully. (9.10a:7/158:8)

3.35. The reason that people nowadays explain everything incoherently is simply that they don't understand thoroughly. (9.10a:8/158:9)

3.36. To appreciate moral principle, you must understand it concretely. Only then will you benefit. If you regard it as somewhat mysterious and strange, you don't fully understand concrete principle. (9.10a:9/158:10)

3.37. Contemporary students do not intimately understand it, but they conjecture about it—this is the vice of "helping it grow."[34] Just observe moral principle calmly, and its significance will naturally become manifest. It's not necessary to have preconceived ideas about it. (9.10b:2/158:13)

32. See Legge, *Chinese Classics*, vol. 3, pp. 23–25; translation from Legge (with modification).

33. The point Chu appears to be making here is that everything in the Classics, even the seemingly most insignificant words, is principle.

34. I.e., forcing it to grow. From *Meng-tzu* 2A/2, where we read: "There was a man from Sung who pulled at his rice plants because he was worried about their failure to grow. Having done so, he went on his way home, not realizing what he had done. 'I am worn out today,' he said to his family. 'I have been helping the

3.38. It's difficult to understand the meaning [of a text]. You must relax the mind and at the same time concentrate it. If the mind isn't relaxed, it cannot perceive the general pattern. If it isn't concentrated, it cannot observe the details of style; but should it become fixated on the literal meaning of words, it will soon fail to see the general pattern. (9.10b:4/158:15)

3.39. Rely on the ideas of the sages and worthies in examining the books of the sages and worthies. Rely on the principle of the universe in examining the affairs of the universe. Men frequently rely on their personal understanding to probe principle. It's simply that what they themselves think is still very far from what was in the minds of the sages and worthies. (9.10b:7/159:1)

3.40. Thinking can be likened to digging a well. If you're not idle, you'll hit clear water. At first the water will certainly be muddy. Dredge it little by little, and it'll naturally become clear. (9.11a:4/159:9)

3.41. Those who earnestly turn to seek it within themselves believe that extensive investigation is to flee toward what's external [and away from the self]. And those who earnestly engage in extensive investigation believe that inner examination is much too limited. Falling into a onesidedness—this is a serious flaw in all students. (9.11b:7/160:2)

---

rice plants grow.' His son rushed out to take a look, and there the plants were, all shrivelled up. There are few in the world who can resist the urge to help their rice plants grow. There are some who leave the plants unattended, thinking that nothing they can do will be of any use. They are the people who do not even bother to weed. There are others who help the plants grow. They are the people who pull at them. Not only do they fail to help them but they do the plants positive harm." Translation from Lau, *Mencius*, p. 78.

Four

On Reading, Part 1
(Chapter 10)

4.1. Book learning is a secondary matter for students. (10.1a:4/ 161:4)

4.2. Book learning is of secondary importance. It would seem that moral principle is originally complete in man; the reason he must engage in book learning is that he hasn't experienced much. The sages experienced a great deal and wrote it down for others to read. Now in book learning we must simply apprehend the many manifestations of moral principle. Once we understand them, we'll find that all of them were complete in us from the very beginning, not added to us from the outside. (10.1a:5/161:5)

4.3. Learning is to focus on what is of vital importance to our selves (i.e., moral principle)—book learning itself is of secondary importance. Moral principle is complete in us, not something added from the outside. Thus when sages tell people that they must engage in book learning, it's because even though they might possess moral principle they must experience it if it is to have any effect. What the sages speak about is what they have experienced of it. (10.1a:9/ 161:8)

4.4. In teaching others, the sages and worthies explained the way of learning quite clearly. Generally speaking, in their reading students should probe to the limit. "The pursuit of learning"[1] is an

---

1. The term *tao wen-hsüeh* is from *Chung-yung* 27/6.

important matter, for one has to understand moral principle to become fully human. Ordinarily, in reading a book we must read and reread it, appreciating each and every paragraph, each and every sentence, each and every word. Furthermore, we must consult the various annotations, commentaries, and explanations so that our understanding is complete. In this way moral principle and our own minds will be in perfect accord. Only then will our reading be effective. In reading, our own moral principle must extend everywhere. Tu Yüan-k'ai [222–284] said: "Put it [the mind] at ease, and you will get it. Keep it satisfied, and you will grasp it. It's as if [the mind], having been immersed in the rivers and seas and soaked in the beneficial rains, had been thoroughly dispelled of its doubts; happily, principle will be understandable. After all this you'll have truly got it."[2] (10.1b:5/162:1)

4.5. Read books to observe the intentions of the sages and worthies. Follow the intentions of the sages and worthies to observe natural principle. (10.2a:3/162:8)

4.6. It's best to take up the books of the sages and read them so that you understand their ideas. It's like speaking with them face to face. (10.2a:4/162:9)

4.7. You must frequently take the words of the sages and worthies and pass them before your eyes, roll them around and around in your mouth, and turn them over and over in your mind. (10.2a:5/162:10)

4.8. When you begin reading, you become aware that you're unlike the sages and worthies—how can you not urge yourself on? (10.2a:6/162:11)

4.9. There is layer upon layer [of meaning] in the words of the sages. In your reading of them, penetrate deeply. If you simply read what appears on the surface, you will misunderstand. Steep yourself in the words; only then will you grasp their meaning. (10.2a:7/162:12)

4.10. When men read a text, they merely read one layer; they don't try to get at the second layer. (10.2a:9/162:13)

2. This quote is from Tu's preface to the *Ch'un-ch'iu ching-chuan chi-chieh* 2a.

4.11. In reading, you must look for an opening in the text; only then will you find the moral principle in it. If you do not see an opening, you'll have no way to enter into the text. Once you find an opening, the coherence of the text will naturally become clear. (10.2a:10/162:14)

4.12. When scholars first look at a text, they see only a confused mass. In the course of time they come to see two or three chunks. But only when they see ten or more chunks will they make progress. It's like Butcher Ting cutting up the ox—it was best when he no longer beheld the whole ox.[3] (10.2b:2/163:1)

4.13. In reading a text, you must be full of vigor. Arouse your spirits, keep your body alert, and don't let yourself grow weary—as if a sword were at your back. You must pierce through each passage. "Strike the head, the tail responds; strike the tail, the head responds."[4] Only then have you read it right. You cannot open a book and fix your mind on it then close it and forget about it. Nor can you when reading the commentary forget about the text or when reading the text forget about the commentary. You must pierce through one passage and only then go on to later ones. (10.3a:3/163:10)

4.14. Here's what is necessary: one blow with a club, one scar; one slap on the face, a handful of blood. Your reading of what other people write should be just like this. Don't be lax! (10.3b:1/164:1)

4.15. The reading of texts should be like a tall or large vessel, going with the wind, its sail hoisted, covering a thousand *li* per day. Then it will be successful. Nowadays, just as [these tall and large vessels] are leaving the small harbor, they run aground—which is of no use at all. When you don't understand a text, such has been your reading. (10.3b:11/164:7)

3. Butcher Ting explained the art of butchering to Lord Wen-hui: "When I first began cutting up oxen, all I could see was the ox itself. After three years I no longer saw the whole ox. And now—now I go at it by spirit and don't look with my eyes." The story of Butcher Ting is found in *Chuang-tzu*, pp. 7–8, and Watson, *Chuang Tzu*, pp. 46–47. The passage here is from Watson's translation, p. 46.

4. I.e., by reading one part vigorously, the other parts will make sense too. This line, with slight modification, is found in *Sun-tzu chi-chu* 11.26b, where it describes the lightning-like response of crack fighting troops. Cf. Griffith, *Sun Tzu*, p. 135.

4.16. In reading, to understand moral principle the mind must be open, unobstructed, and bright. You mustn't be calculating beforehand the gain you'll get from the reading. For once you think about gain, you'll become distressed. And if you're distressed, trivial things will gather in the mind and won't leave. Now you should put aside unimportant matters, stop engaging in idle thought, and concentrate the mind in order to get a real sense of moral principle. In this way the mind will become sharp, and once the mind's sharp, it'll become intimately familiar with moral principle. (10.4a:1/ 164:9)

4.17. In reading, open wide the mind and moral principle will appear. If the mind is anxious and under pressure, moral principle ultimately will have no way of appearing. (10.4a:5/164:12)

4.18. Your reading will be successful only if you understand the spot where everything interconnects—east and west meet at this pivotal point. Simply dedicate yourself to what you're doing at the moment, don't think about the past or the future, and you'll naturally get to this point. But now you say that you've never been able to do it (i.e., read properly), that you fear you're too slow, or fear that you're not up to doing it, or fear that it is difficult, or fear that you're stupid, or fear that you won't remember what you've read— all this is idle talk. Simply dedicate yourself to what you're doing at the moment, don't be concerned whether you're slow or fast, and soon you will naturally get there. Because you have never done it before, exert the right effort now, and make up for past failures. Don't look to your front or back, don't think about east or west, or soon you'll have wasted a lifetime without realizing that you've grown old. (10.4a:7/164:13)

4.19. There are a great many books in the world. If you just read them as you have been, when will you finish with them? You must expend a great deal of effort, for there's nothing in the world that can be done with little effort. But now those texts you should have been reading, you haven't yet read. How much less other texts! (10.4b:1/165:1)

4.20. Read little but become intimately familiar with what you read; experience the text over and over again; and do not think about gain. Keep constantly to these three matters and nothing more. (10.4b:8/165:5)

4.21. Generally, in reading, students should keep to these three [dicta]: (1) read little but become intimately familiar with what you read; (2) don't scrutinize the text, developing your own far-fetched views of it, but rather personally experience it over and over again; and (3) concentrate fully, without thought of gain. (10.4b:9/165:6)

4.22. Best to read less but to become intimately familiar with what you read. That children remember what they've read and adults frequently don't is simply because children's minds are focused. If in one day they are given one hundred characters, they keep to one hundred characters; if given two hundred characters, they keep to two hundred characters. Adults sometimes read one hundred pages of characters in one day—they aren't so well focused. Often they read ten separate pieces when it would be best to read one part in ten. Extend the time you give to your reading; limit the size of your curriculum. (10.4b:11/165:8)

4.23. In reading, keep the curriculum small but the effort you make on it large. If you are able to read two hundred characters, read only one hundred, but on those one hundred make a truly fierce effort. Understand them in every detail, recite them until you are intimately familiar with them. In this way those with weak memories naturally will remember and those without the power of comprehension will be able to comprehend. If you read a great deal, but race through what you read, it will be of no benefit at all. In reading one text, you cannot simultaneously look at those you haven't yet read; you should, however, simultaneously look at those you've read already. (10.5a:7/165:14)

4.24. In reading, don't strive for quantity. Instead become intimately familiar with what you do read. If today you are able to read a page, read half a page; read that half page over and over with all your strength. Only if you read both halves of the page in this manner will you become intimately familiar with the page. And only if you read for the meaning of the ancients will your reading be right. (10.5a:11/166:1)

4.25. In reading, don't strive for quantity. Make sure that you always have a surplus of strength. Cheng-shun[5] said: I wish to read around in the various books. Chu replied: You can't read like that. You must read one book thoroughly, and only then the next. If you read around chaotically in two books at the same time, you will experience great difficulty. It's like shooting a bow. If you have five pecks of strength, you should use a four-peck bow—you can draw it completely and still have strength remaining. Students nowadays don't think about their own strength when reading. I fear that we are not able to handle the reading we set out for ourselves. (10.5b:5/166:5)

4.26. You mustn't want to do everything at once. In a day a man can eat only three bowls of rice; he can't eat ten or more days worth of rice at one sitting. In a day you can read only so much, and your efforts have a limit as well. You mustn't want to do everything at once. (10.6a:1/166:10)

4.27. In your studies read just one text at a time. And only if you read just one paragraph per day will the text begin to become part of you. If you read this text and that, even though they might pass before your eyes, in the end you will not be intimately familiar with them. (10.6a:4/166:12)

4.28. I especially don't want people to skip around as they read. It's essential to focus on each and every paragraph, each and every sentence. (10.6a:9/167:1)

4.29. Reading is one way of apprehending the principle in things. Now we must carefully consider each and every paragraph, over and over again. If in one day or two days we read just one paragraph, this paragraph will become part of us. After gaining a solid understanding of this paragraph, we should read the next one. If we go on like this from paragraph to paragraph, after a while we will understand moral principle in its entirety. What's required here is that we never stop thinking, occasionally turning over and over in our minds what's already become clear to us; then, enlight-

---

5. Wan Jen-chieh, a disciple of Chu's who earlier had studied under Lu Chiu-yüan, Chu's philosophic rival. See *SJCC*, vol. 4, p. 3227, and Ch'en Jung-chieh, *Chu-tzu men-jen*, pp. 248–249.

enment may occur, withour our specially arranging for it. For
though the writing and the meaning of a text may have been explained in a certain way, each reading of it will produce its own
understanding; thus, with some texts, each reading will lead to a
revised understanding. As for those works that have already been
definitively explained, with each reading our understanding will
become still sounder, and much clearer. Hence I have said: "In
reading, don't value quantity, value only your familiarity with
what you've read." In our efforts to understand what we read,
therefore, it's best to advance boldly and not think about retreating. (10.6a:10/167:2)

4.30. In your studies you should read for the meaning of the passage itself. You needn't complicate matters. Read each passage
over and over again until you are thoroughly familiar with it. Only
then will you understand its meaning; only then will you feel
pleased. And only if you're not too eager to proceed to other paragraphs will you get something out of it. People often race ahead
without ever turning back and reflecting. They simply want to read
the next day's material that they haven't yet read; they won't go
back and investigate what they've read already. It's essential to
ponder matters over and over. Only then will you understand. If
your effort is great, your understanding will be superb. And if your
understanding is superb, benefits are assured. He also said: You
can't speak nebulously or too broadly. What's necessary is that the
mind be clear. (10.6b:6/167:7)

4.31. Generally, in reading, you must become intimately familiar
with what you read. Intimate familiarity naturally will lead to complete mastery. And once you master what you read, principle
naturally will become clear to you. It's like eating a piece of fruit.
When you first bite into it, you don't yet know the taste. Then you
eat it. You have to chew it thoroughly, and the taste naturally
emerges. Then and only then do you appreciate whether it is sweet
or bitter—and for the first time you know its taste. He also said: A
gardener waters gardens. One who is good at watering them will
water each vegetable, fruit, and tree according to its needs. Soon
the watering will be sufficient, and the water and soil will be well
mixed; each vegetable, fruit, and tree will be well nourished and
grow naturally. One who isn't good at watering gardens will rush

matters. With bucketfuls of water he'll saturate the vegetables in the gardens. Others might think that he's tending the gardens well, but the vegetation in them won't be properly watered. He also said: As to the way to read, the more you exert yourself, the more far-reaching will be the results. At first you'll find it difficult, but later you will get it. At first it will be a real undertaking, but later you will grasp it. Everything you read is of the same principle. He also said: As to the method of reading, you must exert yourself as you read. If at first you expend a great deal of effort on a text, later not much effort will be necessary: if you expend 100 percent effort on a text at the beginning, later you'll expend 80 to 90 percent, later 60 to 70 percent, and finally 40 to 50 percent. (10.6b:12/167:11)

4.32. At the beginning you think you're able to do a hundred different things; in the end you're unable to do even one. (10.7b:9/168:9)

4.33. Generally speaking, in reading, we must first become intimately familiar with the text so that its words seem to come from our own mouths. We should then continue to reflect on it so that its ideas seem to come from our own minds. Only then can there be real understanding. Still, once our intimate reading of it and careful reflection on it have led to a clear understanding of it, we must continue to question. Then there might be additional progress. If we cease questioning, in the end there'll be no additional progress. (10.7b:11/168:11)

4.34. Books must be read to the point of intimate familiarity. A so-called book is just a book, but our tenth reading of it is different from our first reading, and our hundredth reading, likewise, is naturally different from our tenth. (10.8a:3/168:13)

4.35. To be a man is just to be a man, to read a book is just to read a book. Ordinarily, if a man reads a book ten times and doesn't understand it, he'll read it twenty times. If he still doesn't understand it, he'll read it thirty times. With the fiftieth reading there's sure to be some understanding. If with the fiftieth reading he's still in the dark and doesn't understand, it's that his psychophysical stuff is no good. Nowadays people have yet to read a book ten times, and they say they can't understand it. (10.8a:5/168:15)

4.36. You cannot keep track of the number of times you read a book. When the number's sufficient, stop. (10.8a:11/169:3)

4.37. In a response to a student, Wen-kung[6] explained the way of learning, citing Hsün-tzu's four lines, "[The superior man] recites texts [*sung shu*, literally, "recites number"] in order to penetrate [*kuan*] the Way, ponders in order to understand it, associates with men who embody it in order to make it part of himself, and shuns those who impede it in order to sustain and nourish it."[7] Hsün-tzu's explanation is pretty good. As for the term *sung shu* [literally, "recites number"], I believe that when the ancients recited a text [*sung shu*, literally, "recites a text"] they kept track of the number of times. The character *kuan* means *shu*, "to be intimately familiar with" as in "what we're accustomed to [*hsi-kuan*] becomes second nature to us."[8] It also means *t'ung*, "to understand thoroughly." Only if we're read to the point of intimate familiarity are we able to understand thoroughly. And if we haven't read to the point of intimate familiarity, there is nothing we can possibly ponder. (10.8b:3/169:6)

4.38. In a note to Li Chi-chung,[9] Shan-ku[10] said: "I don't know which of all the Classics and all the histories I'm most intimately familiar with. In general, students are fond of breadth but often lack detailed understanding. They spread themselves over a hundred different books, which isn't as good as having a detailed understanding of one—and if they still had the strength afterward, they could turn to other books. In this way, even if they were to wade and hunt through numerous works, they'd still get the gist. It seems that if our reading of books is based on our capabilities we will benefit from each and every passage, but if the books overwhelm us, even when we're finished with them we'll still be vague

6. Ssu-ma Kuang.

7. See *Hsün-tzu*, p. 3; the translation is from Watson, *Hsun Tzu*, p. 22, with some modification.

8. This phrase, *hsi-kuan ju tzu-jan*, is from *K'ung-tzu chia-yü* 9.7a. This passage may appear puzzling at first to the reader since the transliteration *shu* here is used to represent three different Chinese characters, "number," "text," and "to be intimately familiar with."

9. I can find no biographical information on him.

10. Huang T'ing-chien (1045–1105), a scholar-official best known for his poetry and calligraphy.

about their meaning."[11] The Master took great delight in this comment and felt it would be helpful to his students. (10.8b:7/169:9)

4.39. In reading, to comprehend a passage, you should have a detailed understanding of it. If you don't understand it in detail, your reading of other passages will be muddled too. If you understand one passage in detail, others will be easy to understand. Shan-ku's note[12] explains the method of reading extremely well. (10.8b:11/169:12)

4.40. Students who are overzealous don't understand in detail the meaning of what they read. In reading, you have to be very careful; it's essential that you understand every sentence and every character with certainty. If your effort is lax and you're not given to reflection, you'll simply conclude that there's nothing in your understanding of it that need be doubted; it isn't really that there's nothing to be doubted, but since your understanding isn't complete you just don't realize it. In learning, there's generally a distinction between young and old. When we're young, we have excess energy; it's essential that we leave nothing unread and that we analyze fully the meaning of what we read. By contrast, as we approach old age, we must select out what's important and devote our efforts to it; in reading a particular book, we're aware that later on it will be difficult to summon up the effort to look at it again. We must ponder it deeply and analyze it to its limits, and we'll understand its meaning. It would seem that in the moral principle of the universe there's nothing but right and wrong. Right is right, wrong is wrong, and once we're certain about which is which, though we may not reread a text, the principle in it will naturally infuse us. We'll see it once and never forget it. This may all be compared to eating and drinking. If we chew slowly, the flavor lasts. If we take big bites and big gulps, in the end we don't know the flavor. (10.9a:1/169:14)

4.41. The value of a book is in the recitation[13] of it. By reciting it often, we naturally come to understand it. Now, even if we ponder

11. I have not located this letter in any of the editions of Huang's writings available to me.

12. See the preceding passage.

13. It is clear from context that throughout this passage Chu means by *tu*, "to recite," and not just "to read." Of course, *tu* commonly carries the meaning of "to read aloud."

over what's written on the paper, it's useless, for in the end it isn't really ours. There's value only in recitation, though I don't know how the mind so naturally becomes harmonious with the psychophysical stuff, feels uplifted and energized, and remembers securely what it reads. Even supposing we were to read through a text thoroughly, pondering it over and over in our minds, it wouldn't be as good as reciting it. If we recite it again and again, in no time the incomprehensible becomes comprehensible and the already comprehensible becomes even more meaningful. But if the recitation doesn't reach the point of intimate familiarity, it won't be so meaningful at all. At the moment I'm not even speaking about the recitation of commentaries; let's simply recite the classical texts to the point of intimate familiarity. Whether we are walking or at a standstill, sitting or lying down, if our minds are always on these texts, we'll naturally come to understand them. It has occurred to me that recitation [*tu*] is learning [*hsüeh*]. The Master said: "Learning [*hsüeh*] without thinking is a waste; thinking without learning is dangerous."[14] Learning is reciting. If we recite it then think it over, think it over then recite it, naturally it'll become meaningful to us. If we recite it but don't think it over, we still won't appreciate its meaning. If we think it over but don't recite it, even though we might understand it, our understanding will be precarious. It's just like hiring somebody else to guard our home: because he isn't one of the family, in the end he can't be used as we would use a family member. Should we recite it to the point of intimate familiarity, and moreover think about it in detail, naturally our mind and principle will become one and never shall we forget what we've read. I used to find it hard to remember texts. Then I simply recited them aloud. What I remember now is the result of recitation. Old Su[15] simply took the *Book of Mencius*, the *Analects*, the *Han Fei-tzu*, and the writings of the various sages and for seven or eight years sat quietly reciting them. Afterward he wrote a number of things that were very good. To be sure, his natural abilities couldn't be matched, but still it was essential that he recite as he did. And yet, reciting the texts, he merely wanted to pattern his writing on what was written there. Now if we were to turn our minds and his sort of

14. *Lun-yü* 2/15.
15. Su Hsün (1009–1061), the father of Su Shih and Su Ch'e.

natural ability to the investigation of moral principle, we'd find it right there in the text. Thus we know that the value of a text is in the intimate recitation of it. There is no other way. (10.9a:9/170:3)

4.42. The method of reading is to recite a text, then ponder it over; to ponder it over, then recite it. Oral recitation of a text helps us to think about it. For our minds then hover over the words. If it's just a matter of the mouth doing the reading but the mind doing no thinking, what'll our understanding be like? We won't remember what we've read in any detail. He also said: Because nowadays the number of printed texts is large, people don't put their minds to reading them. As for the Confucians of the Han period, in instructing one another in the Classics, they just recited them from memory. Hence, they remembered them well. But as a result the passages they cited would often contain mistaken characters. For example, in his citations from the *Book of History* and *Book of Poetry*, Mencius was often mistaken. This was because he had nothing to base himself on—he was simply recalling them from memory. (10.10a:1/170:13)

4.43. The reason people today read sloppily is that there are a great many printed texts. The ancients all used bamboo strips to copy out their texts, so only a powerful person could have it done. How could a person of little account manage it? Thus as Wu Hui of the Later Han was about to prepare bamboo strips in order to copy down the *Han History*, his son, Wu Yu, pleaded with him: "If this book is completed, it'll have to be carried about in a cart. Formerly, Ma Yüan was slandered on account of pearl barley. And Wang Yang hoped his pouched clothing would bring him fame."[16] Wu

16. On one of his military expeditions to the south, General Ma Yüan (14 B.C.–A.D. 49) discovered that pearl barley was effective in overcoming malaria, and when he returned north he brought back a cartload with him, intending to cultivate it there. The people of the north saw the cartload of pearl barley and believed the barley to be precious pearls from the south. Consequently, they suspected Ma of accepting bribes; see *Hou Han shu*, vol. 3, 24.846. Wang Yang was fond of carriages and horses and enjoyed wearing new clothes. But when he moved, he took nothing with him but his clothing, which had one pouch in it. The people thus came to believe that Wang was able to manufacture gold. See *Han shu*, vol. 10, 72.3068. Wu Yu's point here is that his father should not incite people's suspicion, such was the labor and expense involved in copying out a text. Wu Yu's comment is from *Hou Han shu*, vol. 8, 64.2099.

Yu's comment makes the point precisely [i.e., that the ancients had to copy out their texts and to do so was difficult]. Huang Pa received the *Book of History* from Hsia-hou Sheng in prison.[17] Only with the passing of two winters was it transmitted. It would seem that the ancients had no written texts, so only if they had memorized a work from beginning to end would they get it. Those studying a text would memorize it completely and afterward receive instruction on it from a teacher. Tung-p'o[18] wrote "An Account of the Collection in Mr. Li's Studio";[19] at that time books were still difficult for one to acquire.[20] Ch'ao I-tao[21] once wanted to get hold of the Kung and Ku commentaries;[22] he searched everywhere for them but came up empty-handed. Later he found one copy of them, and only then was he able to copy them out for his own use. For people today even copying down a text has become bothersome. Therefore, their reading is sloppy. (10.10a:7/171:1)

4.44. When students today read a text, it's just as if they had never read it. When they haven't read it, it's just as if they had. (10.11a:1/171:14)

4.45. Since coming from T'an-chou,[23] I have spoken about nothing else. I haven't stopped telling people to read extremely carefully. (10.11a:10/172:6)

4.46. In reading, simply take what you already understand and read it again and again. (10.11b:11/172:16)

4.47. Nowadays in reading a text, people have yet to read to this point here, and their minds are already on some later passage. And

---

17. Hsia-hou Sheng was a master of the *Book of History* in the Former Han. Huang Pa held various important official positions. They were both imprisoned for protesting Emperor Hsüan's (r. 74–49 B.C.) decision to honor his great grandfather, Emperor Wu (r. 141–87 B.C.).

18. Su Shih. See above, Part One, "Chu Hsi and the Crisis of the Way in the Twelfth Century" and "Chu Hsi and the Transformation of the Confucian Tradition."

19. Found in Su Shih, *Su Tung-p'o ch'üan-chi*, vol. 1, pp. 388–389. Mr. Li is a reference to Li Ch'ang (1027–1090); see *SJCC*, vol. 2, pp. 869–870.

20. Su Shih argues this point in the essay.

21. Ch'ao lived from 1059 to 1129 and wrote a book entitled *Ch'ao-shih k'o-yu*; see Hervouet, *Sung Bibliography*, p. 279.

22. The *Kung-yang* and *Ku-liang* commentaries on the *Ch'un-ch'iu*.

23. Chu was prefect of T'an-chou (modern Hunan) in 1194.

as soon as they do read what's here, they wish to put it aside [and move on]. This sort of reading doesn't aim for a personal understanding of the text. We must linger over what we read, longing to understand it. Only if we don't wish to put it aside will we come to a personal appreciation of it. He also said: Reading a text is like looking at this house here. If you view the house from the outside, then say that you have finished seeing it, there'll be no way to understand it. You must go inside and look around at each and every thing. What's the size and layout of the structure? What's the extent of the latticework? Look through the house once, then again and again. Remember everything, and you'll have understood it. (10.11b:12/173:1)

4.48. Be sure to ponder what you read. Then you'll see the meaning[24] leap right out from the text. (10.12a:8/173:7)

4.49. In reading, you must behold the style and coherence of the writing. (10.12a:10/173:9)

4.50. In reading, don't be obsesssed with finishing. For as soon as you are, your mind will simply fix itself on the blank page at the end of the book, which will be of no benefit. (10.12b:4/173:14)

4.51. A man reading is like a man drinking wine. A man who loves drinking will finish one cup and want still another. A man who doesn't love it will force his way through one cup and stop. (10.12b:9/174:1)

4.52. In reading, you must set a limit beforehand. Managing your reading is like farm work; in farming there are boundary lines. Learning is the same. Beginning students today don't appreciate this principle. At the outset they are extremely zealous, but gradually they become more and more indolent. And in the end they pay no attention at all. This is simply becase they don't set limits at the outset. (10.12b:11/174:2)

---

24. Without much context here it is difficult to know whether to translate *i-li* "meaning" or "moral principle." Chu uses the term in both senses in his works, though, to be sure, much more frequently in the sense of moral principle; I would argue, however, that in the end the "meaning" of the sages' texts was nothing but "moral principle," and thus the two possible translations—at least when Chu is talking about the *i-li* of texts—amount to the same thing. The reader should note that this is not the only passage in these selections that poses this problem.

4.53. These days those who truly read are few, the reason being the pernicious influence of the examination essay. Men make up their minds to seek the unusual in the texts even before they read them— and pay no attention whatsoever to the original meaning. Having got the unusual from them, they imitate it in their examination essays; in the end they're accomplished only at using the unusual in the texts. Even if there were some great ritual at court, they'd still incautiously pick out the unusual from the texts and use it, without realizing that one false move results in a hundred broken pieces. Our elders read these texts too. I once met the elder Tung-lai's[25] older brother. He fully understood the Six Classics and the Three Commentaries[26] and punctuated them himself. In the commentaries [to the Six Classics and Three Commentaries], moreover, he used small circles for punctuation; and where the meaning of the commentaries wasn't adequate, he would write subcommentary in the clerical style using vermilion punctuation. No punctuation or stroke was made in haste. I saw only his *Book of Rites,* and it took this form; so did [his work] on all the other Classics. Previously, the Lüs had been wealthy and honorable. And even though they had held official positions, in most cases they had not presented themselves for the examinations; they had been able to delight in the reading of books. The family pattern that had thus evolved was broken by Po-kung.[27] Since then the Lüs have written the examination essay; and rarely have there been those willing to read in the manner of the elder Tung-lai's older brother. (10.14a:7/175:8)

4.54. People beyond mid-life shouldn't read much; they should simply turn the little they do read over and over in their minds. Then they'll naturally understand moral principle. (10.14b:5/175:15)

25. The "elder Tung-lai" refers to Lü Pen-chung (1084–1145), a noted poet and scholar. See *SJCC*, vol. 2, pp. 1199–1201, and Franke, *Sung Biographies*, vol. 2, pp. 729–735.

26. I.e., the *Kung-yang, Ku-liang,* and *Tso* commentaries on the *Ch'un-ch'iu.*

27. Lü Tsu-ch'ien, Pen-chung's nephew. See above, Part One, "Restoring the Way: Chu Hsi's Educational Activities."

Five

On Reading, Part 2
(Chapter 11)

5.1. As for learning, people strongly desire to acquire it in their minds and embody it in their persons. But if they don't read books, they won't understand what it is their minds are to acquire. (11.1a:4/176:4)

5.2. The books you read, the principle you probe, should be embodied in your person. I don't know whether what you routinely study and probe is on your mind at all times or not. But if it isn't, you're just hurrying through the texts, reading for their literal meaning and taking little pleasure in them. This, I fear, will be of no benefit to you in the end. (11.1a:6/176:5)

5.3. If a person reads constantly, he can pretty much control his mind and thereby keep it constantly preserved. Heng-ch'ü said: "Books are the way to maintain the mind. The moment you put them down is the moment your virtuous nature grows lax."[1] How then can one neglect reading? (11.1a:9/176:7)

5.4. The beginner is sure to have lapses in his inner mental attentiveness. But as soon as he's aware there's been a lapse, he'll arouse his mind. Awareness of the lapse then leads to the resumption of inner mental attentiveness. What I hope is that people, in reading, will grasp moral principle for themselves. If they read all day long,

1. *Chang Tsai chi*, p. 275; cf. Kasoff, *Thought of Chang Tsai*, p. 88.

their minds won't become reckless, but if they get involved in affairs and things, their minds will easily become submerged. If you understand this, then in reading you'll grasp moral principle for yourselves, and you can return [to the right path]. (11.1a:11/ 176:9)

5.5. When one's original mind has been submerged for a long time, and the moral principle in it hasn't been fully penetrated, it's best to read books and probe principle without any interruption; then, the mind of human desire will naturally be incapable of winning out, and the moral principle in the original mind will naturally become safe and secure. (11.1b:3/176:12)

According to Chu Hsi, the distinction between the original or ontological mind (*pen-hsin, tao-hsin*) and the human mind (*jen-hsin*) was first made by Shun in the *Book of History*: "The human mind is precarious, the ontological mind is almost imperceptible. Be discriminating, be undivided, that you may sincerely hold fast the mean."[2] In his "Preface to the *Doctrine of the Mean in Chapters and Verses*," Chu explains what Shun meant by this statement: "The mind—unprejudiced, spiritual, and conscious—is one. But that there is a distinction between the 'human mind' and the 'ontological mind' is because of this: the mind at times arises in the self-centeredness of the psychophysical stuff and at times originates in the perfect impartiality of the moral nature decreed by heaven, so the resulting consciousnesses are different. Hence the mind can be precarious and unsettled, or abstruse and almost imperceptible. Yet all men have a psychophysical form, so even the very wisest will always have a human mind; and all men have a moral nature, so even the very stupidest will always have an ontological mind. If the human mind and the ontological mind become mixed in the heart and one does not know how to control them, the precarious will become even more precarious, the imperceptible will become even more imperceptible, and the impartiality of the heavenly principle in the end will be unable to overcome the selfishness of human desires. 'Be discriminating' means to distinguish between the human and ontological minds so that they do not become mixed. 'Be undivided' means to protect the perfect impartiality of the original mind so that it does not take leave of one. Should one devote oneself without interruption to these matters, making certain that the ontological mind always acts as master of the body and the human mind always obeys its orders, the precarious will become set-

2. *Shang shu* 4.8b; the second sentence of this translation is from Legge, *Chinese Classics*, vol. 3, pp. 61–62.

tled and the almost imperceptible will become manifest. And in activity and tranquillity, in words and actions, one will not err in going either too far or not far enough" (preface to *Chung-yung chang-chü* 1a:7).

5.6. It's essential that preserving the mind and reading books constitute one matter; only then will you succeed. (11.1b:5/177:1)

5.7. In reading, you must keep your mind glued to the text. Only when every sentence and every character falls into place have you done a good job of thinking through the work. In general, the student should collect his mind so that it's completely tranquil and pure and in its normal activity and tranquillity doesn't run wild or become confused. Only then will he understand the text in all of its detail. Reading like this, he'll understand the essentials. (11.1b:8/ 177:3)

5.8. Formerly, Mr. Ch'en Li[3] was distressed that he had no [power of] memory. One day he read the *Book of Mencius*: "The great end of learning is nothing else but to seek for the lost mind."[4] Suddenly, he was enlightened and said: "If my mind is not retrieved, how will I be able to remember a book?" Thereupon he shut his door and engaged in quiet-sitting; for more than a hundred days he didn't look at a book and thereby retrieved his lost mind. He then went to read, and with one glance he absorbed everything. (11.2a:2/177:7)

5.9. It's often because their minds are not present as they read that students don't understand moral principle. The words of the sages and worthies were originally clear of themselves. Simply give a little attention to them and you'll see the moral principle in them. If you were to concentrate, you'd certainly see it. (11.2a:5/177:9)

5.10. When the mind isn't settled, it doesn't understand principle. Presently, should you want to engage in book learning, you must first settle the mind so that it becomes like still water or a clear mirror. How can a cloudy mirror reflect anything? (11.2a:7/ 177:11)

5.11. If your will is not firmly fixed, how are you going to read? (11.2a:9/177:12)

---

3. For a brief biography see *SJCC*, vol. 4, p. 3463.
4. *Meng-tzu* 6A/11; translation from Legge, *Chinese Classics*, vol. 2, p. 414.

5.12. There is a method to book learning. Simply scrub clean the mind, then read. If you don't understand the text, put it down for the moment, wait until your thoughts have cleared, then pick it up and read it again. Now we speak about the need to open up our minds. The mind, how can we open it? We just have to take it and keep it focused on the text. (11.2a:10/177:13)

5.13. In reading, you want both body and mind to enter into the passage. Don't concern yourself with what's going on elsewhere and you'll see the principle in the passage. Take the case of "one who studies widely and with set purpose, who questions earnestly, then thinks for himself about what he has heard"; why is it said that "such a one will incidently achieve goodness"?[5] It would seem that if we're able to preserve our minds at all times, not letting them run wild, we'll naturally come to understand principle. Nowadays people think about other matters at the same time that they're reading. This is just a waste of time; better to put the text aside, wait until the aroused thoughts have quieted down, then read. (11.2b:1/177:15)

5.14. I'm afraid that students often read recklessly because their efforts basically aren't well regulated. It's simply that they read with confused and disordered minds, not clear, settled ones. It would be better if they first nurtured the source. They should turn the moral principle with which they're already intimate over and over in their minds, until it permeates their entire person, and afterward go read the text. Then naturally they'd understand it. This is simply how it is. Old Su[6] described his learning to write, saying: "I took the writings of the ancients and read them. When I first saw the words and ideas of the ancients, I found them so different from mine. With time I read them in greater detail, and my mind suddenly became clear." His words are certainly apt; that the effort he made learning to write led to insight can instruct us on how texts are to be read today. The effort should be very much like this. He also said: After reading a paragraph or two, you should relax the mind so that it is free from anxiety. Don't strive for

---

5. *Lun-yü* 19/6; translation from Waley, *Analects*, p. 225.
6. Su Hsün.

quantity. He also said: Lu Tzu-ching[7] once talked about the way others read. It can indeed be just as he said.[8] (11.2b:6/178:3)

5.15. You can't think about a text for an entire day. To do so, I fear, would be forcing the mind to chase after it. You need to rest a while and nurture your mental energy, and then return to your reading. (11.3a:7/178:11)

5.16. Generally speaking, in reading a text, we must recite it aloud. We can't just think about it. If our mouths recite it, our minds will feel calm, and its meaning will naturally become apparent. When I first began my studies, this is just what I did. There's no other way. (11.3b:3/179:1)

5.17. In reading, students must compose themselves and sit up straight; look leisurely at the text and hum softly; open their minds and immerse themselves in the words; and make the reading relevant to themselves, closely examining their own conduct. He also said: In reading a sentence of text, we must ascertain for ourselves where we might sometime put that sentence into practice. He also said: Right words we absolutely must read; wrong ones too we must read. Refined words we absolutely must read; vulgar ones too we must read. (11.3b:5/179:3)

5.18. In our reading, it's essential to open our minds and to make the reading relevant to our selves. Only by opening our minds are we able to understand the meaning of the sages and worthies. And by making the reading relevant to our selves, the words of the sages and worthies will not be empty. (11.3b:8/179:5)

5.19. In reading a text, you must open your mind. Don't come to the text with preconceived ideas—you'll commit many mistakes in no time at all. He also said: Open the mind and make the reading relevant to yourself. If you open your mind, you'll understand moral principle clearly. If you make the reading relevant to yourself, you'll naturally grasp its meaning for yourself. (11.3b:10/179:6)

7. Chu's philosophic rival, Lu Chiu-yüan.
8. This last comment by Chu about Lu Chiu-yüan is too brief to make much sense of.

5.20. Every word of the sages is heavenly principle and as it should be. Basically, it's easy to be clear about their words, but people don't read them with open minds; they do nothing more than apprehend them superficially. Not understanding the words of the sages, they express their own common ideas and take them as those of the sages. (11.3b:12/179:8)

5.21. Generally speaking, to get moral principle, you must open your mind and read for the true meaning of the classical text. (11.4a:10/179:16)

5.22. Someone asked: In reading, what do you do when you become confused by a multitude of views? The Master replied: You have to open your mind and read through each and every view. Read one view, then another. Read them over and over again, and the right and the wrong, the good and the bad, will all naturally become clear. This can be compared to a person wanting to know if a certain man is good or bad. He should keep his eye on him wherever he goes, following him here and there, observing his words and deeds, and then he'll know whether he's good or bad. He also said: You simply must open your mind. He also said: Wash away the old opinions to bring forth a new understanding.[9] (11.5a:6/180:13)

5.23. To read, you should calm the mind. Generally, you can't bore right through the text you're looking at; you have to proceed from the intelligible passages, not from the obscure ones. The words of the sages and worthies often take the form of conversations with others. If they were lofty and hard to follow, how would the people of that time have understood them? (11.5a:11/180:16)

5.24. Depend on the text to read the text, depend on the object to observe the object. Don't come to the text or the object with preconceived ideas. (11.5b:4/181:4)

5.25. Reading must be an experience meaningful to the self. You can't merely read through the words, nor can you "help them to grow."[10] (11.5b:5/181:5)

9. This is a slight rewording of a statement first made by Chang Tsai. See 3.26.
10. I.e., force them to grow. From *Meng-tzu* 2A/2; see 3.37.

5.26. In reading, we cannot seek moral principle solely from the text. We must turn the process around and look for it in ourselves. Since the Ch'in-Han period, no one has spoken about this; people simply have sought it in the text, not in themselves. We have yet to discover for ourselves what the sages previously explained in their texts—only through their words will we find it in ourselves. (11.5b:9/181:8)

5.27. In learning, we have to read for ourselves, so that the understanding we reach is personally meaningful. Nowadays, however, people read simply for the sake of the civil service examinations. And once they pass the examinations, they read for the sake of [learning to] compose miscellaneous prose. As for the eminent among them, they read for the sake of [learning to] compose ancient-style prose.[11] In all these instances they're reading not for themselves but for other reasons. (11.6b:7/182:7)

5.28. Among the ways to read, there is concentrating on the essentials and the main points; there is coming to an understanding of each and every matter; and then there is explaining the meaning of the words. (11.6b:9/182:9)

5.29. Someone asked about not understanding the importance of what's been read. The Master replied: How is it that one may understand the importance of what one reads? Recently, there's been a kind of student who discards the text, hoping to discover the moral principle in one word or half a sentence. There's another kind who reads widely in the texts without understanding their gist. Neither of these types knows how to learn. One must read intimately and reflect intimately, and after a while one will naturally understand moral principle perfectly. In so doing, one will naturally come to understand what you call the "importance of what's been read." (11.6b:12/182:11)

---

11. *Ku-wen*, or ancient-style prose, had developed, beginning in the T'ang dynasty, as a reaction to the highly stylized prose of the day (*shih-wen*). It was supposed to allow the writer the freedom to concentrate primarily on cultivating the Way, not literary style, in his writing. As this comment suggests, Chu Hsi believed that many of his contemporaries practiced *ku-wen* principally as a means of furthering their reputations.

5.30. In reading, don't force your ideas on the text. You must get rid of your own ideas and read for the meaning of the ancients. In his explanation of "straight, square, and great" [from the *Book of Changes*], Master Ch'eng cited Mencius.[12] It may have been Master Ch'eng's explanation, but in the end it was right on target. (11.9a:7/185:1)

5.31. Whenever you read a text, first come to an understanding of its words, and then read to see if its views accord with principle or not. If they do, they're right, and if not, they're wrong. Nowadays people usually have an idea in their own minds first, then take what other men have said [in the texts] to explain their idea. What doesn't conform to their idea they forcibly make to conform. (11.9a:12/185:5)

5.32. Students mustn't compromise the words of the sages with their own ideas. (11.9b:3/185:7)

5.33. The problem students have with reading is simply that they wish to advance and are unwilling to retreat and reread. The more they advance, the more their reading lacks understanding. It'd be better if they were to retreat but fully comprehend what they read. In general, the problem is that they stick to their opinions and are unwilling to give them up. It's just like hearing litigation: if beforehand the mind supports proposition B, it will simply search for the wrongs in A; and if beforehand it supports A, it will simply discover the wrongs in B. Better to put aside one's views toward A and B and slowly examine them both. Only then will one be able to distinguish right from wrong. Heng-ch'ü said: "Wash away the old understanding and bring forth new ideas."[13] This statement is

---

12. In explaining the passage in *Chou i*, p. 3, which reads, "Six in the second place means: Straight, square, great. Without purpose, yet nothing remains unfurthered" (translation from Wilhelm, *I ching*, p. 13), Ch'eng I said, "Because it is straight, square, and great, it's without purpose and yet nothing remains unfurthered. 'Without purpose' means that it's natural. In the way of *k'un*, nothing activates it, yet it's active; in the sage it effortlessly attains to the Way. 'Straight, square, great' (*chih fang ta*) is what Mencius referred to as 'exceedingly great, exceedingly strong, and straight (*chih-ta chih-kang i chih yeh*).'" Mencius used these words in *Meng-tzu* 2A/2 to describe the "flood-like *ch'i*." For Ch'eng I's comment see *I-ch'uan I-chuan* 1.9b–10a.

13. *Chang Tsai chi*, p. 321.

extremely apt. If one doesn't wash away the old understanding, where will the new ideas arise? Students today have two kinds of flaws: one is that they let themselves be ruled by personal prejudices; the other is that they embrace received theories. Even if they wished to shake free of these, they'd still naturally be troubled by them. (11.10a:3/185:16)

5.34. Students can't simply hold on to what they previously believed. They must get rid of it, and only then will new ideas occur to them. It's like discarding dirty water; afterward clear water will appear. (11.10a:10/186:5)

5.35. When you get to a passage you don't comprehend, you ought to "wash away the old understanding and bring forth new ideas."[14] Still, you should simply follow the text. (11.10a:12/186:6)

5.36. In reading, if you have no doubts, encourage them. And if you do have doubts, get rid of them. Only when you've reached this point have you made progress. (11.11a:1/186:15)

5.37. The problem with men is that they feel the views of others alone may be doubted, not their own. Should they try to reproach themselves as they reproach others, they may come to realize their own merits and demerits. (11.11a:4/187:2)

5.38. Thereupon someone entreated him to transmit it in lectures and discussions. Chu replied: The words of the sages and worthies are luminous, like the sun and the moon [i.e., lectures and discussions are unnecessary]. He also said: People are afflicted with a desire to speed through [what they read]. I once read a collection of poetry with another man. He routinely skipped over the titles of the poems. Not even to read the titles of the poems—what kind of reading of poetry is that? I once saw the inside of Kung Shih-chih's[15] sedan chair. There was but one text to read, which shows he was focused and calm. He added: Normally when a person goes out, he places three or four texts in his sedan chair. He reads one book, and when he gets bored he reads another. What kind of effort is this? (11.11a:6/187:4)

14. Chang Tsai's comment. See 5.33.
15. Kung Mou-liang (1121–1178). See *SJCC*, vol. 5, pp. 4504–4505.

5.39. Someone asked about the various methods of reading the Classics. The Master replied: There is no method. Just read calmly and with an open mind. (11.11b:7/187:13)

5.40. In learning, don't skip steps, and don't be careless. It's a waste of energy. You should follow the proper sequence. And if by following the prescribed method you come to understand one Classic intimately, other texts will be easy to read. (11.11b:8/187:14)

5.41. When we read the Six Classics, it should be just as if there were no Six Classics. We're simply seeking the moral principle in ourselves—this principle is easy to understand. (11.12a:3/188:3)

5.42. In learning, we must first establish the great base: at the outset learning should be concerned largely with what's essential; in the middle stage, largely with breadth; and in the end, with what is essential again. Mencius said: "Learn widely and go into what you have learned in detail so that in the end you can return to the essential."[16] Thus we must first read the *Analects*, the *Book of Mencius*, the *Greater Learning*, and the *Doctrine of the Mean* in order to examine the intentions of the sages and worthies; we must read the histories to examine the traces of dynastic preservation and ruin, order and disorder; and we must read the thinkers of the hundred schools to observe their various faults. There is a proper sequence to these steps; we can't skip over any of them. Nowadays scholars often find pleasure in what is essential but never pursue broad knowledge. I don't know how they can examine what is essential without having first pursued broad knowledge. If a certain person is fond of what's essential, he'll just become a Buddhist priest, concerned with understanding himself alone. There are also scholars who concentrate only on broad knowledge and never return to what's essential. Today they examine one institution, tomorrow another. They merely exert themselves on what's of practical application—their problem is even more severe than that of the essentialists, who ignore broad knowledge. In the end neither type benefits. (11.12a:12/188:10)

5.43. Reading the Classics is different from reading the histories. History is superficial stuff, not important. You can take notes on it

---

16. *Meng-tzu* 4B/15; translation from Lau, *Mencius*, p. 130.

then ask others about it. But should you have questions about a Classic, the affliction will be keen; you'll be like a person who is in pain and wants to alleviate it quickly but can't. It's not at all like reading the histories, where if you happen to have a question you just jot it down on a piece of paper. (11.13b:6/189:14)

5.44. Hao[17] said: Clerk Chao[18] stated, "Once you've come to an understanding on your own, read the Six Classics, the *Analects*, and the *Book of Mencius*. As for the rest, the histories and the miscellaneous writings, there's no need to read them." The idea here is that when you buy gold you must seek out a gold merchant. Where are you going to find gold in a general store?—there's no need to inquire there. Chu replied: Such is the case. But if you have no understanding of the successes and failures, both of antiquity and the present, your learning will be the learning of Ching-kung.[19] There are no books that shouldn't be read. I fear only that we won't have the great strength to read through them all. The Six Classics are the works of the Three Dynasties and earlier and passed through the hands of the Sage—in every respect they are heavenly principle. Post–Three Dynasties texts have strengths and weaknesses, yet heavenly principle inheres in them just the same. Adhering to the standard, we should examine these texts, for they all constitute learning. (11.13b:9/189:16)

5.45. Once principle is clear to you, you will even get something out of reading the works of Shen [Pu-hai] and Han [Fei-tzu].[20] (11.14a:11/190:9)

5.46. To come, through reading, to an understanding of moral principle, we must endure daily hardship, quitting only when we've

17. Kuo Hao, a disciple of Chu's. See *SJCC*, vol. 3, pp. 2115–2116, and Ch'en Jung-chieh, *Chu-tzu men-jen*, pp. 205–206.

18. I have not been able to identify him.

19. I.e., Wang An-shih; see above, Part One, "Chu Hsi and the Transformation of the Confucian Tradition." Wang was deeply devoted to the classical texts, in particular the *Shih ching*, the *Shu ching*, and the *Chou li*, and showed little interest in history or historical texts. Wang, of course, is best known for his program of governmental reforms, which was derived, in part, from his understanding of the *Chou li*. This reform program, in the end, largely failed. Chu's comment here is no doubt intended to be a criticism of both Wang's learning and his reforms, which had not demonstrated the necessary historical sensitivity.

20. Two of the most prominent members of the Legalist school, who lived during the fourth and third centuries B.C., respectively.

grasped it [i.e., moral principle]. Even King Wen worked hard.
How much harder should those of little virtue work! There's a kind
of talk going around these days that makes the younger students
lax. People say things like, "I wouldn't dare criticize my elders," or
"I wouldn't dare engage in reckless talk"—all of which suits the
fancy of those who are lazy. To be sure, we wouldn't dare criticize
our elders recklessly, but what harm is there in discussing the
rights and wrongs of what they did? And to be sure, we mustn't
engage in idle talk, but some parts of our reading pose problems
while some parts are clear, so we have to discuss it. Those who
don't discuss it are reading without dealing with the problems.
Let's compare the essential meaning of a text with the different
explanations of it to find out which explanations are correct. Naturally, some will accord with the essential meaning and some won't.
(11.14b:2/190:11)

5.47. Thereupon he spoke about the method of reading a text,
saying: You should read it ten or more times. Once you've understood 40 to 50 percent of the meaning, look at the annotation. Having understood another 20 to 30 percent, read the classical text
again and you'll understand yet another 10 to 20 percent. Previously, I didn't comprehend the *Book of Mencius* because its paragraphs
were so long. Then I read it in the manner just described, and
although at first its paragraphs were long its meaning nevertheless
cohered from beginning to end. Someone further inquired: In reading, the mind often becomes confused. The Master said: It's that
the mind is difficult to hold on to. Those who understand this problem are few. Previously, I cited the line from the *Doctrine of the Mean*,
"Truthfulness is the beginning and end of all things; without truthfulness, you have nothing,"[21] and explained it to Chih-ch'ing:[22]
"Suppose that you're reading a text of ten lines, and you're intent
on memorizing the first nine of them. If the mind doesn't go astray,
it will fix on these nine lines. This is to be 'truthful' to them; this is
'to have them.' As a result, these nine lines, from beginning to end,

---

21. *Chung-yung* 25/2; translation based on Legge, *Chinese-Classics*, vol. 1, p. 418.
22. Huang Kan (1152–1221), Chu's disciple and son-in-law; see *SJCC*, vol. 4,
pp. 2865–2866, and Ch'en Jung-chieh, *Chu-tzu men-jen*, pp. 261–262.

will be of benefit to you. As for the final line, your mind hasn't fixed on it—here you'll be 'without truthfulness' and 'have nothing.'" (11.14b:8/190:15)

5.48. In reading, as a general rule, people should keep their minds open and read the classical text[23] with a singleness of purpose, until they've become intimately familiar with it. They mustn't come to it with their own ideas about what it will say. They should read it through, then ponder it deeply. Once they've become intimately familiar with it, its words will be their own. Only if they read it in this manner will they understand it. Among today's students one type wants to engage in reading solely that he might learn to compose prose; another type wants his speech to be unusual so that what others say won't compare with what he says. These are serious flaws in the students. The situation may be compared to listening to another person. You should follow every word he utters; don't cut him off and substitute what he's saying with your own ideas. If you do so, you won't understand in the least whether what he's saying is right or wrong. For what is said will merely be your own words. In the end this will be of no help at all. After a while he continued: You must take the classical text and read it till you've become intimately familiar with it. Savor each and every word until you know its taste. If there are passages you don't understand, ponder them deeply, and if you still don't get them, then read the commentaries—only then will the commentaries have any significance. It's like a man who is hungry and then eats or who is thirsty and then drinks—only then does the food or drink have any flavor. If he is not hungry or thirsty and he forces himself to drink or eat, in the end it will be of no benefit to him. He also said: The explanations in my collected commentaries on the *Analects* have all been done carefully. Now I'd like others to read each and every word with the same care I have given them—to ponder them fully. They shouldn't just read through the words mindlessly. He also said: In reading, first and foremost don't come to the text with preconceived ideas. And don't become impatient and stop just as you get the general idea. (11.15a:4/191:5)

---

23. In contrast to the commentaries and explanations of it.

5.49. In reading, students must first read the classical text, keeping the commentary in mind, until they can recite the text with complete mastery. As for what appears in the commentary—the explanations of words, the designations and definitions of affairs and things, the elucidations of the Classic's gist, and the passages tying things together—students are to understand it all, as if they themselves had written it; only then will they be able to appreciate the full flavor of the Classic and advance in their learning, experiencing a breakthrough. If they don't read in this manner, the words will be hollow and learning will not be for their own sake, as is now the case with those preparing for the examinations. Once I met a man who was explaining the *Book of Poetry*. I asked him about the "Kuan-chü" poem.[24] Without any understanding at all of the commentary's explanation of the line or its designations of things, he said: "'There is joy without licentiousness, sorrow without self-injury.'"[25] I continued to speak with him, saying: "You, sir, in speaking now about the *Book of Poetry* needed only these eight characters. Add to them the three characters, 'Having no depraved thoughts,'[26] and with a total of eleven characters you'll have described the whole of the *Mao Book of Poetry*; the three hundred poems [in your hands] become mere dregs." Along the same lines I remember that not many years ago I met Wang Tuan-ming,[27] who said: When Ch'en Yüan-yung[28] asked Ho-ching[29] which passage in I-ch'uan's *Commentary on the Changes* (*I-ch'uan I-chuan*) is the most crucial, Yin responded: "'Substance and function have one source, the manifest and hidden are inseparable.'[30] This is the most crucial passage." Later I reported this to Master Li,[31] who said: "Yin's

---

24. The first poem in the *Book of Poetry*.
25. In *Lun-yü* 3/20 we read: "The Master said, 'In the "Kuan-chü" there is joy without licentiousness, sorrow without self-injury.'"
26. From *Lun-yü* 2/2, where we read: "The Master said, 'In the *Book of Poetry* are three hundred pieces, but the design of them all may be embraced in one sentence—"Having no depraved thoughts."'" Translation from Legge, *Chinese Classics*, vol. 1, p. 146.
27. Wang Ying-ch'en (1118–1176). See *SJCC*, vol. 1, pp. 727–728.
28. Ch'en Hui (1084–1149). See *SJCC*, vol. 1, pp. 679–680.
29. Yin T'un (1071–1142), one of Ch'eng I's foremost disciples. See *SJCC*, vol. 1, pp. 94–97.
30. *I-ch'uan I-chuan*, preface 3a.
31. Li T'ung, Chu Hsi's teacher.

response is certainly good. But one can utter such words only if one has read through the sixty-four hexagrams and the 384 lines and understood them all. If a student didn't yet understand the book in detail and you were to make this statement to him, it would only mislead him." When I heard this, I shuddered. For the first time I realized that my empty and substanceless words up to that point were of no use; and from then on in reading I was ever more thorough.[32] (11.15b:4/191:12)

5.50. Generally, in reading a text, if a person probes to the point where moral principle becomes clear, his mind will be greatly uplifted. Should there be a passage that leaves him in doubt, he must compare the various explanations of it; and when he finds discrepancies among these, the passage ultimately won't rest comfortably in his mind, but he mustn't put it aside. (11.16a:5/192:5)

5.51. Generally, in reading a text, you should examine most closely those passages for which there are differing explanations. Supposing explanation A puts it one way; take firm hold of it, and probe its words through and through. Supposing explanation B puts it another way; take firm hold of it, and probe its words through and through. Once you have probed each of the explanations fully, compare them critically, analyzing them inside and out. Invariably the truth will become clear. (11.16a:8/192:6)

5.52. Because we have commentaries to the Classics, we understand the Classics. Once we have understood the Classics, there's naturally no need for the commentaries. We rely on the Classics simply to understand principle. Once we have grasped principle, there is no need for the Classics. Now if we get stuck on these [the Classics and commentaries], when will we free ourselves from them and reach a thorough understanding [of principle]? Furthermore, "valuing simplicity" doesn't mean we hope the words will be few; rather it refers to whether the words are on target or not. If every sentence is to the point, though there may be a lot of them, what harm can they cause? But if they aren't to the point, the fewer

32. The editors have added the following comment at the end of this passage: "This passage the Master personally wrote out and showed to the students at the school." Cf. *Wen-chi* 71.15b.

there are, the less penetrating they'll be. I once said that in reading a text we must fully understand its meaning, and afterward we needn't bother at all with the commentaries. We must concern ourselves only with the words of the classical text. (11.16a:11/ 192:8)

5.53. Search for the inner meaning of the line. (11.16b:9/192:15)

5.54. Generally, in reading, we must look at the meaning of the surrounding text. We mustn't fixate on the individual character alone. For example, the *Model Sayings of Master Yang* [*Yang-tzu fa-yen*] [says]: "in being *jen* [benevolent] he is yielding, in being *i* [righteous] he is unyielding";[33] but in the *Book of Changes*, unyielding is equated with *jen* and yielding with *i*. For another example, in the *Analects* "to learn without flagging" is *chih* [knowledge] and "to teach without growing weary"[34] is *jen* [benevolence]; but in the *Doctrine of the Mean* it's said that "to bring completion to oneself" is *jen* and "to bring completion to things" is *chih*.[35] In these instances it is essential that we read according to the sense of the original text itself, then there'll be no problems. (11.16b:10/192:16)

5.55. Someone asked how one is to read a word that can be both shallow and profound, trivial and significant. Chu said: You must read the surrounding text. (11.17a:2/193:3)

5.56. In reading, you should look into the meaning of the text and next read the commentaries. People nowadays, however, search outside the meaning of the text. (11.17a:3/193:4)

5.57. Of the commentaries only the ancient ones are not independent essays; they're good to read. They just explain the lines of the Classic, without parting from their intent. This is best. The same can be said of the subcommentaries. Nowadays in explaining texts people attempt to write independent essays; in them they present their own arguments and raise all sorts of questions. Thus what they write, though readable, is a far cry from the intent of the Classics. Master Ch'eng's *Commentary on the Changes* is just such an inde-

---

33. *Yang-tzu fa-yen* 12.1a.
34. From *Lun-yü* 7/2.
35. From *Chung-yung* 25/3.

pendent essay, with much discussion. Thus when people today look at it, they don't read the original Classic with it; they simply study the commentary—which doesn't stimulate them to think [about the Classic]. (11.17a:4/193:5)

5.58. The classical texts of the sages are like the master, the commentaries like the slave. Nowadays people are unacquainted with the master and turn to the slave for an introduction to him. Only thus do they become acquainted with the master. In the end it's not like [turning to] the classical texts themselves. (11.17a:9/193:9)

5.59. Accord with the text in explaining its meaning. (11.17a:11)

5.60. The classical texts contain passages that can't be explained. The only alternative is to offer no explanation; if you insist on offering one, it'll be unintelligent and mistaken in places. (11.17b:1/193:13)

5.61. Those who discuss the Classics these days are usually guilty of one of four vices: raising up what's originally lowly so that it becomes lofty; reading meaning into what's originally shallow so that it becomes profound; pushing away what's originally near at hand so that it becomes remote; and invariably making what's originally clear obscure. These are the great evils plaguing current discussions of the Classics. (11.17b:2/193:14)

5.62. In explaining a text, you must first restore its [original] sentences, next restore its meaning. It doesn't matter if you add unimportant words to it, but don't add repetitious ones. What people nowadays add is precisely these repetitious words. (11.17b:7/194:2)

5.63. The words spoken by the sages and worthies are naturally coherent, each arranged in its proper place—they're nothing like the reckless speech of later men. You need to ponder their meaning; therefore, you can't but discuss them. And in this discussion it's essential that you get the general principles right. Thus you can't but discuss the detail behind these principles as well. It's only because your initial discussion isn't detailed that you don't understand the ideas of the sages and worthies and that later you recklessly hold to certain views, thinking they're right. You'll just go on explaining things recklessly. (11.17b:9/194:4)

5.64. Generally, you mustn't let a student look at a text while he's explaining it. For if he looks at the text, his mind will die right there. Just have him go on explaining it, and his mind will be alive with it. Moreover, he won't forget what he's explained. (11.18a:4/194:10)

5.65. People nowadays have yet to read much in the Classics or thoroughly understand moral principle before they begin reading historical texts, inquiring into the order and disorder of the past and present and studying institutions and the laws. This can be compared to building a dike to irrigate the fields: a dike should be full of water before you open it, then the water will rush out, nourishing all the crops in the field; if you hastily open the dike to irrigate the field just when the dike has accumulated little more than a ladleful of water, not only will this be of no benefit to the field but you'll no longer have even the ladleful of water. Once you've read a lot in the Classics and you've thoroughly understood moral principle, your mind will be completely clear as to the standard of measure; if you don't then turn to the historical texts, inquiring into the order and disorder of the past and present and studying institutions and the laws, it's like having a dike full of water and not opening it to irrigate the field. If you've yet to read much in the Classics or thoroughly understand moral principle but eagerly make reading the histories your first order of business, it's like opening a dike with a ladleful of water to irrigate the field. You can stand there and watch[36] [the water] dry up. (11.18b:5/195:3)

5.66. First read the *Analects*, the *Book of Mencius*, and the *Doctrine of the Mean*. Then read one of the Classics.[37] Then read the histories, which, at that point, will be easy to understand. Read the *Records of the Grand Historian*[38] first. As the *Records of the Grand Historian* and the *Tso Commentary*[39] are mutually inclusive, read the *Tso Commentary* next. Then read the *Comprehensive Mirror for Aid in Government*.[40] And

36. Literally, "wait for."
37. I.e., one of the Five Classics, in contrast to the Four Books.
38. The *Shih chi*, the first great history of China, written by Ssu-ma Ch'ien (145–86 B.C.) of the Han dynasty.
39. One of the so-called Thirteen Classics, the *Tso chuan* is one of the three classical commentaries on the *Ch'un-ch'iu* (*Spring and Autumn Annals*).
40. This annalistic account of China from 403 B.C. to A.D. 959 written by Ssu-ma Kuang was thought to be the most important historical work since the *Shih chi*.

if you still have strength remaining, read the dynastic histories. Simply to read through the histories is not so good as reading through the twists and turns in them with an eye to the present,[41] observing that this is what order and disorder are, this is what victory and defeat are, and that "following the path of orderly government is certain to lead to prosperity, while following the path of disorder is certain to lead to ruin."[42] Do this and you'll understand the sequence of historical events. (11.19a:2/195:8)

5.67. In reading history, you should examine the great moral principles, the great opportunities, and the periods of great order and disorder, success and failure. (11.20b:2/196:15)

5.68. Generally, in reading the Classics and histories,[43] focus on the right and the wrong. As you read the right, look for the wrong. As you read the wrong, look for the right. Afterward you'll understand moral principle. (11.20b:3/196:16)

5.69. In reading a historical text, a person must memorize certain parts of it to understand it. For example, when reading the *Han History*, he should memorize the passage where Kao-tsu declines the Lordship of P'ei, the one where Emperor I [i.e., the King of Huai] sends the Lord of P'ei [i.e., Liu Pang] through the [Han-ku] pass, the one where Han Hsin for the first time persuades the King of Han [to head east],[44] and other things like the historical eulogies and the "Faults of Ch'in."[45] If he simply races through the text, his mind will seem to have it at one moment, and not at the next. Of what use is that? In reading, he must keep his mind on the text at

---

41. The Chinese of this line is awkward; I suspect that characters have dropped out or been misrecorded.

42. From *Shang shu* 8.23a; cf. Legge, *Chinese Classics*, vol. 3, p. 210.

43. Many of the surrounding passages talk about *shih shu*, "historical texts"; it may be that *shu shih* (the Classics and histories), here has been mistakenly transposed.

44. The three passages Chu is referring to here may be found in *Han shu*, vol. 1, 1.9–10, 1.16–17, and 1.30, respectively. These passages deal with important episodes in Liu Pang's struggle with Hsiang Yü for control of the Chinese empire after the fall of the Ch'in dynasty.

45. Pan Ku (A.D. 32–92), the author of the *Han shu*, would record his personal opinions at the end of chapters and introduce them with the stock phrase *tsan yüeh*, "in eulogy we say." "Kuo-Ch'in lun" (The Faults of Ch'in), an essay analyzing the reasons for the downfall of the Ch'in dynasty, was written by the poet and statesman Chia I (201–169 B.C.) and copied into the *Han shu*, *chüan* 31.

all times in order to master it thoroughly from beginning to end.
What's the meaning of this statement? What's the meaning of that
statement? What are the similarities between the statements? What
are the dissimilarities? If he reads it like this, how can he not make
progress? If people today simply did ten days of reading, lowering
their heads and ignoring all unrelated matters, I guarantee that
they'd become transformed people. Even if they were to read for
only a day—no need to speak of ten—they'd see results. And if
they managed to do more than ten years of reading, they'd leave no
text in the world unread. Now you, I'm sure, in an entire year don't
spend even a day giving your whole mind to a text. He also said:
A person must concentrate on whatever he does. Take, for example, Chang Hsü and his study of cursive calligraphy. He watched
Lady Kung-sun perform the sword dance and became enlightened
[about calligraphy];[46] if he hadn't been giving his whole mind
to it, how could he have become enlightened? (11.21a:7/197:10)

46. Chang Hsü and Lady Kung-sun lived in the eighth century. Chu probably
has the lines from Tu Fu's (712–770) preface to his poem "Kuan Kung-sun ta-
niang ti-tzu wu-chien-ch'i hsing" (A Poem on Seeing the Sword Pantomime
Dance of the Pupil of Lady Kung-sun) in mind here. Hung, *Tu Fu*, p. 251, trans-
lates these lines: "Formerly, Chang Hsü of Wu district, well known for skill in
cursive calligraphy, saw frequently in Yeh District the West River Pantomime and
the Sword Pantomime dances of Madame Kung-sun First, and from then on his
cursive calligraphy made rapid progress." Chu's remark is similar to one found in
the Ch'eng brothers' *I-shu*, p. 207.

Six

Holding On to It (Chapter 12)

6.1. Since antiquity, sages and worthies have all considered the mind to be the root. (12.1a:4/199:4)

6.2. The myriad words of the sages and worthies ask only that people not lose their original minds. (12.1a:5/199:5)

The original mind (*pen-hsin*) refers to the mind man is born with; it is one with the mind of heaven. On the relationship between this mind and the so-called human mind, see 5.5.

6.3. If the mind is not preserved, your entire person will be without a master. (12.1a:7/199:7)

"The mind is the dwelling of intelligence and the master of the whole body" (*YL* 98.9a:6/vol. 7, 2514:10).

6.4. As soon as you leave your gates, there's a host of twists and turns. If you are without a master, how will you find your way? (12.1a:8/199:8)

6.5. If the mind is present, your recklessness will naturally recede and fall into line with its orders. (12.1a:9/199:9)

6.6. Man simply has a mind. But if he doesn't control it, what sort of man will he be? (12.1a:10/199:10)

6.7. Man's spirit flies about, like dust. If the mind be not present in his body,[1] harm will result. (12.1a:12/199:12)

---

1. Literally, "inside the shell."

6.8. A man confused isn't lucid; it's only as he begins to acknowl-edge his confusion that lucidity sets in. (12.1b:5/200:2)

6.9. If a man's mind is always clear, his body will follow the accepted rules without any external compulsion. It's only because there are times when man's mind becomes distracted that we set up the many rules to regulate it. If we are ever vigilant, so that our bodies follow the accepted rules, our minds will not become lost and will endure in their brightness. To keep the mind constantly alert, then to regulate it with rules as well, is the way to nurture the mind both from within and without. (12.1b:6/200:3)

6.10. In antiquity the blind music instructor chanted from the *Book of Poetry*; his intent was to warn and admonish others. Never did these warnings and admonitions cease—they were a constant dis-turbance. The result was that men couldn't but be stirred. General-ly, in learning, we must be vigilant, like the monk Jui-yen,[2] who every day routinely asked himself whether his master [i.e., his mind] was alert or not and then supplied the answer himself, saying that it was. Students today, however, don't do this. (12.1b:12/200:7)

6.11. A person in possession of his mind is aware that he has a body. A person in the dark isn't aware that he has a mind. He is like a person who, sleeping, isn't aware that he has a body; though he's asleep, should someone awaken him his body, of course, will be right there with him. The mind is just like this. As soon as someone awakens the person from his darkness, his mind will be present there. (12.2a:7/200:12)

6.12. The mind is simply one mind. One doesn't control this mind with another mind. What is meant by "preserving it," what is meant by "retrieving it," is simply to awaken it. (12.2b:1/200:16)

6.13. Each person has only one mind that serves as master. It must be kept awake at all times. (12.2b:3/201:1)

6.14. If a person doesn't know his own faults, it's because he has never personally examined and become conscious of them. (12.2b:5/201:3)

---

2. A reference to Jui-yen Shih-yen, Buddhist mendicant who lived during the Five Dynasties period (907–960). See entry in *Zengaku daijiten*, vol. 1, p. 628.

6.15. Try to concentrate your mental energy, and whatever is obscure to you and whatever evil thoughts you might have will disappear. T'ai-tsu [r. 960–976], in a poem about the moon, said: "Not yet out of the sea, the thousand mountains are black / Reaching into the heavens, the myriad kingdoms are bright."[3] When the sun isn't yet up, blackness extends everywhere. As soon as there's a ray of light, the road becomes bright. (12.2b: 10/201: 7)

6.16. A person should gather in his mind at all times so that mental energy is present at all times. It's like carrying a hundred-catty load. One must steel one's body to carry it. (12.3a: 1/201: 9)

6.17. In learning, before inquiring into what constitutes true knowledge and vigorous action, a student should collect his mind and give it a place to settle. If in gathering it in he places it in the midst of moral principle, it'll be largely free of reckless thoughts, and after a while it'll weigh light with material desire and heavy with moral principle—it's essential that moral principle outweigh material desire in the mind: it's like a scale that fluctuates between a low and a high end. And once he understands moral principle absolutely clearly, though he may want to stop, he won't be able to; as for material desire he of course won't have the time for it. But if in "holding it fast and letting it go, preserving it and losing it,"[4] he is without a master [i.e., a collected mind], even though we might explain [true knowledge and vigorous action] to him, it'd be of no use. (12.3a: 12/201: 16)

6.18. Students must seek their lost minds. Afterward they'll understand the goodness of their natures. Man's nature is in all instances good; it's simply because man has let go of his mind that he falls into evil. "What heaven has conferred is called human nature" means that the heavenly mandate exists in man and that he's completely good. "When the feelings have been aroused, and they attain their due measure and degree"—this is goodness.[5] When the feelings don't attain their due measure and degree—this is evil. Man's nature is perfectly complete. Never can what's been allotted

---

3. This poem may be found in *Sung-shih chi-shih* 1.1b.
4. This phrase derives from *Meng-tzu* 6A/8; cf. Legge, *Chinese Classics*, vol. 2, p. 409.
5. These quotes are from *Chung-yung* 1/1 and 1/4.

to man by the *yin* and *yang* psychophysical stuff and the five
agents contain evil. It's simply because man himself doesn't move
toward the good that he becomes evil. Han Yü argued that with the
death of Mencius "it was no longer handed down."[6] This was for
the simple reason that later students didn't give any attention to
the mind. The tradition of Yao and Shun discussed "the human
mind and the ontological mind" and "being discriminating, undivided, and holding on to the mean."[7] Under heaven there are merely two alternatives—good and evil. For example, when *yin* and *yang*
are present in the realm of heaven and earth, the wind will be gen-
tle and the sun warm, and the ten thousand things will send forth
shoots—this is the meaning of good. But when *yin* is in power, the
ten thousand things will wither. Evil has the same effect in man.
The principle of heaven and earth is sure to restrain the *yin*
psychophysical stuff, normally preventing it from gaining the upper
hand. Still, it's important that in those places where good and evil
have become mixed students disentangle them; they mustn't let the
shoots of goodness that grow in even the smallest patch of evil be
cut down. If in their ordinary lives they're always conscientiously
examining themselves, preserving and nourishing it [the mind], in
time they'll naturally become cultivated. (12.4b:4/203:2)

For Chu Hsi it is the responsibility of the mind to realize the good nature
with which one is born. Following Chang Tsai, Chu Hsi believed that
"the mind governs the nature and the feelings" (e.g., *YL* 5.11b:12/93:14).
Should the mind permit the feelings to get out of control, the nature will
become obscured; but if the feelings are kept in check, so that "they attain
their due measure and degree," the nature will remain undisturbed and
manifest. Hence, the mind, with its will, must be bent on actualizing,
through learning, the goodness within oneself.[8]

---

6. Han Yü, the great prose stylist of the T'ang dynasty, is often given credit for
the revival of Confucianism in the T'ang, a revival that led to the prominence of
Neo-Confucian teachings in the Sung. Chu Hsi here is referring to Han Yü's discussion of the transmission of the Confucian Way, found in *Chu Wen-kung chiao
Ch'ang-li hsien-sheng wen-chi* 11.3b.

7. A paraphrase from *Shang shu* 4.8b, which Chu understood as follows: "The
human mind is precarious, the ontological mind is almost imperceptible. Be discriminating, be undivided, that you may sincerely hold fast the mean." For the
importance of this *Shang shu* statement to Chu Hsi see 5.5.

8. On the centrality of the mind in Chu Hsi's thought see Gardner, "Transmitting the Way," particularly pp. 163–172.

6.19. Someone asked about "preserving the mind." Chu replied: "Preserving the mind" isn't just something you write down on a piece of paper. You should fully understand the sort of thing the mind is. The sages and worthies explained it extremely clearly. Fearing that later men wouldn't understand, Mencius went on to explain "the four germs" as well.[9] Mull over what they said carefully. (12.5b:1/204:1)

6.20. Just preserve it for a moment, and right away its pleasure, anger, sorrow, and joy will become well regulated. (12.5b:6/204:5)

Since "the mind governs the nature and the feelings," an attending mind will naturally keep the feelings under control.

6.21. For the person [whose mind] is bright, it's bright. Others must nurture it. Nurturing it isn't to hammer and chisel away at it laboriously. It's simply to keep the mind open and calm, and in time it'll become bright of itself. (12.5b:12/204:10)

6.22. It's best if in responding to affairs the mind of man is always just as it is when it has nothing to respond to. (12.6a:5/204:14)

6.23. In ordinary life it should be solemn, as if in thought. (12.6a:6/204:15)

6.24. Generally speaking, you needn't be too concerned with unrefined psychophysical stuff. If the mind is calm, the psychophysical stuff will naturally become tranquil. It's just that a coarse mind is a common failing among students. Heng-ch'ü said: "Yen-tzu didn't become a sage; his mind was still coarse."[10] If you do not preserve it with every breath, it'll become coarse. The important thing is to reflect carefully on matters and make clear distinctions between them in order that principle may become clear and righteousness apparent in all its subtlety; and if in preserving and nurturing it [the mind] there isn't a moment's interruption, heavenly principle will be constantly preserved and human desire will disappear. This, indeed, is to approach perfection. (12.6b:2/205:5)

9. In *Meng-tzu* 2A/6 we read: "The heart [*hsin*, 'heart' or 'mind'] of compassion is the germ of benevolence; the heart of shame, of dutifulness; the heart of courtesy and modesty, of observance of the rites; the heart of right and wrong, of wisdom. Man has these four germs just as he has four limbs." Translation from Lau, *Mencius*, p. 83.

10. Cf. *Chang Tsai chi*, p. 274; cited in Kasoff, *Thought of Chang Tsai*, p. 99.

6.25. If a person is able to preserve his mind so that it is exceptionally clear, he'll naturally be capable of merging with the Way. If in addition he brings to bear the meritorious effects of study and inquiry, [his achievement] will be immeasurable! (12.6b:6/205:8)

6.26. Man's mind is originally bright. It's just that it gets covered over by things and affairs and can't get out from under them; hence, illuminating principle is difficult. Let's strip away the things covering over the mind, and wait for it to come out and be itself. Since it's called the mind, it'll naturally know right from wrong and good from evil. (12.6b:8/205:9)

6.27. You should always be sure the mind has a master. When it has yet to finish one thing, it mustn't go on to another. The mind is vast like heaven and earth, unprejudiced and clear like the sun and the moon. If you seek quiescence but the mind nonetheless isn't quiescent, it's because it's chasing after things. If you don't seek quiescence but the mind is quiescent nonetheless, it's because it has a master [keeping it under control]. (12.7a:1/205:12)

6.28. A person must examine his mistaken mind with his unmistaken mind. The unmistaken one is the original mind; the mistaken one is the original mind lost. (12.7a:3/205:14)

6.29. Only when the mind attains its proper balance is it capable of appreciating the goodness of human nature. (12.7a:5/205:15)

6.30. The effort required of students entails pruning away superficial and extraneous ideas. (12.7a:7/206:1)

6.31. Generally speaking, in order to learn you must first brighten the mind. Only afterward are you capable of learning. It's comparable to lighting a fire: you must first fan the flame and afterward add the firewood; then the flame will become bright. If you add the firewood first, and only then fan the flame, the flame will go out. Take our contemporaries for example: without even looking into the Six Classics, they probe into the examination form of essay. (12.7a:12/206:5)

6.32. Keep firm hold over the road to life and death [i.e., the mind]. (12.7b:5/206:9)

6.33. The words of the sages and worthies for the most part seem dissimilar. Yet they've always been interconnected. For example, the Master said: "Do not look, listen, speak, or move, unless it be in accordance with the rites";[11] "when abroad, behave as though you were receiving an important guest, and when employing the services of the common people, behave as though you were officiating at an important sacrifice";[12] and "be loyal and true in your every word, serious and mentally attentive [*ching*] in all that you do."[13] Mencius then said: "Seek for the lost mind,"[14] and "preserve the mind and nourish the nature."[15] The *Greater Learning* then treated what is called "the apprehension of the principle in things, the extension of knowledge, setting the mind in the right, and making the thoughts true."[16] Master Ch'eng then concentrated on elucidating the word *ching*. If you simply read all this, it may seem like a hodgepodge, utterly confused. But in fact it's all of the same principle. Tao-fu[17] said: Drifting around in the texts, I felt they were all different. It's only when I really applied myself that the principle running through them all became apparent. Chu said: That's right. Just concentrate your efforts on one spot; all the rest inheres in that spot. The Way of the sages and worthies is like a house. Though there are different doors, you'll be able to enter it approaching it from one direction only. I'm just afraid that you won't make the effort. (12.8b:1/207:7)

6.34. Now that we're talking about this,[18] it seems hazardous to talk about it. This is why Master Chou simply said: "Singleness means to be free of desire."[19] But these words were lofty and in the end extraordinarily hard to pin down: what was it that the ordinary

11. An abbreviation of what appears in *Lun-yü* 12/1; translation based on Lau, *Confucius: The Analects*, p. 112.

12. *Lun-yü* 12/2; translation based on Lau, *Confucius: The Analects*, p. 112.

13. *Lun-yü* 15/6; translation based on Waley, *Analects*, p. 194.

14. *Meng-tzu* 6A/11; translation from Legge, *Chinese Classics*, vol. 2, p. 414.

15. *Meng-tzu* 7A/1.

16. *Ta-hsüeh*, "Classic of Confucius," para. 4. Translation based on Gardner, *Chu Hsi and the Ta-hsueh*, p. 92.

17. Chu's disciple Yang Tao-fu; see *SJCC*, vol. 4, pp. 3184–3185, and Ch'en Jung-chieh, *Chu-tzu men-jen*, pp. 272–273.

18. The topic being talked about would seem from context to have been the ideal state of mind.

19. Chou Tun-i, *T'ung-shu*, chap. 20, p. 165.

person was supposed to do to become "free of desire"? Therefore, I-ch'uan simply talked about inner mental attentiveness, letting people work it out for themselves; having a pretty firm grasp of it, they'd have a point from which to begin. And though they might not succeed [at what they did], they wouldn't fail either. Essentially, both Chou and Ch'eng hoped people would understand the mind clearly, and then they'd naturally succeed. But all those who nowadays speak of inner mental attentiveness are eloquent about external matters; they don't know to seek results directly from the mind, and consequently they end up distressed and unhappy. Their approach is not so effective as seeking the lost mind from right under their noses, thereby saving themselves a great deal of trouble. It's an extremely simple matter: just arouse the mind and prevent it from growing dim, and in one or two days you'll see the results. It'll be easy and save you trouble. It's simply a state somewhere between thinking and not thinking. Why is it that you find it difficult and don't do it? (12.10b:2/209:6)

6.35. Learning is extraordinarily complicated for people. They can't possibly do without some basic [guiding] principle. This is the reason for Master Ch'eng's phrase "hold on to inner mental attentiveness," which simply means to arouse the mind so that it becomes bright and thus understands all affairs. Over time it naturally will become vigorous and strong. (12.10b:12/209:13)

6.36. Master Ch'eng's contribution to later students lies mostly in his development of the concept of inner mental attentiveness: if a man practices inner mental attentiveness, his mind and nature will be preserved at all times; if he doesn't practice inner mental attentiveness, they won't be preserved. The Buddhists and Taoists are able to hold on to inner mental attentiveness, but they recognize only higher matters and not lower ones. Our students[20] nowadays make the effort, but only on lower matters—I fear that they disregard higher ones. These higher ones, however, are fundamental.[21] (12.11a:6/210:1)

---

20. Reading *chüeh* as a misprint for *hsüeh-che*, which seems justified given the context, particularly the reference to *hsüeh-che* in the first line of the passage.

21. The meaning of this passage is not altogether clear. The idea here would seem to be that one must be mentally attentive in both abstract *and* concrete matters.

6.37. Practicing inner mental attentiveness is of the greatest importance to the Confucian school. From beginning to end there mustn't be even a moment's interruption. (12.11b:2/210:6)

6.38. Practice inner mental attentiveness and the myriad manifestations of principle will be complete in you. (12.11b:6/210:9)

"The mind is the intelligence of man and thus embraces the myriad manifestations of principle and responds to the myriad affairs" (Chu Hsi's commentary on *Meng-tzu* 7A/1, in *Meng-tzu chi-chu* 7.1a:3).

6.39. Inner mental attentiveness will overcome the hundred moral depravities. (12.11b:8/210:11)

6.40. Just practice inner mental attentiveness and your mind will become one. (12.11b:9/210:12)

6.41. If a person's able to remain mentally attentive, his mind will be perfectly clear and heavenly principle bright. At no place does he make even the slightest effort, yet at no place is even the slightest effort left unmade. (12.12a:1/210:16)

6.42. Inner mental attentiveness is something that props a person up. If a person's dissolute and lazy and he begins to practice inner mental attentiveness, it'll prop up his mind. And if he can remain attentive at all times, though there might be the occasional reckless or depraved thought, it'll retreat and fall into line [with the mind's orders]. (12.12a:3/211:1)

6.43. Someone asked about inner mental attentiveness. Chu replied: If for even one thought it is not maintained, it is an interruption; if for even one matter it goes astray, it is an interruption. (12.12b:1/211:10)

6.44. Someone asked how to work at inner mental attentiveness. Chu replied: It's simply to have no wild ideas within, no wild behavior without. (12.12b:2/211:11)

6.45. To explain "holding on to inner mental attentiveness" doesn't require many words. Just appreciate fully the flavor of these phrases [of Ch'eng I]—"be ordered and solemn," "be dignified and grave,"[22] "change your countenance," "set your thoughts in

22. From *I-shu*, pp. 167, 188.

order,"[23] "regulate your dress and dignify your gaze,"[24]—and make a concrete effort at [doing what they say]. Then what is called [by Ch'eng I] "correcting ourselves within" and "concentrating on one thing" naturally will entail no additional measures: the mind and body will become reverent, and the manifest and the hidden, one. (12.12b:6/211:14)

6.46. "Sit as though you were impersonating an ancestor, stand as though you were performing a sacrifice."[25] The head should be upright, the eyes looking straight ahead, the feet steady, the hands respectful, the mouth quiet and composed, the bearing solemn[26]— these are all aspects of inner mental attentiveness. (12.13a:2/ 212:4)

6.47. What nowadays is referred to as "holding on to inner mental attentiveness" doesn't mean to make the words "inner mental attentiveness" into some great object you clutch to your bosom. It's important only that the mind be constantly possessed of the intention [to practice inner mental attentiveness], not the term. (12.13a:4/212:5)

6.48. In times of activity, you must regulate yourself; in times of quiescence, you must regulate yourself. [I], Fang,[27] asked whether inner mental attentiveness is a thread running through activity and quiescence. Chu replied: In the final analysis, every word used by man runs like a thread through [both] activity and quiescence. (12.13b:4/212:13)

6.49. For the most part, not to seize it [i.e., the mind] firmly is not to be benevolent. The mind of man—clear, open, and settled—is the essence of benevolence. If one doesn't seize it firmly, selfish desires will get hold of it and shake it till it's confused. But to seize it firmly, what other way is there than faithfully holding on to inner mental attentiveness? (12.14a:11/213:10)

---

23. From *I-shu*, p. 165.
24. From *I-shu*, p. 205.
25. From *Li chi* 1.8a.
26. This description, in a slightly different order, is found in *Li chi* 30.23a–b.
27. Chu's disciple Yang Fang (*chin-shih* 1163); see *SJCC*, vol. 4, pp. 3098–3099, and Ch'en Jung-chieh, *Chu-tzu men-jen*, pp. 267–268.

6.50. Someone asked about how to develop truthfulness and inner mental attentiveness and to rid oneself of desires. Chu replied: This is the ultimate. To be true to oneself is to do away with all falsehoods; to be mentally attentive is to do away with all laxness. As for desires, they must simply be restrained. (12.14b:7/213:15)

6.51. "Practicing inner mental attentiveness" is like tending a field and keeping it well watered. "Subduing oneself"[28] is to remove the weeds from it. (12.15a:3/214:5)

6.52. Someone asked about "holding on to inner mental attentiveness" and "subduing oneself." Chu replied: "Practicing inner mental attentiveness" is to nurture it [i.e., the mind] and take firm hold of it so that it doesn't go awry. "Subduing oneself" is to wipe it clean to the very root. There was also a question about "Admonitions of the Studio of Inner Mental Attentiveness" [Ching-chai chen].[29] Chu replied: This is a listing of the practices of inner mental attentiveness; it speaks of its many different aspects. (12.15a:4/214:6)

6.53. Someone inquired: I once learned how to "hold on to inner mental attentiveness." When I read, my mind would fix on the text; when I dealt with matters, my mind would fix on those matters. It thus seemed that I had become somewhat good at it. And yet when I closed my eyes and practiced quiet-sitting, I couldn't expel my thoughts. Someone remarked: It's just that when you closed your eyes you began to get wild ideas. When you were reading, your mind fixed on the text; when you were dealing with matters, your mind fixed on those matters—merely because you had collected the mind. But you didn't yet understand the substance of inner mental attentiveness. Chu said: If when you practice quiet-sitting you are unable to expel your thoughts, it's because you are

28. This term is from *Lun-yü* 12/1, where we read: "To subdue oneself and return to propriety, is perfect virtue." Translation from Legge, *Chinese Classics*, vol. 1, p. 250.

29. In 1176, Chu returned to his native Wu-yüan County where he took his lodgings with Wang Ch'ing-ch'ing (*hao*, Ching-chai); Chu wrote this brief set of admonitions on practicing inner mental attentiveness on Wang's studio wall. "Ching-chai chen" may be found reproduced in *Wen-chi* 85.6a–b. For Wang Ch'ing-ch'ing see *SJCC*, vol. 1, p. 724, and Ch'en Jung-chieh, *Chu-tzu men-jen*, p. 131.

not practicing inner mental attentiveness as you do your quiet-sitting. Inner mental attentiveness is simply inner mental attentiveness! What "substance of inner mental attentiveness" are you going to look for? If you fragment inner mental attentiveness like this, your problems will become even greater, and you'll never make an effort to practice it. You'll just end up monkeying with words. (12.15b:3/214:13)

6.54. As for inner mental attentiveness, don't think of it as some matter [outside yourself]. It's simply to collect your own mental energy and concentrate it on a certain spot. Now it seems to me the reason none of you are making progress is that you only know how to talk about "apprehending the principle in things" but are lacking in the fundamentals. Unconcentrated as your mental energy and your thoughts are, your effort is unpenetrating. It's not that certain matters in particular distract your thinking—just enjoying the scenery leads your mind far astray. How can this compare to maintaining it within at all times? To have absolutely no interest in the inconsequential matters of the world may seem unfeeling at first, but, in fact, it's best if this is the case. (12.16b:8/215:16)

6.55. There's a dead inner mental attentiveness, and there's a living one. If you simply hold on to inner mental attentiveness, concentrating on one matter, but fail, when some other matter arises, to rescue it with righteousness and to discriminate between right and wrong—this isn't living inner mental attentiveness. Once you're good at it, inner mental attentiveness will always be accompanied by righteousness and righteousness always by inner mental attentiveness. In quiescence, you'll examine whether you're mentally attentive or not; in activity, you'll examine whether you're righteous or not. How can you "behave when away from home as though you were in the presence of an important guest or deal with the common people as though you were officiating at an important sacrifice"[30] if you don't practice inner mental attentiveness? Or how can you "sit as though you were impersonating an ancestor, stand as though you were performing a sacrifice,"[31] if you don't practice inner mental attentiveness? It's essential that inner mental

30. *Lun-yü* 12/2; translation based on Lau, *Confucius: The Analects*, p. 112.
31. From *Li chi* 1.8a.

attentiveness and righteousness sustain each other, with one following upon the other ad infinitum. Then inner and outer will be thoroughly interconnected. (12.17a:2/216:4)

6.56. To nourish yourself, you must practice inner mental attentiveness. To manage affairs, you must accumulate righteousness. (12.17a:7/216:7)

6.57. Inner mental attentiveness and righteousness are simply one matter. It's like our two feet: firmly planted they are inner mental attentiveness, but as soon as they move they are righteousness. Or our eyes: when closed, they are inner mental attentiveness, but open and looking at things they are righteousness. (12.17a:8/216:8)

6.58. Before encountering matters, all we can say is, "practice inner mental attentiveness to straighten the inner life." But once matters and things come our way, we ought to distinguish right from wrong.[32] It doesn't do simply to practice inner mental attentiveness. Inner mental attentiveness and righteousness are not two different matters. (12.17a:10/216:9)

6.59. "Inner mental attentiveness" means to stick to this without wavering; "righteousness" means to do with that whatever is appropriate. (12.17a:12/216:11)

6.60. In practicing inner mental attentiveness, you have to look back. To be righteous, you have to look forward. (12.17b:1/216:12)

6.61. Ming-tao[33] taught people to practice quiet-sitting. Master Li[34] also taught people to practice quiet-sitting. It seems that if one's mental energy is not settled, principle has no place to lodge. He also said: You must practice quiet-sitting; only then will you be able to gather in the mind. (12.17b:3/216:14)

6.62. Someone asked: It doesn't matter whether you are engaged in quiet-sitting or responding to affairs, you must concentrate your

32. A phrase from *Chou i*, p. 4, often cited by the Ch'eng brothers and Chu Hsi, reads: "Practice inner mental attentiveness to straighten the inner life; practice righteousness to order the external life."

33. Ch'eng Hao.

34. Li T'ung.

mind, right? Chu replied: In practicing quiet-sitting, you mustn't sit in Ch'an-like contemplation, cutting off all thought. Just gather in the mind; don't let it run wild with idle thought, and it will be at peace and of itself concentrated. Then, when affairs arise, it will respond to them as it should. Once the affairs have passed, it will again be at peace. You mustn't rouse two or three additional affairs when dealing with the first one, or you'll become confused and directionless, and then how will you achieve a state of concentration? If you simply observe that in the case of King Wen, "Full of harmony was he in his palace; / Full of reverence in the ancestral temple. / Out of sight he still felt as under inspection; / Unweariedly he maintained [his virtue],"[35] you'll understand that practicing inner mental attentiveness is just as I've said. The ancients, from the time they were children, made this sort of effort; this is why in sprinkling and sweeping[36] they performed rituals for sweeping. Whether studying poetry, music and dance, or recitation, you have to concentrate the mind. For example, in studying archery, if the mind is not present, how will you be able to hit the mark? Or, in studying charioteering, if the mind is not present, how will you manage the horses? It's the same in calligraphy and mathematics. Now, if you never did it [i.e., concentrate the mind] when you were young, there's nothing you can do about that now; only if you do it from here on out might you achieve any success. If you don't make the effort, though you may want to read and understand moral principle, it'll be just like wanting to build a house when there's no foundation for it or place to erect the supports. Now let's talk about whether a restless mind is able to enter into moral principle, and whether it's compatible with the mind of the sages and worthies. That we nowadays seek after the mind is precisely because we want to establish a foundation. Once the mind is bright and there's a place to preserve it, in learning we'll know the proper direction in which to go, without any mistakes. But should the mind be confused and muddled, we won't know what direction to take. In learning, then, where will we begin? And, moreover, where will we end? It's precisely for this reason that Master Ch'eng found it

35. *Shih ching* 240/3; translation from Legge, *Chinese Classics*, vol. 4, p. 447.
36. Sprinkling and sweeping were part of the program of lesser learning. See the annotation to 1.1.

necessary to tell others to be diligent in practicing inner mental attentiveness. (12.17b:11/217:5)

6.63. Someone asked whether quiescence is often required in the preservation and nurturing of it [i.e., the mind]. Chu replied: Not necessarily; but Confucius taught people that whenever it was required to make a real effort at it. Nowadays we may talk about making quiescence our ruling principle, but that doesn't mean we should discard things and affairs in the pursuit of it. As human beings we naturally serve sovereign and kin, have intercourse with friends, care for wives and children, and manage servants. We cannot cast things aside, simply shut our gates and practice quiet-sitting, and then, when things and affairs come our way, say, "I'm waiting to preserve and nurture it." Neither can we simply pursue things and affairs limitlessly. We must consider bringing an end to these two types of practices, and only then might we enjoy some success. A short time later he continued: In times of activity, quiescence is right there. In times of activity, there's quiescence as well—respond to affairs in accord with principle, and though there may be activity, there's quiescence too. Thus it is said: "Knowing where to come to rest, one becomes steadfast; being steadfast, one may achieve a quiescence."[37] When things and affairs come your way, if you don't respond to them in accord with principle, but keep yourself distantly aloof from them in search of quiescence, your mind will be incapable of achieving quiescence. Yet if in times of activity you're able to accord with principle, in times when there's nothing to do you'll be able to achieve quiescence. And if in times of quiescence you're able to hold on to it [the mind], in times of activity you'll be capable of acting. In times of activity, you must make the effort; in times of quiescence, you must make the effort—the two efforts do not depend on each other.[38] Never let up in your effort, and you'll be successful. If there are no interruptions, in times of quiescence you'll be truly quiescent, and in

---

37. *Ta-hsüeh*, "Classic of Confucius," para. 2. Translation from Gardner, *Chu Hsi and the Ta-hsueh*, pp. 90–91, with modification.

38. I would guess that something is missing from this brief phrase here. The meaning I now tease out of it is: Your effort in times of activity isn't enough; no matter how great it is, you must also make the effort in times of quiescence—and vice versa.

times of activity the mind will be inactive—in activity there'll be
quiescence as well. But if no effort is made, in times of activity
you'll be truly active, and in times of quiescence, though you may
wish to become quiescent, you'll be unable to—in quiescence
there'll be activity as well. Activity and quiescence are like a boat in
water: as the tide comes in, it becomes active; as the tide goes out, it
stops. When there's something that must be done, it [the mind]
becomes active; when there's nothing to be done, it becomes quiescent. Be that as it may, activity and quiescence have no sharp
boundaries; there's no principle strictly separating one from the
other. It's like a man's breath: he sucks it in and there's quiescence,
he blows it out and there's activity; in conversation he responds
and there's activity, he pauses and there's quiescence. Everything
is like this. As for nurturing [the mind] and extending knowledge,
with which does one begin? And yet students must choose a starting point for themselves. Master Ch'eng in learning placed the extension of knowledge before all else. It was knowledge that came
first. But he also said that it's impossible to extend knowledge without abiding in inner mental attentiveness. Inner mental attentiveness, then, comes first as well; from here one pushes outward. This
is just how it is. (12.18b: 10/218: 3)

6.64. Before encountering some affair, the mind must be quiescent.
Only when the affair's at hand should it be employed, then it'll
have the strength to respond. If it isn't quiescent when it ought to
be, its thoughts will become confused, and when the affair's at hand
it'll already be weary. The passage in which I-ch'uan explains
quiescence as concentration [goes on to] say, "If [in quiescence] it
doesn't concentrate, [in activity] it'll be unable to follow the
right."[39] At rest gather it in; then in doing things, you'll have the
mental energy. (12.19b:4/218: 15)

6.65. Quiescent, it's settled. Cultivated, it's penetrating. (12.19b:
10/219:4)

6.66. There's activity in quiescence, as when an idea arises in the
mind. And there's quiescence in activity. Each one entrusts itself to
the other. (12.20a: 1/219:6)

---

39. *I-shu*, p. 142.

6.67. Someone asked about activity and quiescence. In the course of a day people spend very little time in quiescence and a great deal of time in activity. Chu said: The sage, in activity, is quiescent. By contrast, the multitude, in activity, is confused and disturbed. When people today want to do something, they're never capable of concentrating on it or dealing with it efficiently and without confusion. For as they deliberate on it, they want to do this and at the same time want to do that. This is why in times of activity there isn't that quiescence. (12.20a:4/219:9)

6.68. If you practice quiet-sitting for a long time, you'll become muddled and weary, incapable of thinking. When you get up, you'll feel agitated and won't think calmly.[40] (12.21a:12/221:1)

40. Even though he emphasized the value and importance of quiet-sitting in the Confucian self-cultivation process (e.g., 6.61), Chu here is cautioning his students against exaggerating its importance, as he felt the Buddhists did.

Seven

Energetically Putting
It into Practice
(Chapter 13)

7.1. Studying it extensively isn't the same as knowing its essentials, and knowing its essentials isn't the same as actually practicing it. (13.1a:4/222:4)

7.2. Goodness is over there, so we go there to practice it. When we've practiced it for a long time, it becomes one with us. And when it becomes one with us, we've truly acquired it. If we're unable to practice it, goodness will be goodness, and we will be we. (13.1a:5/222:5)

7.3. If we need not practice it personally but only have to talk about it and that's all, then the seventy disciples studying under Confucius would have required a mere two days to talk about it and been done. Why would they have followed Confucius for so many years, never leaving his side? And if it wasn't that they needed the time to put it into practice, then all of Confucius's disciples must have been foolish and incompetent, and I doubt that that's the case. The ancients day and night without stop gave assiduous attention to the mind; and when it came to conducting their business, they simply did as their abilities permitted. For example, Yu with decisiveness alone, Ssu with understanding alone, and Jan Ch'iu with versatility alone could serve in office.[1] They

---

1. Confucius makes this comment about his disciples Tzu-lu, Tzu-kung, and Jan Ch'iu in *Lun-yü* 6/8.

needed nothing else. If it is important business, have great sages and worthies do it; if it is minor business, have lesser worthies do it. Each person does what his abilities allow. How can anyone be forced [beyond that]? (13.1a:10/222:9)

7.4. If a person isn't able to put moral principle into practice, it's simply because the moral principle within him has yet to be fully realized. He shouldn't complain that he can't put it into practice; rather he should turn within and try to bring the Way there to full realization. (13.1b:6/223:1)

7.5. Recently, I've spent less time talking and more time practicing. As far as matters are concerned, you yourselves must go care for them, examine them, and nurture them. As far as books are concerned, you yourselves must go read them. And as far as moral principle is concerned, you yourselves must go investigate it. I'm just one who guides and corroborates: if you have questions or difficulties, we'll discuss them together, but that's it. (13.2a:3/223:7)

7.6. It's because his heels do not touch the ground that a man drifts about carelessly and does not firmly establish himself. (13.2a:9/223:12)

7.7. To engage in learning is like climbing a pagoda. If you climb one story after another, you'll personally get to know the top story, without inquiring of anyone else. If you don't actually walk up it but just fantasize about it, you'll be incapable of understanding even the lowest story. (13.2a:10/223:13)

7.8. What are the percentages of heavenly principle and human desire? Heavenly principle is originally large. Human desire, then, operates from within the heavenly principle. And even though it is human desire, human desire naturally contains heavenly principle. Someone asked: Isn't it that originally it was all heavenly principle? Chu replied: At birth a person's all heavenly principle; human desire is produced later, without cause. (13.2b:4/224:2)

7.9. As for the mind of man, if heavenly principle is preserved, human desire will disappear. But should human desire prevail, heavenly principle will be blotted out. Never do heavenly principle and human desire permeate each other. The student must fully realize this and be watchful over himself. (13.2b:7/224:4)

7.10. Generally speaking, if a person is capable of standing firmly on the threshold between heavenly principle and human desire, he'll make great progress. (13.2b:9/224:6)

7.11. The boundary between heavenly principle and human desire is a shifting one. Thus Master Chou spoke simply of "incipient movements not yet visible outside."[2] But in distinguishing between the two, we must be quick. Thus Heng-ch'ü always spoke of "anticipating." (13.2b:10/224:7)

7.12. A person possesses heavenly principle and human desire. When this one excels, that one retreats; when that one excels, this one retreats. There is no such thing as a neutrality in which there's no advancing and retreating; as a rule, if people don't advance, they retreat. It may be compared to the confrontation between Liu [Pang] and Hsiang [Yü] that took place between Ying-yang and Ch'eng-kao.[3] When that one advanced a step, the other retreated a step; when this one advanced a step, the other retreated a step. Beginning students must dig in their heels and resist the other [i.e., human desires]. Having resisted it even a bit, they'll go on resisting it bit by bit. If their minds don't retreat, they're sure to be victorious in the end. How grand things will be with victory. (13.3a:9/224:16)

7.13. A person has only one mind. If it is right today and wrong tomorrow, it isn't that he takes a wrong mind and substitutes it for the right one. If it's bad today and good tomorrow, it isn't that he takes a good one and substitutes it for the bad one. For there is only one mind; it just depends on the waxing and waning of heavenly principle and human desire. The mind from start to finish has always operated together with heaven and earth. For there is only one mind. In reading, don't bother to bring corroborative evidence to bear. To become thus entangled is simply for the sake of others. If you're truly reading for yourself, you have to test what you read against your own mind, understanding that what the sages and worthies said is no different from your own mind today. This is the proper effort. (13.3b:2/225:3)

---

2. The translation of *chi* here is from Graham, *Two Chinese Philosophers*, p. 35.

3. The confrontation between Liu Pang and Hsiang Yü over the territory between Ying-yang and Ch'eng-kao (present-day Honan), which occurred in 204–203 B.C., is described in *Han shu*, vol. 1, 1. 40–45.

7.14. Moral principle is what the body and mind naturally possess. Yet when you lose it, you don't know how to recover it. Wealth and position are things external to the body. Yet you seek them, fearing only that you will not get them. Even supposing you did get them, they wouldn't do your body or mind the slightest bit of good; moreover, you can't be certain of getting them. Now if you were to seek moral principle, you'd get it;[4] and, if you were capable of not losing what you had, you'd become a sage or a worthy. What's beneficial and what's harmful are extremely clear then. As for the impartiality of the human mind, it's always obscured by selfish desire. Thus you mustn't let go of it [i.e., the mind] but must always be vigilant about these two things [i.e., the beneficial and the harmful]. Once you come to understand them, you are sure to reflect seriously on the one and anxiously rid yourself of the other. (13.4a:8/225:14)

7.15. All matters, be they large or small, possess righteousness and profit. Just now you've done something good; but it involved some private gain as well. This is what is meant by "doing it with goodness, without understanding the Way." (13.6a:6/227:13)

7.16. Benevolence and righteousness are rooted in the original endowment of man's mind. The mind of profit is engendered by the urge we have to keep up with each other. (13.6b:2/228:4)

7.17. In people there's simply impartiality and partiality. In the universe there's simply heterodoxy and truth. (13.6b:3/228:5)

7.18. To deal with matters in accord with the true and geat moral principle under heaven is to be impartial; to deal with them in accord with our own personal ideas is to be partial. (13.6b:4/228:6)

7.19. In all matters examine into the right and wrong. Supposing you did something today; if you yourself are comfortable with it and have no doubts about it, it was the right thing to do. But if you yourself have doubts about it, it was wrong thing to do. (13.6b:8/228:9)

---

4. The phrase *ch'iu tse te chih* ("seek and you'll get it") comes from *Meng-tzu* 7A/3, as does much of the sentiment in this passage.

7.20. Discussion is absolutely essential. But then you must go and personally make the effort. If you simply talk about a matter, within a day or two you'll be done. It's the effort that's difficult. Take the person who knows a certain act is wrong and that he mustn't do it but for no particular reason again suddenly thinks about doing it, or in the midst of an act knows it isn't righteous and that he shouldn't do it but nonetheless proceeds to do it without even being aware of it. What's to be done? Or, there's some good act, and his mind initially is set on doing it but in the end is unwilling to do it. What's to be done? It would seem that man's mind is originally good. The moment that it sees good and wants to do it is the seed of the true mind manifesting itself. But as soon as it becomes manifest, it's immediately obstructed by the psychophysical endowment and the material desires, which prevent it from remaining manifest. One must examine it, preserve it, and nurture it personally. To understand this requires the greatest effort. (13.6b:12/228:13)

7.21. There was a question about loving and hating. Chu said: Loving and hating are emotions. Loving good and hating evil are human nature. It's part of human nature to love good and hate evil; to love or to hate without basis is partiality. (13.8a:8/230:6)

7.22. Buddhist scripture says: "The Buddha appears in the world because of the one great causal event."[5] The sage likewise appears because of this one great event. Moral principle is originally in all men, but only in the sage does it become as brilliantly manifest and grand as it does: "What you don't understand, I will explain for you here so that you will understand.[6] And what you don't know how to do, I will provide an example here for you to follow. All I want is for moral principle to be sustained so that it stands upright in the world forever—its top leaning against the sky and its bottom leaning against earth, without wavering. If for even a day there's no one to uphold it, it'll fall down flat, and in no time its feet will be leaning against the sky and its head leaning against earth; it'll be completely topsy-turvy and confused, and all will be ruined."

5. Chu's comment here is a paraphrase of *Miao-fa lien-hua ching*, vol. 9, p. 7a. This translation is based on that found in Yampolsky, *Platform Sutra*, p. 166.

6. This line, and the next few that follow, would seem to be from the point of view of the sage-instructor and serve as an elaboration of the passage from the *Shang shu* that immediately follows.

Therefore it is said: "Now heaven, to protect the people down below, made for them rulers, and made for them instructors, that they
might be able to assist Shang-ti, and secure the tranquillity of the
four quarters of the empire."[7] Heaven simply engendered you, en-
trusting you with moral principle. Whether you take on the task or
not is simply up to you. Doing it well depends on you; doing it
poorly likewise depends on you. Thus heaven sets up the rulers/
instructors to help you along. And once they have nurtured you
and guided you through education, there isn't one among you who
won't fully realize his nature. This is what happened in the time of
Yao and Shun; it was a time in which truly "the tranquillity of the
four quarters of the empire had been secured." For just as soon as
any of the bad people or unmanageable affairs of the world met up
with Yao and Shun, they became calm and settled. Thus, to say
that they were "able to assist Shang-ti" is perhaps to say that they
helped Shang-ti do what he hadn't done himself. Since the Ch'in-
Han period, exposition of the proper learning [i.e., the Way] hasn't
been clear. The world's rulers have indeed done their job as their
abilities and wisdom have permitted, but there has been no one
who has appreciated the matters of the "inborn luminous Virtue"
and "renewing the people":[8] the way of the ruler has every now and
then enjoyed some success; but the way of the instructor has been
altogether absent. (13.8a: 11/230:8)

7.23. A sage doesn't know that he himself is a sage. (13.10a:7/
232:5)

7.24. In teaching and guiding the younger generation, you must be
stern and untiring. But only if you're able to inspire and enlighten
them as well will you be successful. If you're simply stern with
them, restraining them and that is all, it'll be of no help. (13.13a:
6/235:5)

7.25. I've said that today's ways of teaching and guiding others all
miss the point. There isn't a person who is clear [about the way to

---

7. From *Shang shu* 11.6a; translation from Legge, *Chinese Classics*, vol. 3, p. 286,
with modification.

8. These two terms come from the first line of the *Ta-hsüeh*: "The way of greater
learning lies in keeping one's inborn luminous Virtue unobscured, in renewing the
people, and in coming to rest in perfect goodness." See Gardner, *Chu Hsi and the
Ta-hsueh*, pp. 88–90.

teach and guide others]. Those who explain moral principle explain it all wrong; their explanations follow an errant path. Those who write essays just learn to write those bad essays. Those who write poetry don't recognize good poetry. Those who discuss Ch'an don't discuss the Ch'an of the original Buddha. And those who cultivate and nurture the [Taoist] way don't cultivate and nurture the way of Lao and Chuang. There isn't a one who has got it right. (13.13a:8/235:6)

7.26. There exists this principle, and only then does there exist this thing or matter. It's like the grass and the trees: only when there exists a seed will the grass or the trees grow. And it's like a person: only when he has the mind to accomplish a certain matter will he succeed at that matter. Without this mind how would he be able to succeed at it? (13.14a:1/236:2)

7.27. Everything is a matter of learning. (13.14a:3/236:4)

7.28. Somebody said that matters are many. Chu replied: The matters in the world are infinite. Don't bother with matters that are large but unimportant; neither should you bother with those that are small and unimportant. [Of what remains] dispense first with the obvious, then with the subtle. Polish one layer, then the next. This is how the matters of the universe should be treated. It says in the *Doctrine of the Mean*: "[The superior man] is cautious over what he does not see and apprehensive over what he does not hear."[9] Only if he first deals with what he sees and what he hears and afterward applies himself to what he does not see and does not hear can he be meticulous [in his endeavor]. These days people always skip a step as they proceed; without first applying themselves to what they see and what they hear, they proceed directly to what they don't see or hear. We can assume that they won't manage successfully and that in the end everything will be spoiled. It's like working in the darkest room in the house. How can one work there? Only if one starts in a place "seen by ten eyes, pointed at by ten hands"[10] [i.e., an obvious place], will one be successful. (13.14a:4/236:5)

---

9. *Chung-yung* 1/2; translation from Chan, *Source Book*, p. 98.
10. *Ta-hsüeh*, "Commentary of Tseng Tzu" 6.3; translation from Gardner, *Chu Hsi and the Ta-hsueh*, p. 106.

7.29. You must establish a rough foundation, then make the appropriate effort on the fine points. Nowadays people freely utter words that lack moral principle and freely do things that lack moral principle. This is because they seek the profound and abstruse before establishing a rough foundation. And even if they were to understand the profound and abstruse, what effect would it have on them? (13.14a:12/236:10)

7.30. Often we wish to accomplish something without appreciating that if we ourselves aren't established yet we'll be absolutely incapable of seeing the matter through. For should even the slightest selfish thought remain in a man's mind, it's enough to ruin matters. If there's the slightest blemish above [in the mind], there'll be a conspicuous one below [in the matter]. If there's the slightest error above, there'll be a sizable one below. Now, if we fully understand 100 percent of some matter but are diverted from it in the end by something else, we'll only be able to do 50 or 60 percent of it. And if we were to understand only 40 or 50 percent of it now, in the end then what? (13.14b:3/236:12)

7.31. The mind that wants to do the good thing is the true one. The mind that wants to do the bad thing is the false one. If within [the mind] the false one mixes with the true one, it will ruin the true one as well. (13.14b:10/236:16)

7.32. You must have trust in it. This matter may be unusual, but if you don't trust in it, you'll run into trouble.[11] (13.14b:12/237:1)

7.33. People today, before they understand something, impulsively act on it—without understanding it in the least. Once they do understand it, they realize that what they've already done is often reason to be horrified. (13.15a:5/237:5)

7.34. If as you do things you're concerned with profit and loss, in the end you're bound to suffer loss. (13.15a:9/237:8)

7.35. Do nothing beforehand; hope for nothing afterward.[12] (13.15a:10/237:9)

---

11. Lack of context makes this passage unintelligible. In fact, it can be punctuated in any number of ways.

12. The grammar here is clear, but the meaning is vague. I suspect that the passage means something like don't do anything before you've thought it through, and once you've done it don't expect any gain.

7.36. In their dealings, the ancients would seek to be accommodating only if important affairs of state were involved: in matters of life and death, preservation and destruction, there were times when they couldn't act directly on their [good] impulses but had to weigh things carefully, then act. Nowadays people behave like this in all their affairs—they're bent on being accommodating. "If gain be got by bending the yard to straighten the foot, may we likewise do that?"[13] It doesn't make any sense to me.[14] (13.15a:11/237:10)

7.37. People really can't be understood. There are men who are extremely frugal with themselves, who carry out the principles they hold,[15] who above eat dry earth and below drink from the yellow springs,[16] but who covet official rank. And there are men who live in uncorrupted poverty but who are fond of women. It's simply that these men are unable to subdue their selfish desires. In their dealings, they see only what's important to them [i.e., official posts and women] and nothing else. Someone else said: It seems that these persons would rank higher than those even baser. Chu replied: You can't put it like this. For as soon as they become tainted, they're no good at all—you really can't rank them. Merely coveting official rank, they'd dare even to kill their fathers and sovereign. (13.16a:9/238:9)

7.38. As for the honored ones of antiquity, the better they were served, the better the virtue they nurtured became. Those who since have been served and well nurtured have merely been corrupted by it. (13.16b:11/239:2)

7.39. What your physical being expends is simply a "guest" energy [i.e., it's yours only temporarily]. If you just spoke about and immersed yourself in human nature and principle, there'd naturally be a difference in your dealings with matters. (13.17a:3/239:5)

7.40. Compassion and kindness must be the foundation. As for bravery and determination, though we cannot be without them, their use is restricted to certain occasions. (13.17a:5/239:6)

13. From *Meng-tzu* 3B/1; cf. Legge, *Chinese Classics*, vol. 2, p. 262.
14. This is criticism of the Chekiang school of "utilitarianism"; cf. Tillman, *Utilitarian Confucianism*, p. 149.
15. From *Meng-tzu* 3B/10.
16. From *Meng-tzu* 3B/10.

7.41. Discussion that sidesteps and avoids the issue is most harmful to matters. (13.17a:7/239:7)

7.42. To go beyond what is appropriate in matters is mere pretense. (13.17a:8/239:8)

7.43. If you avoid the commonplace, it's only because you don't fully understand. (13.17a:12/239:11)

7.44. Shu-meng[17] asked: Master Ch'eng said that as for "'consciously avoiding suspicion,' the worthy man mustn't do it, how much less the sage."[18] Now if there is some matter in which one should be indirect and cannot proceed straightforwardly—this can't be considered "consciously avoiding suspicion." Chu said: That seems right. But if one's "consciously avoiding suspicion," fearful of what other people might say—this is selfish thinking. It's like not doing what one knows fully well one should do—it's selfishness.[19] It's also "consciously avoiding suspicion." Only after having made considerable effort and having examined himself at some length will a person understand this. For instance, if someone presents you with a thoroughbred horse, even though you don't accept it, when later you're recommending people [for office] you'll not have forgotten the incident, and in the end you won't recommend that person. Not recommending him, of course, is all right. But it's because in your heart you've never forgotten the matter and [still] find the thought of accepting a gift unbearable—this is "selfish thinking." It's like being an official at court these days and recognizing clearly that this is a good person whom you should recommend. But because you and he in the past have had friendly relations—and I'm not talking about a relative here, for of course it's against the law to recommend relatives—but simply because the two of you have been well acquainted, you "consciously avoid suspicion" and don't recommend him. It's also like having a person who has always been on bad terms with you; when you become an official, though there is some matter for which he ought to be

17. Chu's disciple, Chiang Shu-meng; see Ch'en Jung-chieh, *Chu-tzu men-jen*, pp. 337–338.

18. From *I-shu*, p. 258. This is cited by Chu Hsi in his commentary on *Lun-yü* 5/2.

19. This line is puzzling; I suspect that the phrase *shih-ch'i yü pu-ch'i* is a highly idiomatic expression, one that I do not fully understand.

punished, you fear that others will say you are punishing him be-cause of the earlier emnity, and so you forget about it. In all these cases the mistake is great. (13.17b:7/239:16)

7.45. Someone then said that the mind of man mustn't be narrow. In dealing with other people and things, the mind mustn't first separate what's to be treated well from what's to be treated poorly. Chu said: Only the superior man is able to connect with the will of all under heaven, opening up [his mind] so that its scope becomes vast, thus allowing everyone to feel a sense of plenitude in their hearts. How content they'll be! (13.18a:6/240:7)

7.46. Someone asked: In dealing with other people and things, should we respond to them according to the strength of our feelings toward them? Or should we treat them generously regardless of our feelings? Chu replied: If we know the way whereby to regulate our minds and preserve ourselves, in dealing with other people and things we'll naturally be possessed of a standard. (13.18a:9/240:9)

7.47. There are those matters that one ought not to tolerate. One can't learn to tolerate everything. (13.18a:12/240:11)

7.48. Learning to tolerate everything results in baseness and dis-honesty. (13.18b:1/240:12)

7.49. Students must be punctilious [literally, "have angular walls"], then they can support weighty matters. Take Tzu-lu, for example. Even when there were no longer problems in the world, he wouldn't directly "enter into association with one who in his own person was guilty of doing evil."[20] (13.18b:2/240:13)

7.50. The reason people become distressed about poverty and humble status and anxious about wealth and honor is simply that they don't understand moral principle. If they understood moral principle, poverty and baseness would be incapable of doing them harm, and wealth and honor would add nothing to them. They need only to understand moral principle. (13.19a:10/241:10)

7.51. When people shower one another with small favors, we know the spiritual climate is no good. (13.20a:4/242:8)

---

20. A reference to *Lun-yü* 17/6; Legge, *Chinese Classics*, vol. 3, p. 321.

7.52. Even before you begin doing things, your mind is set on finishing them, and thus you always rush right through them. (13.20a:9/241:12)

7.53. Moral principle is something all minds share; it's easy for people to investigate it. Preparing for the examinations is something external to oneself; by contrast, it's difficult to do. What a pity that preparing for the examinations has ruined so many people. (13.21a:6/243:10)

7.54. Scholars must first distinguish between the examinations and studying—which is less important, which is more important. If 70 percent of their determination is given to study and 30 percent to the examinations, that'll be fine. But if 70 percent is given to the examinations and 30 percent to study, they're sure to be overcome by the 70 percent—how much more if their determination is completely given to the examinations! Thus in growing old, they'll have nothing at all to draw on, for they've never been concerned with self-improvement. What the Sage taught others was nothing but self-improvement. (13.21a:8/243:12)

7.55. As for the person who specializes in writing the examination-style essay, what he says is always what the sages and worthies have said. Take, for instance, when he speaks of incorruptibility; he is able to do so eloquently. And when he speaks of righteousness, he again is able to do so eloquently. Yet in his own behavior he naturally is neither incorruptible nor righteous. This is because he takes so many words and merely expresses them on paper. Incorruptibility is something he explains in response to a posed question; the same with righteousness. Neither are matters of personal concern at all. (13.21b:9/244:5)

7.56. Chu told someone: It appears that today people's minds are of one of two types. How is it that the mind that fixes on fame and prosperity turns against the right mind and not toward moral principle? You have gone to the examinations for several years now. Your writing, I thought, must be refined; and because you single-mindedly focused on writing the examination-style essay, it seemed that with but one try you would win a high place on the list of successful candidates and then assume an illustrious position in government and that would be that. But now you still haven't suc-

ceeded. From this we can see that success and failure aren't necessarily what we might expect. You have immersed yourself in them
[i.e., the examinations], but have never stood out; in the end you're
just going to ruin yourself. Put them aside and try to understand
moral principle, because it's essential; and later you might even
achieve fame. Mencius said: "With those who do violence to themselves, it is impossible to speak. With those who throw themselves
away, it is impossible to do anything. To disown in his own conversation propriety and righteousness, is what we mean by doing
violence to one's self."[21] "To disown propriety and righteousness"
is to say expressly that propriety and righteousness are bad. In the
world there's the sort of person who hates for others to do good
deeds and simply says, "Why do others bother to do so many exemplary things?" This is because he's done the violence to himself that
he has. You can't even talk to him. As for "those who throw themselves away," they themselves say, "Moral principle is good. I've
heard what others say and furthermore accept it. I'm just unable to
do it; no matter what you do, I'm unable to do it." This is to
"throw themselves away." In the end "it is impossible to do anything with them." Therefore I-ch'uan said: "Those who do violence to themselves resist it, utterly lacking trust in it. Those who
throw themselves away sever themselves from it, practicing it not at
all."[22] "Resist it, utterly lacking trust in it," is simply to say they
are without moral principle. "Sever themselves from it, practicing
it not at all," is to say that they know moral principle exists but
they cut themselves off from it, unwilling to practice it. "Those who
do violence to themselves" implies imperiousness. "Those who
throw themselves away" implies timidity and weakness. (13.22a:1/
224:8)

7.57. He said to someone: You say not to study but only to read the
examination-style essays a bit. In the end what sort of person do
you hope to become? You'll take the examinations and fail repeatedly; and in old age you'll just be melancholy, drifting from one

21. From *Meng-tzu* 4A/11; translation from Legge, *Chinese Classics*, vol. 2,
p. 301.
22. *I ch'uan I-chuan* 4.11b–12a.

village to another. But if as a result of the examination-style essay you were to become an official, you'd just be brash; you'd never say that you wanted to serve the country and the people, to promote what's beneficial and abolish what's harmful, or to acquit yourself in office as well as possible. You'd always be thinking simply that you wanted to advance, obsequiously following behind others and intriguing to get ahead. In seeking promotion and recommendation, there's nothing you wouldn't do. (13.22b:4/245:2)

7.58. There are some scholars who have a slight understanding of the direction in which to head. However, that side [i.e., the examinations] is so important to them that they can't forget about it. How can they come to know the affairs of this side [i.e., self-improvement]? Now even if they were to concentrate their minds and reflect quietly for days and months on end, they'd still understand only one matter today and one matter tomorrow, never reaching a comprehensive understanding. How much more difficult it is since confusion reigns in their minds and never, for even a day, do they devote themselves to this [i.e., self-improvement]. (13.23a:4/245:10)

7.59. Chu was talking about the relative importance of cultivating the self and competing in the examinations. He then said: Nowadays men are unrestrained in their disloyalty and unfiliality, violate their integrity and sense of shame, and disregard regulations totally. It's not just the men themselves who don't regard their behavior as unusual; the authorities don't regard it as unusual either. Even the village neighborhoods don't regard it as unusual. I don't understand how customs have fallen into such disrepair. It's dreadful— I'm completely horrified by it. (13.23a:8/245:13)

7.60. Not sitting for the examinations is a small matter. But these days when people say they aren't going to sit for the examinations, they regard it as some fantastic achievement. The way I see it, if they were to put their minds to understanding moral principle, soon the other side [i.e., the examinations] wouldn't matter at all to them; and without realizing it, they'd come to regard wealth, honor, prosperity, and success as completely inconsequential. Take Kuo Tzu-i, for example. He served as the secretariat director for twenty-four years[23] and made a great name for himself—still he was just like this [looking upon wealth, etc., as completely inconsequential].[24] (13.23a:12/245:16)

7.61. Someone asked whether preparing for the examinations interferes with one's efforts at true learning. Chu said: Master Ch'eng has said that one shouldn't fear that it will interfere with one's efforts at true learning but only that it will rob one of one's will to learn. If one spends ten days of every month preparing for the exams, one still has twenty days to cultivate true learning. But if one's will to learn is shaken by the preparation for the exams, then indeed there's no cure.[25] (13.23b:6/246:5)

7.62. If you believe that the civil service examinations are for your family's sake and therefore don't engage in learning for your own sake, it's simply that you lack the determination. And if you believe preparing for the examinations interferes with true learning—I don't know that it interferes with your eating and drinking—it's simply that you lack the determination. (13.23b:9/246:7)

7.63. Preparing for the examinations doesn't harm one's studying. Previous generations, when did they ever refrain from taking the examinations? It's simply because people today don't settle their minds that harm is done. As soon as their minds become fixed on success or failure in the examinations, their understanding of the words they read is all wrong. (13.24a:3/246:12)

7.64. He was once discussing the examinations and said: It isn't that the examinations are a trouble to men, it's that men become troubled by the examinations. A scholar of superior understanding reads the texts of the sages and worthies and on the basis of his understanding of them writes the essays required in the examinations. He places aside considerations of success and failure, gain

23. More literally what this line means is that Kuo Tzu-i (697–781) was rated or evaluated twenty-four times in his position as secretariat director (at the time, officials were rated annually; see Guisso, *Wu Tse-t'ien*, p. 92, and des Rotours, *Le traité des examens*, pp. 50–55, 231–233). During the T'ang, the secretariat director normally served a maximum of four years; that Kuo served twenty-four years suggests the degree of his dedication and the esteem in which he was held.

24. For Kuo's biography see *Hsin T'ang shu*, vol. 15, 137. 4599–4609.

25. Ch'eng's comment, paraphrased here by Chu, can be found in *Honan Ch'eng-shih wai-shu* 11.5a.

and loss, so even if he were to compete in the examinations every day he wouldn't be troubled by them. If Confucius were born again in today's world, he wouldn't avoid competing in the examinations, and yet they wouldn't trouble him in the least. There are, of course, those who because of their natural dispositions are not troubled by things so needn't exert themselves in mastering them. Ever since I was young, I've viewed the examinations lightly; and it's not that I understood what they were about and so took them lightly. It's just like a person who by natural disposition doesn't like to drink— when he sees wine, he instinctively hates it; it isn't that he realizes the harm wine does. There's also the person who by natural disposition isn't fond of pleasures of the flesh; it's not that he has an understanding of why, but just that by natural disposition sees such pleasures as unimportant. If one were like this, one could save much effort in mastering this thing [i.e., the examination process]. Nowadays perhaps we're not capable of being like this—only if we exert ourselves may we successfully master things. (13.24a:5/ 246:14)

7.65. I-chih[26] said: Hsü Shu-chung[27] is too eager in preparing for the examinations. Chu replied: His family is impoverished and his parents old—he can't avoid competing in the examinations. It's best to let him prepare for them. Preparing for the examinations does no harm. It's only if one first fills one's mind with thoughts of success and failure that injury is done to the Way. (13.24b:2/ 247:4)

7.66. Someone asked about studying for the examinations. Chu said: Preparing for the examinations does not interfere with true learning. Just use the examinations as an instrument to straighten your own moral principle.[28] It'd be best if you didn't deliberately follow the fashions of the times or deliberately avoid them. (13.24b:6/247:7)

7.67. Formerly, in writing examination-style essays, people expressed themselves in a crude but straightforward manner. What

26. Probably Yang Yu-i; see *SJCC*, vol. 4, p. 3159.
27. I have not been able to identify him.
28. I.e., just use the preparation for the examinations as an opportunity to cultivate your own moral principle.

they wrote was full of meaning, as well as full of vitality. Recently, the examination-style essays have become roundabout and highly refined. In no time people have gotten caught up in this style, and we see that the spirit of the essays has decayed. It's because our culture has weakened, and our customs have fallen into ruin. We've come to this, now what do we do? (13.25a:3/247:14)

7.68. Nowadays people are unable to cultivate themselves. Once they become literati, they struggle to acquire office. And having taken office, they again become distressed that they don't advance [literally, "the pay doesn't increase"]. They run around in haste, without a day's rest [seeking promotion]. How can they compare with the humble scholar living in a mountain retreat? The Way and righteousness fill his body. And once the Way and righteousness fill his body, what can possibly hamper him? (13.25a:6/247:16)

7.69. As an official, do not shirk matters; likewise do not usurp matters. (13.25b:3/248:6)

Glossary

This list excludes common place-names and most of the names and titles in the Bibliography.

Ai, Duke 哀
ai 礙

Ch'an 禪
Ch'an-yüan ch'ing-kuei 禪苑清規
Chang-chou 漳州
Chang Hsü 張旭
Chang Shih 張栻
Chang Tsai, Heng-ch'ü
   張載, 橫渠
Ch'ao I-tao 晁以道
Chao-shih k'o-yü 晁氏客語
Ch'en Fu-liang 陳傳良
Ch'en Hui, Yüan-yung 沈晦, 元用
Ch'en Li 陳烈
Ch'en Liang 陳亮
Ch'en Shan 陳善
Cheng-ho wu-li hsin-i 政和五禮新儀
ch'eng 誠
Ch'eng Chien 成覸
Ch'eng Hao, Ming-tao
   程顥, 明道
Ch'eng I, I-ch'uan 程頤, 伊川
Ch'eng-kao 成皋
"Ch'eng-shih chia-shu tu-shu fen-

nien jih-ch'eng" 程氏家塾
   讀書分年日程
Ch'eng Tuan-li 程端禮
chi 幾
ch'i 氣
Ch'i 齊
Ch'i-tiao K'ai 漆雕開
Chia I 賈誼
Chia-li 家禮
Chiang Shu-meng 蔣叔蒙
Chiang Wen-ch'ing 江文卿
Chien-yang 建陽
chih (arrive) 至
chih (knowledge) 智
chih (will) 志
chih chih (extension of knowledge)
   致知
chih chih (knowing it) 知之
chih fang ta 直方大
chih-ta chih-kang i chih yeh
   至大至剛以直也
Chin 金
ch'in 欽
Ch'in 秦
chin-shih 進士

Chin-ssu lu 近思錄

Ch'in Kuei 秦檜

ching (inner mental attentiveness) 敬

ching (quiescence) 靜

"Ching-chai chen" 敬齋箴

ching-tso 靜坐

ch'ing 情

ch'iu tse te chih 求則得之

ch'iung li 窮理

Chou 周

Chou, Duke of 周

Chou i 周易

Chou-i pen-i 周易本義

Chou-i ts'an-t'ung-ch'i k'ao-i 周易參同契考異

Chou-kuan 周官

Chou li 周禮

Chou Tun-i 周敦頤

Chu Hsi 朱熹

Chu Sung 朱松

Chu-tzu ta-ch'üan 朱子大全

Chu-tzu yü-lei 朱子語類

Chu-tzu yü-lei chi-lüeh 朱子語類輯略

Ch'u 楚

Ch'u-tz'u chi-chu 楚辭集注

chüan 卷

Chuang 莊

chüeh 覺

Ch'un-ch'iu 春秋

chung-ho 中和

Chung-yung 中庸

Chung-yung chang-chü 中庸章句

"Chung-yung chang-chü hsü" 中庸章句序

Fu Hsi 伏羲

Fu Yüeh 傅說

Han 漢

Han Fei-tzu 韓非子

Han Hsin 韓信

Han-ku 函谷

Han shu 漢書

Han T'o-chou 韓佗冑

Han Yü 韓愈

Ho-nan Ch'eng-shih i-shu 河南程氏遺書

Ho-nan Ch'eng-shih wai-shu 河南程氏外書

hsi-kuan 習貫

hsi-kuan ju tzu-jan 習貫成自然

Hsi-ming 西銘

Hsi-ming chieh-i 西銘解義

Hsia-hou Sheng 夏侯勝

Hsiang Yü 項羽

hsiang-yüeh 鄉約

Hsiao ching 孝經

Hsiao-ching k'an-wu 孝經刊誤

Hsiao-hsüeh 小學

Hsiao-tsung, Emperor 孝宗

Hsieh Liang-tso 謝良佐

Hsieh Shang-ts'ai hsien-sheng yü-lu 謝上蔡先生語錄

hsin 心

hsin-hsüeh 心學

hsing 性

Hsing-li ching-i 性理精義

Hsing-li ta-ch'üan 性理大全

hsü 虛

hsü-hsin 虛心

Hsü Shu-chung 許叔重

Hsü Yü 徐寓

Hsüan, Emperor 宣

hsüeh 學

hsüeh-che 學者

"Hsüeh-hsiao kung-chü ssu-i" 學校貢舉私議

hsüeh-kuei 學規

Hsün-tzu 荀子

Hu Hsien 胡憲

Huai 懷

Huai-hai 懷海

Huang Kan, Chih-ch'ing
　黃榦, 直卿
Huang Pa　黃霸
Huang Shih-i　黃士毅
Huang T'ing-chien, Shan-ku
　黃庭堅, 山谷
*Hui-an hsien-sheng Chu Wen-kung
　wen-chi*　晦庵先生朱文公文集

i (doubt)　疑
i (righteous)　義
I, Emperor　義
I ching　易經
I-ch'uan I-chuan　伊川易傳
I-hsüeh ch'i-meng　易學啓蒙
i-li　義理
I-li ching-chuan t'ung-chieh
　儀禮經傳通解
I-lo yüan-yüan lu　伊洛淵源錄

Jan Ch'iu　冉求
jen　仁
jen-hsin　人心
Jen-tsung, Emperor　仁宗
Jurchen (Ju-chen)　女真
Jui-yen Shih-yen　瑞巖師彥

K'ang-hsi, Emperor　康熙
Kao-tsu, Emperor　高祖
ko wu　格物
Ku-liang　穀梁
ku-wen　古文
kuan　貫
"Kuan-chü"　關雎
Kuan Chung　管仲
"Kuan Kung-sun ta-niang ti-tzu
　wu-chien-ch'i hsing"
　觀公孫大娘弟子舞劍器行
Kuan-tzu　管子
k'un　坤
kung　恭
Kung-ming I　公明儀

Kung Mou-liang, Shih-chih
　龔茂良, 實之
Kung-sun　公孫
Kung-yang　公羊
"Kuo-Ch'in lun"　過秦論
Kuo Hao　郭浩
Kuo Tzu-i　郭子儀

Lao　老
li (a measure)　里
li (principle)　理
Li Ch'ang　李常
Li chi　禮記
Li Chi-chung　李幾仲
li chih　立志
Li Ching-te　黎靖德
li-hsing　力行
li-hsüeh　理學
Li T'ung　李侗
Lin Yung-chung, Tse-chih
　林用中, 擇之
Liu Ch'ing-chih　劉清之
liu-i　六藝
Liu Mien-chih　劉勉之
Liu Pang　劉邦
Liu Tzu-hui　劉子翬
lo chih　樂之
Lo Ts'ung-yen　羅從彥
Lu Chiu-yüan, Tzu-ching
　陸九淵, 子靜
Lu Tzu-shou　陸子壽
Lü Pen-chung, Tung-lai
　呂本中, 東萊
Lü Ta-chün　呂大鈞
Lü Tsu-ch'ien, Po-kung
　呂祖謙, 伯恭
Lun-yü　論語
Lun-yü chi-chu　論語集注

Ma Yüan　馬援
Meng-tzu　孟子
Meng-tzu chi-chu　孟子集注

Ming　明
Ming-ch'en yen-hsing lu　名臣言行錄
Mo Ti　墨翟

Nan-k'ang　南康
Ning-tsung　寧宗

Ou-yang Hsiu　歐陽修

Pai-chang ch'ing-kuei　百丈清規
Pan Ku　班固
pang　榜
P'ei　沛
pen-hsin　本心
Ping-fa　兵法

san-she fa　三舍法
Shang　商
Shang shu　尚書
Shang-ti　上帝
she-ts'ang　社倉
Shen Pu-hai　申不害
Shen-tsung, Emperor　神宗
shih　士
Shih chi　史記
Shih chi-chuan　詩集傳
shih-ch'i yü pu-ch'i　十起與不起
Shih ching　詩經
shih shu　史書
shih-wen　時文
shu　熟
Shu chi-chuan　書集傳
Shu ching　書經
Shu-i　書儀
Shu-meng　叔蒙
shu shih　書史
Shun　舜
Ssu-ma Kuang, Wen-kung
　司馬光, 溫公
Ssu-shu　四書
Ssu-shu chi-chu　四書集注
Ssu-tzu　四子

Su Ch'e　蘇轍
Su Hsün　蘇洵
Su Shih, Tung-p'o　蘇軾, 東坡
Sung　宋
sung shu (recites number)　誦數
sung shu (recites text)　誦書

Ta-hsüeh　大學
Ta-hsüeh chang-chü　大學章句
"Ta-hsüeh chang-chü hsü"
　大學章句序
Ta-hui Tsung-kao　大慧宗杲
T'ai-chi t'u-shuo　太極圖說
T'ai-chi t'u-shuo chieh　太極圖說解
T'ai-chou　台州
T'ai-tsu, Emperor　太祖
T'ai-tsung, Emperor　太宗
T'an-chou　潭州
T'ang Chung-yu　唐仲友
tao　道
tao-hsin　道心
Tao-hsüeh　道學
tao wen-hsüeh　道問學
T'eng　滕
"Ti-tzu chih"　弟子職
"T'i hsiao-hsüeh"　題小學
T'ien Chi　田忌
t'ien-li　天理
Ting, Butcher　丁
Ts'ai Ch'en　蔡沈
tsan yüeh　贊曰
Ts'ao Shu-yüan, Ch'i-yüan
　曹叔遠, 器遠
Tseng Tien　曾點
Tseng Tzu　曾子
Tso chuan　左傳
tsu-k'ao lai ko　祖考來格
tsun te-hsing　尊德性
tu　讀
Tu Fu　杜甫
tu-shu fa　讀書法
Tu Yüan-k'ai　杜元凱

Tung Chung-shu 董仲舒

t'ung 通

T'ung-an 同安

T'ung-shu chieh 通書解

Tzu-chih t'ung-chien 資治通鑑

Tzu-chih t'ung-chien kang-mu
資治通鑑綱目

Tzu-kung, Ssu 子貢, 賜

Tzu-lu, Yu 子路, 由

Tzu-ssu 子思

Wan Jen-chieh, Cheng-shun
萬人傑, 正淳

Wang An-shih, Chieh-fu, Ching-
kung 王安石, 介甫, 荊公

Wang Ch'ing-ch'ing, Ching-chai
江清卿, 敬齋

Wang Tzu-ch'ung 王子充

Wang Yang 王陽

Wang Ying-ch'en, Tuan-ming
江應辰, 端明

wei-chi chih hsüeh 為己之學

Wei-hsüeh 偽學

wei-jen chih hsüeh 為人之學

wen 文

Wen, Duke 文

Wen, King 文

Wen-hui, Lord 文惠

wen yi kuan tao 文以貫道

Wu, Emperor 武

Wu Hui 吳恢

Wu Ting, King 武丁

Wu Yu 吳祐

Wu-yüan 婺源

yang 陽

yang-ch'i 陽氣

Yang Chu 楊朱

Yang Fang 楊方

Yang Shih 楊時

Yang Tao-fu 楊道夫

Yang-tzu fa-yen 揚子法言

Yang Yu-i, I-chih 楊由義, 宜之

Yao 堯

Yen Hui, Yen-tzu 顏回, 顏子

yin 陰

yin-ch'i 陰氣

Yin T'un, Ho-ching 尹焞, 和靖

Ying-tsung, Emperor 英宗

Ying-yang 滎陽

Yu-ch'i 尤溪

Yu Tso 游酢

Yü 禹

yü-lei 語類

yü-lu 語錄

Yüan 元

"Yüeh-chi" 樂記

Yung-chia 永嘉

Works Cited

Biot, Edouard. *Le Tcheou-li, ou rites des Tcheou.* 2 vols. Paris: Imprimerie Nationale, 1851.

Bol, Peter K. "Chu Hsi's Redefinition of Literati Learning." In *Neo-Confucian Education: The Formative Stage,* ed. Wm. Theodore de Bary and John W. Chaffee. Berkeley: University of California Press, 1989.

Brokaw, Cynthia. "Determining One's Own Fate: The Ledgers of Merit and Demerit in Sixteenth- and Seventeenth-Century China." Ph.D. diss., Harvard University, 1984.

Bruce, J. P. *The Philosophy of Human Nature, by Chu Hsi.* London: Probsthain and Co., 1922.

Carter, Thomas. *The Invention of Printing in China and Its Spread Westward.* New York: Columbia University Press, 1925.

Chaffee, John W. "Chu Hsi and the Revival of the White Deer Grotto Academy, 1179–1181." *T'oung Pao* 71 (1985): 40–62.

———. "Chu Hsi in Nan-K'ang: *Tao Hsüeh* and the Politics of Education." In *Neo-Confucian Education: The Formative Stage,* ed. Wm. Theodore de Bary and John W. Chaffee. Berkeley: University of California Press, 1989.

———. "Education and Examinations in Sung Society (960–1279)." Ph.D. diss., University of Chicago, 1979.

———. *The Thorny Gates of Learning in Sung China: A Social History of Examinations.* Cambridge: Cambridge University Press, 1985.

Chan, Wing-tsit. "Chu Hsi and the Academies." In *Neo-Confucian Education: The Formative Stage,* ed. Wm. Theodore de Bary and John W. Chaffee. Berkeley: University of California Press, 1989.

———. "Chu Hsi's Completion of Neo-Confucianism." In *Etudes Song: In memoriam Etienne Balazs,* ed. Françoise Aubin, ser. 2, no. 1. The Hague: Mouton, 1973.

———. "The *Hsing-li ching-i* and the Ch'eng-Chu School of the Seventeenth Century." In *The Unfolding of Neo-Confucianism*, ed. Wm. Theodore de Bary. New York: Columbia University Press, 1975.

———. *Instructions for Practical Living by Wang Yang-ming*. New York: Columbia University Press, 1963.

———. "Patterns for Neo-Confucianism: Why Chu Hsi Differed from Ch'eng I." *Journal of Chinese Philosophy* 5.2 (June 1978): 101–126.

———. *Reflections on Things at Hand*. New York: Columbia University Press, 1967.

———. *A Source Book in Chinese Philosophy*. Princeton: Princeton University Press, 1963.

Chang Chien 張健. *Chu Hsi te wen-hsüeh p'i-p'ing yen-chiu* 朱熹的文學批評研究. Taipei: Commercial Press, 1969.

Chang Li-wen 張立文. *Chu Hsi ssu-hsiang yen-chiu* 朱熹思想研究. Peking: Chinese Academy of Social Sciences, 1981.

Chang Tsai 張載. *Chang Tsai chi* 張載集. Peking: Chung-hua Shu-chü, 1978.

Ch'ang Pi-te 昌彼得, Wang Te-i 王德毅, Ch'eng Yüan-min 程元敏, and Hou Chün-te 侯俊德, eds. *Sung-jen chüan-chi tzu-liao so-yin* 宋人傳記資料索引. 6 vols. Taipei: Ting-wen Shu-chü, 1974–1976.

Ch'en Jung-chieh 陳榮捷 (Wing-tsit Chan). *Chu-hsüeh lun-chi* 朱學論集. Taipei: Student Book Co., 1982.

———. *Chu-tzu men-jen* 朱子門人. Taipei: Student Book Co., 1982.

Ch'en Shan 陳善. *Men-shih hsin-hua* 捫蝨新話. *Ts'ung-shu chi-ch'eng* edition.

Ch'eng Hao 程顥 and Ch'eng I 程頤. *Ho-nan Ch'eng-shih i-shu* 河南程氏遺書. *Kuo-hsüeh chi-pen ts'ung-shu* edition.

———. *Ho-nan Ch'eng-shih wai-shu* 河南程氏外書. In *Erh-Ch'eng ch'üan-shu* 二程全書. *Ssu-pu pei-yao* edition.

Ch'eng I. *I-ch'uan I-chuan* 伊川易傳. In *Erh-Ch'eng ch'üan-shu*. *Ssu-pu pei-yao* edition.

———. *I-ch'uan wen-chi* 伊川文集. In *Erh-Ch'eng ch'üan-shu*. *Ssu-pu pei-yao* edition.

Ch'eng Tuan-li 程端禮. "Ch'eng-shih chia-shu tu-shu fen-nien jih-ch'eng" 程氏家塾讀書分年日程. *Ssu-pu ts'ung-k'an* edition.

Ch'ien Mu 錢穆. *Chu-tzu hsin hsüeh-an* 朱子新學案. 5 vols. Taipei: San-min Shu-chü, 1975.

Chou i 周易. Harvard-Yenching Institute Sinological Index Series, supplement no. 10.

Chou li 周禮. *Shih-san ching chu-shu* (I-wen reprint) edition.

Chou Ta-t'ung 周大同. *Chu Hsi* 朱熹. Taipei: Commercial Press, 1968.

Chou Tun-i 周敦頤. *T'ung shu* 通書. In *Chou-tzu ch'üan-shu* 周子全書. Taipei: Commercial Press, 1978.

Chu Hsi 朱熹. *Chu-tzu yü-lei* 朱子語類. Ed. Li Ching-te 黎靖德. Ch'uan ching t'ang edition, 1880.

———. *Chu-tzu yü-lei*. Ed. Li Ching-te. Peking: Chung-hua Shu-chü, 1986.

———. *Chu-tzu yü-lei chi-lüeh* 朱子語類輯略. Ed. Chang Po-hsing 張伯行. *Ts'ung-shu chi-ch'eng* edition.

———. *Chung-yung chang-chü* 中庸章句. In *Ssu-shu chi-chu* 四書集注. *Ssu-pu pei-yao* edition.

———. *Hui-an hsien-sheng Chu Wen-kung wen-chi* 晦庵先生朱文公文集. *Ssu-pu tsung-k'an* edition.

———. *Meng-tzu chi-chu* 孟子集注. In *Ssu-shu chi-chu*. *Ssu-pu pei-yao* edition.

———. *Ta-hsüeh chang-chü* 大學章句. In *Ssu-shu chi-chu*. *Ssu-pu pei-yao* edition.

———. *Ta-hsüeh huo-wen* 大學或問. In *Ssu-shu ta-ch'üan* 四書大全. Japanese edition of 1626 based on Yung-lo edition of 1415.

Chu, Ron-Guey. "Chu Hsi and Public Instruction." In *Neo-Confucian Education: The Formative Stage*, ed. Wm. Theodore de Bary and John W. Chaffee. Berkeley: University of California Press, 1989.

Chuang-tzu 莊子. Harvard-Yenching Institute Sinological Index Series, supplement no. 20.

Chung-yung 中庸. References are to standard chapter and verse numbers. See James Legge, *The Chinese Classics*, vol. 1, *The Doctrine of the Mean*.

Collcutt, Martin. *Five Mountains: The Rinzai Zen Monastic Institution in Medieval Japan*. Cambridge: Harvard University, Council on East Asian Studies, 1981.

de Bary, Wm. Theodore. *The Liberal Tradition in China*. Hong Kong: Chinese University Press, 1983.

———, ed. *Sources of Chinese Tradition*. Vol. 1. New York: Columbia University Press, 1960.

des Rotours, Robert. *Le traité des examens, traduit de la Nouvelle histoire des T'ang*. Paris: Librairie Ernest Leroux, 1932.

Ebrey, Patricia, ed. *Chinese Civilization and Society, a Sourcebook*. New York: Free Press, 1981.

———. "Education through Ritual: Efforts to Formulate Family Rituals during the Sung Period." In *Neo-Confucian Education: The Formative Stage*, ed. Wm. Theodore de Bary and John W. Chaffee. Berkeley: University of California Press, 1989.

Fan Shou-k'ang 范壽康. *Chu-tzu chi ch'i che-hsüeh* 朱子及其哲學. Taipei: K'ai-ming Book Co., 1964.

Franke, Herbert, ed. *Sung Biographies*. 4 vols. Wiesbaden: Franz Steiner Verlag, 1976.

Freeman, Michael D. "Lo-yang and the Opposition to Wang An-shih: The Rise of Confucian Conservatism, 1068–1086." Ph.D. diss., Yale University, 1973.

Gardner, Daniel K. *Chu Hsi and the Ta-hsueh: Neo-Confucian Reflection on the Confucian Canon*. Cambridge: Harvard University, Council on East Asian Studies, 1986.

———. "Principle and Pedagogy: Chu Hsi and the Four Books." *Harvard Journal of Asiatic Studies* 44.1 (June 1984): 57–81.

———. "Transmitting the Way: Chu Hsi and His Program of Learning." *Harvard Journal of Asiatic Studies* 49.2 (June 1989): 141–172.

Giles, Herbert A. *A Chinese-English Dictionary*. 2 vols. Reprint. New York: Paragon Book Reprint Corp., 1964.

Goodrich, L. C. "The Development of Printing in China." *Journal of the Hong Kong Branch of the Royal Asiatic Society* 3 (1963): 36–43.

Gōyama Kiwamu 合山究. "Shu Ki no Sogaku hihan, josetsu" 朱熹の蘇学批判, 序說. *Chūgoku bungaku ronshū* 3 (1972): 25–36.

Graham, A. C. *Two Chinese Philosophers: Ch'eng Ming-tao and Ch'eng Yi-ch'uan*. London: Lund Humphries, 1958.

Griffith, Samuel B. *Sun Tzu: The Art of War*. London: Oxford University Press, 1963.

Guisso, R. W. L. *Wu Tse-t'ien and the Politics of Legitimation in T'ang China*. Bellingham: Western Washington University, Program in East Asian Studies, 1978.

Han shu 漢書. Peking: Chung-hua Shu-chü, 1962.

Han Yü 韓愈. *Chu Wen-kung chiao Ch'ang-li hsien-sheng wen-chi* 朱文公校昌黎先生文集. *Ssu-pu ts'ung-k'an* edition.

Hartwell, Robert M. "Demographic, Political, and Social Transformations of China, 750–1550." *Harvard Journal of Asiatic Studies* 42.2 (December 1982): 365–442.

———. "Historical Analogism, Public Policy, and Social Science in Eleventh- and Twelfth-Century China." *American Historical Review* 76.3 (June 1971): 690–727.

Hatch, George. "Su Shih." In *Sung Biographies*, ed. Herbert Franke. Wiesbaden: Franz Steiner Verlag, 1976.

———. "The Thought of Su Hsün (1009–1066): An Essay in the Social Meaning of Intellectual Pluralism in Northern Sung." Ph.D. diss., University of Washington, 1972.

Hervouet, Yves, ed. *A Sung Bibliography*. Hong Kong: Chinese University Press, 1978.

Hou Han shu 後漢書. Peking: Chung-hua Shu-chü, 1965.

Hsin T'ang shu 新唐書. Peking: Chung-hua Shu-chü, 1975.

Hsün-tzu 荀子. Harvard-Yenching Institute Sinological Index Series, supplement no. 22.

Hu Shih 胡適. "*Chu-tzu yü-lei* te li-shih" 朱子語類的歷史. In *Chu-tzu yü-lei*. Kyoto: Chubun Shuppansha, 1979.

Huang I-chou 黃以周. *Hsü Tzu-chih t'ung-chien ch'ang-pien shih-pu* 續資治通鑑長編拾補. In Li T'ao 李燾, *Hsü Tzu-chih t'ung-chien ch'ang-pien* 續資治通鑑長編. Taipei: Shih-chieh Shu-chü, 1974.

Hung, William. *Tu Fu: China's Greatest Poet*. Cambridge: Harvard University Press, 1952.

Hymes, Robert P. *Statesmen and Gentlemen: The Elite of Fu-chou, Chiang-hsi, in Northern and Southern Sung*. Cambridge: Cambridge University Press, 1986.

Ichikawa Yasuji 市川安司. "*Shushi gorui* zakki" 朱子語類雜記. *Jinbun kagakuka kiyō* 人文科學科紀要 21 (1959): 137–184.

Kasoff, Ira. *The Thought of Chang Tsai (1020–1077)*. Cambridge: Cambridge University Press, 1984.

K'ung-tzu chia-yü 孔子家語. *Ssu-pu ts'ung-k'an* edition.

Lau, D. C. *Confucius: The Analects*. Harmondsworth: Penguin, 1979.

———. *Mencius*. Harmondsworth: Penguin, 1970.

Lee, Thomas. *Government Education and Examinations in Sung China*. Hong Kong: Chinese University Press, 1985.

Legge, James. *The Chinese Classics*. Rev. edition. 5 vols. Hong Kong: Hong Kong University Press, 1960.

———. *The Li Ki*. 2 vols. Vols. 27–28 in *The Sacred Books of the East*, ed. F. Max Müller. Oxford: Clarendon Press, 1885.

Levering, Miriam. "Ch'an Enlightenment for Laymen: Ta-Hui and the New Religious Culture of the Sung." Ph.D. diss., Harvard University, 1978.

Li chi 禮記. *Shih-san ching chu-shu* (I-wen reprint) edition.

Li, Dun J. *The Essence of Chinese Civilization*. New York: Van Nostrand Reinhold, 1967.

Li T'ao 李燾. *Hsü Tzu-chih t'ung-chien ch'ang-pien* 續資治通鑑長編. Taipei: Shih-chieh Shu-chü, 1974.

Liu, James T. C. *Reform in Sung China: Wang An-shih (1021–1086) and His New Policies*. Cambridge: Harvard University Press, 1959.

Lo Ken-tse 羅根澤. *Chung-kuo wen-hsüeh p'i-p'ing shih* 中國文學批評史. 3 vols. Shanghai: Ku-tien Wen-hsüeh Ch'u-pan She, 1957–1961.

Lo, Winston Wan. *The Life and Thought of Yeh Shih*. Hong Kong: Chinese University of Hong Kong, 1974.

Lu Chiu-yüan 陸九淵. *Hsiang-shan hsien-sheng ch'üan-chi* 象山先生全集. *Ssu-pu ts'ung-k'an* edition.

Lun-yü 論語. Harvard-Yenching Institute Sinological Index Series, supplement no. 16.

Lynn, Richard. "Chu Hsi as Literary Theorist and Critic." In *Chu Hsi and Neo-Confucianism*, ed. Wing-tsit Chan. Honolulu: University of Hawaii Press, 1986.

March, Andrew. "Self and Landscape in Shu Shih." *Journal of the American Oriental Society* 86.4 (October–December 1966): 377–396.

Meng-tzu 孟子. Harvard-Yenching Institute Sinological Index Series, supplement no. 17.

Meskill, John. *Academies in Ming China, a Historical Essay*. Tucson: University of Arizona Press, 1982.

Miao-fa lien-hua ching 妙法蓮華經. In *Taishō shinshū daizōkyō* 大正新修大藏經, vol. 9. 1927. Reprint. Tokyo: Taishō Shinshū Daizōkyō Kankō Kai, 1960–1978.

Morohashi Tetsuji 諸橋轍次 and Yasuoka Masahiro 安岡正篤, eds. *Shushi gorui* 朱子語類. Vol. 6 in *Shushigaku taikei* 朱子學大系. Tokyo: Meitoku Shuppansha, 1981.

———, eds. *Shushigaku taikei* 朱子學大系. 14 vols. Tokyo: Meitoku Shuppansha, 1974–1983.

Murck, Christian. "Su Shih's Reading of the *Chung-yung*." In *Theories of the Arts in China*, ed. Susan Bush and Christian Murck. Princeton: Princeton University Press, 1983.

Nivison, David. "Protest against Conventions and Conventions of Protest." In *The Confucian Persuasion*, ed. Arthur Wright. Stanford: Stanford University Press, 1960.

Okada Takehiko 岡田武彦. "*Shushi gorui* no seiritsu to sono hampon" 朱子語類の成立とその版本. In *Chu-tzu yü-lei*. Kyoto: Chubun Shuppansha, 1979.

Peterson, Willard J. "Another Look at *Li*." *Bulletin of Sung-Yüan Studies* 18 (1986): 13–31.

Pulleyblank, E. G. "Chinese Historical Criticism: Liu Chih-chi and Ssu-ma Kuang." In *Historians of China and Japan*, ed. W. G. Beasley and E. G. Pulleyblank. London: Oxford University Press, 1961.

Sariti, Anthony William. "Monarchy, Bureaucracy, and Absolutism in the Political Thought of Ssu-ma Kuang." *Journal of Asian Studies* 32.1 (November 1972): 53–76.

Schirokauer, Conrad. "Chu Hsi and Hu Hung." In *Chu Hsi and Neo-Confucianism*, ed. Wing-tsit Chan. Honolulu: University of Hawaii Press, 1986.

———. "Chu Hsi as an Administrator, a Preliminary Study." In *Etudes Song: In memoriam Etienne Balazs*, ed. Françoise Aubin, ser. 1, vol. 3. The Hague: Mouton, 1976.

————. "Chu Hsi's Political Career: A Study in Ambivalence." In *Confucian Personalities*, ed. Arthur Wright and Denis Twitchett. Stanford: Stanford University Press, 1962.

————. "Neo-Confucians under Attack: The Condemnation of *Weihsüeh*." In *Crisis and Prosperity in Sung China*, ed. John Winthrop Haeger. Tucson: University of Arizona Press, 1975.

Schwartz, Benjamin I. "Some Polarities in Confucian Thought." In *Confucianism in Action*, ed. David Nivison and Arthur Wright. Stanford: Stanford University Press, 1959.

————. *The World of Thought in Ancient China*. Cambridge: Harvard University Press, 1985.

Shang shu 尚書. *Shih-san ching chu-shu* (I-wen reprint) edition.

Shih ching 詩經. References are to standard Mao ode and verse numbers. See James Legge, *The Chinese Classics*, vol. 4, *The She King, or the Book of Poetry*.

Ssu-ma Ch'ien 司馬遷. *Shih chi* 史記. Peking: Chung-hua Shu-chü, 1959.

Su Shih 蘇軾. *Su Tung-p'o ch'üan-chi* 蘇東坡全集. 2 vols. Taipei: Ho-lo T'u-shu Ch'u-pan She, 1975.

————. *Tung-p'o t'i-pa* 東坡題跋. *Ts'ung-shu chi-ch'eng* edition.

Sun-tzu chi-chu 孫子集注. *Ssu-pu ts'ung-k'an* edition.

Sung-shih chi-shih 宋詩紀事. Taipei: Ting-wen Shu-chü, 1971.

Sung, Z. D. *The Text of Yi King: Chinese Original with English Translation*. Shanghai: Modern China Education Co., 1935.

Ta-hsüeh 大學. References are to standard chapter and verse numbers. See Daniel K. Gardner, *Chu Hsi and the Ta-hsüeh*, and James Legge, *The Chinese Classics*, vol. 1, *The Great Learning*.

Terada Gō 寺田剛. *Sōdai kyōikushi gaisetsu* 宋代教育史概說. Tokyo: Hakubunsha, 1965.

Tillman, Hoyt C. *Utilitarian Confucianism: Ch'en Liang's Challenge to Chu Hsi*. Cambridge: Harvard University, Council on East Asian Studies, 1982.

Tomoeda Ryūtarō 友枝龍太郎. *Shushi no shisō keisei* 朱子の思想形成. Rev. edition. Tokyo: Shunjusha, 1979.

Tu Yüan-k'ai 杜元凱. *Ch'un-ch'iu ching-chuan chi-chieh* 春秋經傳集解. *Ssu-pu ts'ung-k'an* edition.

Twitchett, Denis. *Printing and Publishing in Medieval China*. New York: Frederic C. Beil, 1983.

Übelhör, Monika. "The Community Compact (*Hsiang-yüeh*) of the Sung and Its Educational Significance." In *Neo-Confucian Education: The Formative Stage*, ed. Wm. Theodore de Bary and John W. Chaffee. Berkeley: University of California Press, 1989.

————. "Mr. Lü's Community Pact, with Additions and Deletions by Chu Hsi." Paper presented to the International Conference on Chu

Hsi, University of Hawaii, July 1982.

Waley, Arthur. *The Analects of Confucius*. New York: Vintage, 1938.

Wang An-shih 王安石. *Lin-ch'uan hsien-sheng wen-chi* 臨川先生文集. *Ssu-pu ts'ung-k'an* edition.

Wang Mou-hung 王懋竑. *Chu-tzu nien-p'u* 朱子年譜. *Ts'ung-shu chi-ch'eng* edition.

Watson, Burton. *Chuang Tzu: Basic Writings*. New York: Columbia University Press, 1964.

————. *Hsun Tzu: Basic Writings*. New York: Columbia University Press, 1963.

————. *Records of the Grand Historian of China*. 2 vols. New York: Columbia University Press, 1961.

Welch, Holmes. *Taoism: The Parting of the Way*. Boston: Beacon Press, 1957.

Wilhelm, Richard. *The I ching, or Book of Changes*. 3d edition. Princeton: Princeton University Press, 1967.

Williamson, H. R. *Wang An Shih: A Chinese Statesmen and Educationalist of the Sung Dynasty*. 2 vols. London: Arthur Probsthain, 1937.

Yampolsky, Philip. *The Platform Sutra of the Sixth Patriarch*. New York: Columbia University Press, 1967.

Yang Hsiung 揚雄. *Yang-tzu fa-yen* 揚子法言. *Ssu-pu ts'ung-k'an* edition.

Yeh Shih 葉適. *Shui-hsin hsien-sheng wen-chi* 水心先生文集. *Ssu-pu ts'ung-k'an* edition.

Zengaku daijiten 禪學大辭典. 3 vols. Tokyo: Taishukan Shoten, 1977.

Index

Academies: as challenge to Buddhism's influence, 28–29; and Chu, 20, 28–31, 77. *See also* White Deer Hollow Academy
"Admonitions of the Studio of Inner Mental Attentiveness" (*Ching-chai chen*), 173
Analects (*Lun-yü*): Chu's commentaries on, 8, 155; in Chu's curriculum, 39, 40, 43–44, 152, 160; cited, 99, 112–13, 158; and Confucian school turn toward, 78–79; reading, 153; and Su Hsün, 138; views of learning in, 13, 58. *See also* Four Books
Apprehending principle, 75, 169, 174; in book learning, 128; and Ch'eng I, 53n.68, 66, 73; and Chu, x–xi, 9, 52–53, 53n.68, 73–74, 88n.2, 117–18; and Confucian Classics, 38; and extension of knowledge, 41, 117; in greater learning, 88; and inner mental attentiveness, 52–53; and Lu Chiu-yüan, 74; reading as way of, 53–56, 133; and self-cultivation, 117–18. *See also* Principle, or moral principle; Probing principle
Art of War, 107–8, 108n.34
"Articles of the White Deer Hollow Academy," 5, 29–31

Book of Changes (*Chou I, I ching*), 8; Ch'eng I and, 73; in Chu's curriculum, 39; cited, 112, 150, 150n.12, 158; and *yin* and *yang*, 125. *See also* Five Classics
Book of Filial Piety (*Hsiao-ching*), 32
Book of History (*Shu ching*), 8; in Chu's curriculum, 39, 58; and Huang Pa and Hsia-hou Sheng, 140; and Mencius, 139; on original vs. human mind, 144;

and principle, 125–26; and Wang An-shih, 60, 153n.19. *See also* Five Classics
Book of Master Kuan (*Kuan-tzu*), 94–95
Book of Mencius (*Meng-tzu*): Chu's commentary on, 8; in Chu's curriculum, 39, 40, 43–44, 152, 160; Chu's reading of, 154; cited, 99, 145; and Confucian school turn toward, 78–79; reading, 153; and Su Hsün, 138. *See also* Four Books
Book of Poetry (*Shih ching*), 8, 156, 164; in Chu's curriculum, 39; in Confucius's curriculum, 58; in lesser learning, 94; and Mencius, 139; and Wang An-shih, 60, 153n.19. *See also* Five Classics
Book of Rites (*Li chi*), 8; in Chu's curriculum, 39; commentary on, 142. *See also* Five Classics
Bruce, J. P., ix
Buddhism, 26, 72, 108, 109, 152, 170, 184; and Buddha-nature, 115; and Ch'eng brothers, 12n.5; and Chu, 4, 12, 21, 68; and Confucian Way, 21; and learning, 21; popularity of, 11–12; and printing, 21; quiet-sitting in, 179n.40; and Sung Confucianism, 78. *See also* Ch'an Buddhism
Butcher Ting, 130, 130n.3

Ch'an Buddhism, 12, 186. *See also* Buddhism
Ch'an-yüan ch'ing-kuei. See *Ch'an-yüan Code*
Ch'an-yüan Code (*Ch'an-yüan ch'ing-kuei*), 94, 94n.15
Chang Hsü, 162, 162n.46
Chang Po-hsing, xi, xin.1
Chang Shih, 5, 14n.14, 121n.17

Compositor: Asco Trade Typesetting Ltd.
      Text: Baskerville
   Display: Baskerville